Andrew Thompson
University of Glamorgan.
March, 2000

After Britain

Also by Tom Nairn

The Left Against Europe
The Break-up of Britain
The Enchanted Glass: Britain and its Monarchy
Faces of Nationalism: The Modern Janus Revisited

After Britain

New Labour and the
Return of Scotland

TOM NAIRN

Granta Books
London

Granta Publications, 2/3 Hanover Yard, London N1 8BE

First published in Great Britain by Granta Books 2000

A CIP catalogue record for this book is available
from the British Library.

1 3 5 7 9 10 8 6 4 2

ISBN 1 86207 050 4

Typeset by M Rules

Printed and bound in Great Britain
by Mackays of Chatham plc

Contents

For Anthony
and the Next Time

Preface

The inspiration I owe for most of this book appears on every page of it in one way or another, but is worth repeating again here. It is to Anthony Barnett, who has put me right about something or other relating to it practically every day since I began writing, either through his own writing (especially his *This Time*) or via the telephone, and his unceasing and incisive commentary upon the collapse of the United Kingdom. So this is really his book in an unusual sense, and I hope he doesn't mind too much.

Most of it is new, but one or two chapters require comment. Chapter Two, for example, was originally a talk at a political party commemoration in January 1999. I have deliberately left it as such, without much rephrasing or alteration, and acknowledging the organizers. The party was the Scottish National Party, and the event was its seventieth birthday, just four months before the reconvening of the Scottish Parliament by Winifred Ewing. As such, it occurred very much as part of the whole book's ongoing debate (and it has not been published anywhere else). Keeping it as it was is also a way of indicating where this book is coming from. It tries to avoid the bias of nationalism, but also that of a presumptuous and unjustified internationalism – the sort which is almost always metropolitan dominance, either in disguise or in waiting. There is no fail-safe navigation-chart for passing between Scylla and Charybdis – in this case, I suppose one should imagine them as the once-lovely nymph of Britishness, against the dread whirlpool of ethnic nationalism. One just has to try, and also to accept the loneliness measured by the cries of outrage coming from both banks of the channel.

An earlier version of Chapter Three appeared in the *New Left Review* in 1997, after being given as a seminar at Birkbeck College, London. It tries to take the story of Scottish 'suppressed statehood' back beyond the present day, to the moment of the original Union, the one between the crowned dynasties of Scotland and England. Chapter Four started life as a contribution to a conference on constitutional reform in late 1997 held by Edinburgh University and its publication *Scottish Affairs*, in association with British Telecom (Scotland). Chapter Five was first launched as an article for the special Scotland issue of the *Independent on Sunday*'s supplement in September 1998.

As usual, I am indebted for all kinds of support to Ray and Kay Burnett of the Dícuil Foundation, to colleagues at the University of Edinburgh, especially David McCrone, Tony Cohen, Paul Lalor, Lindsay Paterson and Stewart Sutherland, as well as to Sue Grant, Helen Berry and all my students in the Graduate School for Social and Political Studies. Paul Henderson Scott, Rob Brown of the *Sunday Herald*, William Storrar and other colleagues of Common Cause, Terence Brown of Trinity College and Keith Dixon of the Stendahl University at Grenoble have also helped me to keep going. I am grateful to Wolfgang Natter, Jonathan Allison and Cynthia Irvin for their hospitality and stimulation at the University of Kentucky in Lexington, in 1998. A good deal of it reached final form here, in *Henk's huis* in County Roscommon, with an awful lot of daily support and sustenance from Millicent, Greig and Rachel. They were bearing me onwards, even when they seemed to be interfering with 'mar book'.

The Old Rectory, Kilmore, Ireland
July 1999

Introduction

The people of these islands have seldom been united, politically or culturally. Efforts were made to unite them from the 12th century onwards, but they only came under the same monarch in 1603, and the complete political union, which was at last achieved in 1801, endured only till 1922. Since then the process has been reversed . . .

Hugh Trevor-Roper (Lord Dacre) 'The Unity of the Kingdom', in *The English World* (1982)

Break-up to Aftermath

Twenty-two years ago I published a book of essays called *The Break-up of Britain*. During the 1990s it came to be more read, but circumstances prevented its republication to satisfy (particularly) a growing demand from students in faculties of social science and politics. By the time this became possible, it was too late. The process I had guessed about in the seventies was not only occurring, but had gone too far for the book to reappear without a burdensome apparatus of comment, updating or qualification.[1] During the last period of the present book's composition that process has accelerated to the point where each passing month – and finally, almost every new day – has demanded updating or review.

Anarchy Unloosed?

There was another reason for not causing the title to reappear. In 1977 Great Britain was still gripped by the Cold War, a glacial epoch of great-power confrontation within which national struggles and independence movements were severely constricted. The climate of international relationships allowed (and indeed officially approved) liberation-politics among the ex-colonial or Third World countries – even though these polities discovered that 'freedom' normally entailed conscription into one of the new imperia. Choice was effectively limited to one or other big-brotherly enclosure. Inside the fraternal redoubts of the First and Second 'worlds' it was not sanctioned at all. There, nationality-aspirations were circumscribed to (respectively) administrative autonomy and the 'cultural' display-modes of transcended inheritance – 'traditions' redefined so as not to interfere with serious politics.

Under those conditions, 'break-up' was inevitably a speculative idea. No one had much idea of what it might mean in practice. However, from 1988 onwards, the world soon learned what it could mean. The collapse of undemocratic imperia like Yugoslavia, the USSR and Ethiopia produced episodes of pandemonium and civil war, as nations rediscovered themselves with the means available – revived but serious traditions of myth-blood and revenge. The worst episode of this post-glacial crisis occurred in Central Africa, with the massacre of the Tutsi population in Hutu-dominated Rwanda, and the spreading of the conflict into its neighbouring states. Was such ethnic cleansing to become characteristic of a globe no longer 'controlled' by restraining ideological blocs?

I have argued elsewhere that this has been neither inevitable nor even characteristic.[2] However, crises give rise to crisis-scenarios none the less. And in these nationalism has often been cast in a diabolical role. In the 1990s such millennium-style prophecies continued to have some bearing on the British-Isles archipelago, primarily because of the persisting war in Northern Ireland. There, the worst single atrocity would not take place until the summer of 1998, in the Omagh town-centre bombing. Under such conditions 'break-up' could all too easily be given the sense of bloody or helpless fragmentation, and imply a descent into ethnically-regulated conflict – something better restrained, obviously, by almost any outside or multinational power. However biased and anachronistic, such labels have a life of their own: language does speak through those who use it, even if they can sometimes talk back, or alter it. Where an accompanying ideological imputation is so persistent, change of use becomes the sole way of contesting meanings.

Fits and Starts of Dissolution

Ulster is a good example here. The Omagh massacre occurred, in fact, within an utterly different context – one not at all easy to label or dismiss. This was a complex, long-drawn-out process of negotiated change – the 'Peace Process' – aimed at setting up a form of communal self-government in the former British Province of Northern Ireland. Founded upon fifteen years of diplomacy and consultation, this was evidently much more a managed breakdown of the former United Kingdom than any kind of 'break-up'. Indeed it was a conscious attempt to overcome the fatality of the latter. In 1998 it won overwhelming popular support from both parts of Ireland in referenda. Changes to the constitutions of both the Irish Republic and Great Britain were needed, and the strong support for the deal from both the

United States and the European Union countries indicated its potential significance for international relations.

All this indicates that the parameters of British 'break-up' are now quite different from those of scaremongering prophecy. But they are different also from what anyone could have imagined twenty years ago. A dissolution of the old multi-national state is indeed under way, and there is now almost no one who believes otherwise. There are simply different formulae being debated over the outcome: 'devolution', 'independence in Europe', an 'association of British states', all-English or regionalized-English representation – and so on. In the 1970s, the old unitary Crown-state was taken for granted. In 1999 it still figures in such calculations – but as an inheritance (some would say a curse) rather than as part of the future. Indeed the Belfast Agreement of Easter 1998 included its own 'official' new-age forecast of Britishness. 'Strand Three' of that Agreement proposes the foundation of a British-Irish Council ('Council of the Isles') to coordinate or supervise the future business of the archipelago. This is perhaps the most accurate single gauge of the real distance now traversed. On a terrain formerly the prerogative of cranks and dreamers, Ministers and bureaucrats were at the beginning of 1999 busy planning offices and allotting provisional budgets to a spectral body intended to profoundly modify – and possibly even to succeed – the United Kingdom.

One implication of the actual trajectory post-Britain seems to be following is a complexity unsuspected by anyone twenty years ago. The grand simplicities of Britain's *ancien régime* encouraged over-simple ideas of its collapse. Absolute Parliamentary Sovereignty, the glamorous concentration-effect of Monarchy, the dominance of a single huge metropolitan area, and a primitive two-party, simple-majority electoral system – all these led to instinctive previsions of an equivalently unitary end-game. The theatre of imperium fostered over-dramatic notions of its own demise. Such expectations were reinforced by history, and to some extent by current politics in the 1990s. Previous multinational polities had in fact 'collapsed' relatively quickly and acrimoniously: the Romanov and Hapsburg empires, for example, or the Ottoman Sultanate – not to speak of contemporary successors like the USSR and Yugoslavia.

However, these catastrophes were the by-product of wars and their associated revolutions (including the Cold War). Reflection on them did not take account of the possibly slow or staged decline of empire, under more fortunate circumstances which might exempt it from military defeat and violent societal upheavals. But this has turned out to be exactly the case of the British United Kingdom. It is an imperium which has steadily contracted while avoiding foreign disasters. It was refounded upon an early-modern form of parliamentarism in the years from 1688 (the Glorious Revolution) to 1707 (the Treaty of Union with Scotland). Thus fortunate geography and overseas conquests alone did not explain its 19th century eminence. A primitive civic state also conceded just enough popular representation to avert subsequent revolution.

But in a longer time-arc this democracy-by-stages has become dissolution-by-stages, through the erosion and qualification of a once unified Sovereignty. In the accelerating mill-race of modernity, no other empire would be given the chance of such prolonged adaptation. In the British case belated and piecemeal adaptations have conserved the kernel of an élite unitary state right to the end of the second millennium – and this process is still going on. The Irish Peace Process is a vital part of it. And so is the parallel negotiation now launched with Scotland. Assimilation or subordination of the non-English periphery was a necessary condition of Britain's great-power phase and imperial ambitions. Their desubordination is an equally necessary accompaniment of that phase's end (as Lord Dacre conceded long ago, in the passage quoted above).

In short, comparison with the decease of past imperia implies less direct juxtaposition than trying to think what might have happened to (e.g.) Austria-Hungary, had it been granted similar time and fortunate external circumstances. This is what I have attempted below in the chapter about the strange phenomenon of 'Blairism'. In its own promotional material Blair's New Labour government ranks as a radical new beginning, indeed a world-historical example of post-socialist or 'third way' rejuvenation. But it can also be perceived as merely a farther chapter of decline and fall – accompanied by ever-wilder self-deceptions which are really compensations for a certain inescapable and shameful weakness of state following upon 'Thatcherism'.

It was the persistence of an unreformed empire-state which led to Mrs Thatcher's convulsive parody of reform. She understood, correctly, that 'radical' changes were indispensable to contest decline. However, the cumulative socio-economic transformations undertaken by her governments were (in the absence of political revolution) merely ways of undermining the former ruling class and state. By reaction these produced a successor and substitute – Blair's recast and over-regimented Party machine. In this perspective New Labour can be read as a terminal form of archaism: the last gasp, continuing to proclaim itself a new and unheard-of birth.

But the advantage of such a terminal condition is that it must negotiate. A polity near the end of its tether has to manoeuvre incessantly, in order to maintain itself. This is surely preferable to the Thatcherite intransigence whose finest hour was the South Atlantic War. For all its absurdity, the fanfare of Millenium Dome public relations must be better than the bewitchment of the old Monarchy. The new corruption ('sleaze') of a replacement élite is less damaging than the structural and chronic deformation of its traditional predecessor ('class'). The social caste structure of the Anglo-British Empire was an ancestral curse; what we confront today is little more than its episodic aftermath. And the latter's weakness renders possible what a combative ancestral strength would never have considered.

The End of 'Kith and Kin'

During the first two years of the New Labour régime these features have been shown above all on the periphery. It is the state's revised treatment of its minority nationalities and problems which has disclosed its altering nature. Ireland has already been mentioned, and has rightly occupied the foreground of attention in 1997 and 1998. Ending the war in Ulster entailed a fundamental re-articulation of the United Kingdom's unitarist tradition, founded on a post-Thatcher recognition that – in the language of the 'Downing Street Declaration' – Britain no longer retained 'a selfish strategic interest' in retaining control over any part of Ireland.

That altering nature made the Belfast Agreement and the Peace Process possible. However, such alteration has so far been neither rapid nor drastic enough to make sure the Peace Process would be successful. The weak link in the new politics was all along on the Westminster side. Blair's rhetoric of radicalism, and his impressive personal commitment to a new deal for Ulster, were simply never matched by *real* changes to the central state. That touches on a central theme of this whole book: for an undefeated anachronistic state, self-preservation is always likely to be the determining issue. It was one thing for Britain to nobly renounce 'selfish strategic interest'; quite another for it to turn itself a polity redefined by other, and more modest, aspirations – a 'down-sized' state, as it were, reconciled to more ordinary and middle-range purposes at some distance from the historic centre stage. At the same moment as Blair's government was manoeuvring towards a civic settlement in Northern Ireland, it found itself striving to reoccupy precisely that centre stage position with Robin Cook's Ethical Foreign Policy and the Prime Minister's bid for leadership of NATO in a new Balkan war. Thus the future of a remote province was eclipsed by the glamour of appearing to bestride the world once more.

Great Britain was herself once more, in other words (if only for a few weeks, and with ambiguous effects). Yet this also had some direct impact upon the agonized province. The Protestant Unionist community there could not help feeling reassured by such a reassertion of Britishness: it had in the past defined its own identity by alignment with imperial causes and blood-sacrifices like the Battle of the Somme during World War I.

Yet on Thursday, 15 April 1999 its first day of existence turned out to be its last – a 'farce' (in Gerry Adams's words on Good Friday the previous year) as grotesque and disappointing as its dawn had appeared marvellous. Since then many stiff upper lips have insisted that Good Friday can never die, and that there really remains no alternative to patient persistence along broadly the same path. These crestfallen verdicts are understandable, but probably useless. For they are also ways of avoiding the main question: what was really wrong with the Peace Process?

Such a catastrophic fall must have had some serious flaw built into it. Camp-followers of both sides had their ready answers, of course: Republican Nationalists are incurable snakes (the *Telegraph*, *The Times* and *The Scotsman*) or else

Unionists are obdurate blockheads (the *Guardian* and most others). There certainly was a weak link in the chain. But it was on the British side – that is, the side of the UK state (rather than of the Ulster Unionists alone). Endless praise had by then been heaped upon the tireless devotion of Prime Minister Blair to the Process, as upon that of Bertie Ahern, Mo Mowlam, Senator Mitchell, Seamus Mallon and many others. No disparagement of any of their efforts is implied in pointing out that other factors were always involved.

A great game of state was also being played out. That game goes back to the 17th century, and its rules were pre-democratic – primitive-modern rather than post-modern. They came from the world of conquest and justifying faith, and to some extent the individual actors of 1998 and '99 could not help still being their agents. In a well-remembered phrase in 1998 Blair said he felt history's hand on his shoulder – 'I really do . . .' he continued in the familiar boyish style, as if the idea had just come to him over breakfast. He was right, surely – though it might have been more accurate to say that even then the relentless fury of Ireland was on his back. The negotiated Peace Process was made to look initially like a miraculous escape from deep-set historical patterns; yet in the end it broke the back of Blair's all-round Devolution project, and signalled the disintegration of the United Kingdom even more loudly than before.

That 'project' was the preservation of the world's oldest multinational state through cautious, negotiated reform controlled from the centre. In 1997 it appeared a lot more radical than it actually was, partly through hype and partly by contrast with the political rigor mortis of the preceding Conservative régime. It sought renewal at a safe distance: change round the edges, so that Middle-English Sovereignty could continue at the centre – dynamic modernization, but without overmuch pain or revolution for England herself. However preferable Blairism has been to Thatcherism politically, it remains another version of the same deeper purpose. Its 'radicalism' too was in the service of the heartland's continuity – suitable new departures *for them* (out there and down below) so that *we* may remain in England's due place, undiminished upon the centre stage of the world.

In other words, New Labour's project has retained an unavoidable archaism in its genetic code – and Ulster-Unionist atavism has survived (and even renewed itself) by its intimate link to that code. It depends upon symbiosis with the older core of the Anglo-British identity – the part which regresses to William and Mary, the Battles of the Boyne and Culloden Moor. For all Blair's personal sincerity, this is what really betrayed the Peace Process. Part of it necessarily depended on the support of the highly-organized tribal culture of Northern Irish Protestantism – the descendants of settlers in whom the ancient grandeur remains strong, and is still nourished by the terroristic parades of every Marching Season. In other parts of the UK symbolism may have worn out – but not here. As Ruth Dudley Edwards has shown in *The Faithful Tribe* (1999), Orangeism has many redeeming features; but it also remains based upon instinctive attunement to the most backward-looking core of Britishism – Monarchy, imperial Sovereignty and a kind of spiritual racism. They have consistently got the better of this beast because they are so at home with it: they go on assuming (in the old phrase) that they are its 'kith and kin'.

By the middle of 1999, Unionism was feeling more confident about the old rapport. Devolution had been enacted in Scotland and Wales without too much trouble, and modern constitutionalism (the worst threat) had been rejected for the centre. Britain was looking safer – safe enough to revert to the old rules, in fact. After the breakdown both sides bellowed

loudly about how the other one had flouted democratic principles. But at bottom democracy had nothing to do with it.
England-Britain preserves its Northern Irish protectorate not
by a vote but by historical *noblesse* whose customary obligations
Blair merely inherited in 1997 – and thought he could use to
reinforce his scheme of all-round (but not too drastic) renovation. Solving the Irish Question would have been a notable
trophy of British grandeur regained. At the same time, any *democratic* verdict by the electorates of Scotland, Wales and
England itself would have broken that old code instantly. The
peoples of the mainland have become far more modern than
their state. They need to be liberated from Britain. This is why
the Unionists dread liberation, and labour to keep up their col-
lusion with whatever seems most likely to salvage past
grandeur and keep the old game going. Without the obligations of 'kith and kin' *or* a nationalism of their own, this
community would cease to exist.[3]

Revising a Treaty

But important as the Northern Ireland problem is, it cannot be
reckoned the crucial passage for the unmaking of the United
Kingdom. The decisive step must lie in establishing a different
relationship with the Scots.

The latter are the largest minority in the UK, representing
nearly 10% of its population and occupying about a third of its
territory. By the summer of 1999 they had their own elected
parliament with extensive authority over most domestic affairs,
and some representation in the European Union. However, the
awkward problem they pose to Great Britain does not – contrary
to a widely-held and quite natural opinion – lie in their status as
a persecuted or unjustly assimilated national minority. Rather, it

is located in Scotland's status as an imperfectly absorbed *state*. Indeed assimilation has never been seriously on the agenda in this episode of Great Britain's formation. The 1707 Treaty of Union may have been the keystone of British unity for nearly three centuries; but it was – and I would argue, has always at bottom remained – just what the historical term indicates. It was a treaty between states, and not an act of conquest, subjugation, or colonization. Its purpose was subordination, not elimination. 'Incorporation' – the term actually used in 1707 – bore the sense of what occurred more accurately than any later substitute. The English state and parliament wished to take over their neighbours' state, not to extirpate them as a race. Once taken over at that level, they could be forgotten about – such was the long-standing (but now vestigial) great-power purpose of 'Great Britain'.

But of course the agreement has never been accepted with that sense in Scotland. How could it be? A statified 'people' cannot forget itself. Even though its educated élite urges it to be content with a lower profile, and to accept a humbler rôle within some greater glory, the task remains very hard. On another level, communities defend themselves. Such self-defence is a part of collective reproduction, and of all figurative kinship beyond the literal family. Preserved in this case by nationwide institutions as well as by tenacious popular memory, such customary attitudes have endured and acquired a life of their own. From the time of Walter Scott onwards, these roots of statehood were endowed with the glamour of a lost kingdom, and the tantalizing sense of redemption which always informs nostalgia. Although mocked from the outset as wilful and unreasonable, this display-identity has in truth proved incomparably stronger than every one of its philistine adversaries. Colonial empire, Liberalism, the heavy-industrial workshop of the world, British Socialism and Thatcherism have all in turn become as Nineveh and Tyre; while the eclipsed state-land of the Scots has run beneath and outlasted each ruin in turn, until ready to resume its interrupted existence. This has been concealed from general understanding by something obvious, and yet consistently disregarded. There was after May 1707 no collective political voice of what remained (by the provisions of the Treaty itself), a different society. That was the point of the deal. A Scottish ruling class threw in its lot with the English Empire, convinced that the forfeiture would be in the (separate) interest of its nation. The larger partner might dominate the merger, yet for the lesser it would remain a kind of partnership – permanently distinct from mere colonization or assimilation. For the 80% majority such notions ceased to be of any importance once the ink was dry on the 1707 scrolls. But they have remained of significance for the diverse, voiceless social order in the North – a significance which has steadily increased since mid-century, and is now unlikely to stop short of reclaiming independence.

'Voiceless', that is, until this year. Voice is very important for both nation-building and (the Scottish example) nation-retention, or reconstitution. But it is *constitutive* of a state. The assumption here, argued in a number of ways throughout this book, is that it is a mistake to view the resumption of self-government by Scotland as either an episode of colonial 'national liberation' or as simply another chapter in the extension of European 'regional government'. In practice, it is most likely to involve a rewriting of the Treaty of Union and (as a precondition of doing so effectively) a redefinition of statehood. Resuming a former independence is unlike attaining it for the first time. The recovery of collective will by an already constituted nation is not at all the same as 'nation-building' in the sense made familiar through the annals of ethnic nationalism and decolonization.

Furthermore, there may be big advantages to this contrast. As features surface which have been for so long 'occluded' by the uniqueness of the Scotland-England relationship, it may well be that British and other statesmanship falls back upon them with relief. The very things relegated to the museum by imperial Union may yet provide a constructive way forward. And, again contrary to much opinion of the moment, that way may have few threatening implications for other national or regional dilemmas in the European Union.

In an Old House

I mentioned earlier the sheer complexity now involved in sub-dividing the old house of Britain. The Northern Ireland issue itself exhibits a concentration of ethnic, political and interna-tional motifs which has constantly baffled observers and politicians alike. The problem of Scotland, however, is most likely to be resolved by a reassertion of civic nationalism, which it is now difficult to imagine stopping short of 'inde-pendence-in-Europe' (even if this category remains ill-defined). The landscape confronting the new Welsh National Assembly is different again: it does have a 'nation-building' task closer to that of 19th and 20th century tradition – and correspondingly closer to many other 'buried' or half-assimilated minorities in Europe. Beyond the familiar Scotland-Ireland-Wales triad there now lies the question of Cornwall, and of the very small territories, the Isle of Man, Jersey and Guernsey, which were simply ignored by traditional all-British political reflection – too insignificant to figure, as it were, in its dazzling image of greatness and global reach. No one ignores them now. Alongside many other norms, scale has changed its meaning within the much less blinding image implicit in 'really existing' globalization – and its corollary, a more realistic and self-conscious localism.

As if this range of situations were not enough, they all revolve around one very large and still more puzzling one: the question of England. In this regard, all too little has altered since 1977. Now as then, what happens after Britain must depend very largely upon a redefinition of that majority identity – upon the people who, in the famous phrase, 'have not spoken yet' or even acknowledged the need to do so as a separate political entity. While the Republic of Ireland has turned into another country and the UK periphery has been launched on a course of accelerating difference and novelty, the English heartland remains by contrast almost unchanged.

Unchanged, that is, in a deep-political sense: it continues to behave and feel *as if* Great Britain and its unitary state still existed. The United Kingdom was such a convenience for the English that they seem, perhaps naturally, still disinclined to give it up and construct a successor constitution and identity. Yet as long as such inertia endures, no one can be sure of the larger outcome. The English were the main builders of the old archipelago; they can hardly avoid being the architects of the new – and so far, neither the other island minorities nor their 'partners' in European Union appear to be having much influence upon them.

This gathering complexity and differentiation mean it is now very difficult to write a single successor volume to *Break-up*. The present book tries to deal only with the present UK constitution, 'Blairism' and Scotland. In a second study I hope to write something about the development of the other territories, England itself, and the outlook for a 'Council of the Isles', 'Association of States' (or whatever the body is finally called).[4]

Europe has also to be ever-present in both studies. It is impossible to look at the recent evolution of Ireland (South and

North), for example, without understanding how this has been quietly yet also thoroughly reconfigured by European influence. The long history of emigration, Catholic anti-communism, the ambitions of successive US Presidents, and the activities of American pro-IRA groups have all placed Transatlantic influence in the foreground of the Peace Process. Yet it was the landscape behind which proved truly decisive. It was this utterly transformed hinterland – the new prosperity of the South, the Common Agricultural Policy, and the confidence of a modernized Irish political élite – which enabled 1998's great popular vote for such a decisive break with the past. Not long after the Belfast Agreement the European common currency came into existence – the precursor, surely, of equally vast social and political mutations in the century to come. That also was a quiet revolution, *une révolution tranquille* as the Quebeckers said of their own emergence in the 1960s and '70s. But are not tranquil revolutions as lasting and important as those of barricades and bombs? Do they not also require a state-level transformation to be complete, and to establish their meaning in the world – and hence, their long-range meaning for themselves?

Yet there is also a primarily English climate of opinion, hard-nosed and myopic, which has set itself ever more against this immense transformative power. In the conjoined names of neo-liberalism and Britain's great-power past it created in the 1990s the weird hippogriff of 'Euro-scepticism', which was to dominate the fag-end years of Conservative rule. It is anything but extinct today. If such a proto-nationalist mythology does indeed become the matrix for popular heartland resentment at decline and loss, and is farther aggravated by failure or marginalization, then of course serious problems could be posed. However, the most important cause of these will not be 'Europe' or the misbehaviour and self-assertiveness of minorities: it will be the failure and belatedness of central constitutional reform. Not that this will be much consolation to those caught up in the consequences.

As for Scotland, I think it will soon become clear that not only the Scottish National Party but most of the new Parliament takes 'independence in Europe' seriously. It is likely to have as little time for Euro-scepticism as for the relics of Marketolatry and Great-Power nostalgia. European Union is not (as some critics have asserted) just a convenient replacement for the United Kingdom – a way of sidestepping 'real independence' or even 'real nationalism'. Rightly or wrongly, those involved do not perceive it as a repetition of the self-subordination of 1707, but as a new way of obtaining independence in the post-imperial and post-Cold War world. In that world 'independence' is being redefined by global conditions going far beyond trade matters and the power (or weakness) of business corporations. Of course no small edge-land of five million people can itself do much to change such parameters. On the other hand, it can more reasonably hope to contribute something to them, by affirming its own new existence within the great changes of 2000 and after.

August 1999

CHAPTER ONE

Blair's Britain

Where are the wonderful structures with which the men of these days were lifted to the skies, rising above the clouds? These marvellous things are to us little more than the fables of the giants and the old gods that walked upon the earth, which were fables even to those whom we call the ancients.

After London; or, *Wild England* (1885) by Richard Jefferies, Part I, 'The Relapse into Barbarism'.

A State of Possession

Since May 1997, the archipelago which was once the homeland of British Empire has been resonating with a rhetoric of new beginnings. It has been given almost daily visions of departure and new starts – images of a New Britain inhabiting a new millennial time. The accession of Anthony Blair's New Labour Party to office in May 1997, brought with it a circus of Magi and fairground pundits who all denounced the dingy decay of John Major's Conservatism (1992–97) and looked forward to an era of the contrary: radical modernization and renovation in every direction, style instead of grunge, youthful confidence instead of senility disguised as 'stability'. Major's rhetoric had echoed that of the old Christian Democrats in Italy, who after twenty years in office promised '*Progresso senza avventure*' – progress without risks, no rash adventures into the unknown. The Blairites seemed initially to be declaring just the opposite. Genuine progress requires some risks, they appeared to mean – hence the courage must be found to take them.

So one house seemed to be being abandoned for another, in the summer of that year. Even then, however, a more cautious or historically-minded observer might have had some doubts. Eighteen years before – quite a short time by United Kingdom standards, or at least by its mists-of-time rhetoric – Mrs Thatcher too had moved into No. 10 Downing Street amid dazed bits of poetry and euphoric promises. The dawn chorus of '79 had been surprisingly like that of '97. Twenty-five years before that, Blair's predecessor Harold Wilson had taken office, also swearing allegiance to an ultra-modern, radical Britain, poised to startle the world with its transformation in the 'white heat' of the new technology. And another eighteen years before him, when Attlee's post-war Labour régime had swept Winston Churchill from power, it had pledged no less than a Jerusalem upon the British earth. Breaks with the past, people-power, industrial reconversion, renewed world-leadership, giving youth a chance, the overdue end of everything fuddy-duddy: however welcome, it could not really be claimed in 1997 that such formulae were novel.

The truth is that the 'fusty customs' (etc.) of the aged British Kingdom already included a fairly middle-aged tradition of new mornings, appeals to youth, hormone-implants and some-what exaggerated New-Age resolutions. True, few seemed bothered by this at the time. But that may simply have been because, by 1997, the prevalent popular mood was one of pro-found revulsion against the prolonged rundown of the previous radical spasm: 'Thatcherism'. The mood was so general that not many could bear to think of 'all that' continuing, and was in fact of a profundity revealed only with some retrospect. In 1999 (for example) a convinced Tory could write in *The Times*:

> I voted to re-elect the scoundrels . . . (but) they have no
> conception of the loathing with which the country held and
> still holds them. That public hostility is wholly appropriate.
> The last Tory administration was an utterly miserable expe-
> rience . . . It was easily the least attractive government of the
> century.[1]

Very few voters wanted to see that government reborn in still
another form (even if, for reasons to which I will return, it was
to be an important part of what they actually got). And also, the
public-relations of the incoming party were extremely loud,
stylish and well-organized. So there was an irresistible combination, powerful enough to last for some time: a public which
needed to believe, and the techniques of belief-cultivation,
being deployed from above as never before.

However, I suspect that this understandable transition concealed another. There was indeed a 'break with the past' going
on. Only it was not (or not quite) the one publicized by the new
government and its think-tanks. A house was in fact being
abandoned; but it was not simply that of the long Tory hegemony of 1979–97, or even that of the post-World War II era as a
whole. It was 'Britain' itself – the historical 'United Kingdom'.
Full state-titles are not often used; but perhaps the era's conclusion is an appropriate moment for them to be unfolded.
What was really at issue here was the residue of Empire days,
that 'United Kingdom of Great Britain and Northern Ireland'
still inscribed on Her Majesty's passports, together with her
few surviving 'dependencies and possessions'.

The intention of the New Labour régime was in fact to
change and to preserve this state inheritance. No other 'project'
was really possible – or at least, it would have to rest upon this
fundamental one. But within the latter, which was more important – change or preservation? Generally speaking, some

preservation is a condition of reform, in the usual sense of this term. A framework is conserved, so that alterations can be made to or within it. The point is a banal one, of course: the most total revolutions have preserved vital parts of their countries, and sometimes rigid conservatives have been unable to avert sea-changes. However, particular circumstances can render the contradiction meaningful. A given government has to choose one emphasis or another, more or less determinedly: sometimes a 'framework' itself (institution or state) has to be altered, or even destroyed utterly, for social, economic or other changes to happen at all.

At the outset the Blair government's rhetoric gave the appearance of such determination. It stressed change both widely and unilaterally, to convey a sense of contrast with the sepulchral state-mortis of John Major's period in office. It soon became evident, however – even in the first months – that preservation was at least equally important to it. During that summer the impact of Princess Diana's death already had a more than emblematic importance. It indicated how very far from revolutionary was the inner instinct of New Labourism. Confronted with incipient popular revolt against the prime symbolism of that time-worn Constitution it so wished (in rhetoric) to modernize, the government seems to have found itself calculating from the first instant how to save Monarchical face. And as time passed, the gloomy shade of another 'Progress without adventure' has loomed ever larger.

The absence of dissent from that moment, and its continued repression by Blair's apparatus of conformity, poses a profound question. What if the Kingdom had already reached a condition where the two ambitions – conservation and 'radical' change – really are incompatible? What if 'Britain' was already at an ebb-level, from which no returning of the historic tide was possible? In that case, reform would inevitably be overwhelmed by the need to preserve, or to keep going at all costs. Societies and peoples do not of course 'die' or become residual pools in this sense. But states can do so. And where, as is undoubtedly the case in England, state and nation have grown into prolonged and mutually dependent fusion, 'reform' is likely to be unusually of a piece, and unusually difficult.

Only part of this underlying question is explored in this book. Here, the argument is that the old British State is also a state of possession, in a more than metaphorical sense. It has to a remarkable extent configured the nationalities it controlled, and above all the heartland-nation, England. A modernity of military victories and of freedom from internal revolution had built up a practically boundless confidence in that configuration. From 1997 forward, such self-confidence permitted both recklessly rhetorical 'radicalism' and a shameless fall-back upon the changeless verities of common sense, empiricism and British traditionalism. It encouraged Blair, for example, to believe that 'devolution' was possible, and that its difficulties would cause no problems of principle or substance to the enduring centre. To the latter there still adhered in fact a kind of eternity – the predominant family values, as it were, capable of regulating the vast majority through (or eventually, against) upsets, conflicts and the rawer side of radical innovation. In practice the British state and most of its 'nation' remains in thrall to what it still cannot help apprehending as a long, even an immemorial, past. Such houses do not let themselves be abandoned so easily. They tend to possess the souls of those who inherit them, and at no time has this been plainer than in the two years since Tony Blair's government took office.

For over 80% of the old home's occupants, the country on the other side of the 2000 threshold is bound to be England. But in spite of the pyrotechnics of recommencement and radicalism, they don't (or do not yet) appreciate what that means, in the sense of feeling or assessing the deeper impact such changes may have. It is easier to dream (as in the Belfast Agreement and the 'Council of the Isles') of moving house than to actually do it. Even when the inhabitants pretend otherwise, the shade may continue to possess the collective soul. What has been a genuinely *longue durée* cannot be transformed overnight, or without a struggle.

The Coolness of Death

Different parts of countries decay (or revive) at different rates. It may be possible for a state to go on decaying while a nation revives. But in England, where state and nation have been for too long fused together like one being, there can then be such confusion that nobody knows what's going on. Something of this struck me quite unexpectedly just before the Easter of 1998. Some readers may recall that was the moment when the Prime Minister, after escorting a group of Chinese leaders around the 'Powerhouse UK' Portakabins briefly erected on Horse Guards Parade, gave fuzzily breathless endorsement to a number of 'Best-of-British' inventions intended for the Greenwich Millenium dome. These included (it was reported) 'an orthopaedic overshoe for cattle and a device for trapping cockroaches in talcum powder'. Nothing was said of the Chinese reaction to Mr Blair's disclosure.

It was just then I felt a very distant warning bell begin to ring. But I couldn't make out where – it was something like a remote smoke-alarm going off in a distant part of the house, most likely with a faulty battery. The sensation persisted none the less, an irritating half-reminiscence from some buried source. Then a day or two later I woke suddenly about three in the morning and it was on the surface: of course – '*The Man*

Without Qualities'. Spin-doctors be damned: what Britain now
has is a quasi-President-Without-Qualities, together with a
quasi-courtly régime straight out of the pages of a seventy-
year-old novel from the Hapsburg Empire. When trying to form
their theory of Blairism, commentators have naturally made
comparisons with roughly similar Atlantic-area régimes of the
present day. But may there not be a time warp in operation
here? In certain respects the historic State Blair has inherited is
not contemporary with post-World War II European states at
all. It belongs in a different age.

An hour or so later I got up and poked around in the garage
until I found Robert Musil's three-volume epic. Damp and
dust had not been kind to it, but Parts One and Two were perfectly legible. By breakfast time I had rediscovered all the
famous characters: Count Leinsdorf ('After all, my boy, we're
all Socialists at heart . . . !'); the insufferable mover and shaker
Countess Diotima (who suddenly looked like Peter
Mandelson's great-grandmother); and looming in the background, the old Royal Waxwork show which before 1914 most
people had sniggered at, while uneasily feeling that it somehow
remained indispensable, and just had to be kept going.

Reading on, I could see how since 1997 some things in *The
Man Without Qualities* now register much more strongly. Musil
was terribly scathing about the Austrian worship of everything
'cool', for instance. The term itself had not been invented, but
the attitudes are unmistakable: obsession with form as a substitute for content, and an accompanying dread of anything
naff or lumpen. Having deteriorated into a kind of Stately
confidence-trick, Europe's most ancient régime had at the
beginning of the century come to rely wholly on daily injec-
tions of confidence. It was everyone's duty to be utterly
brilliant at all times. Off-message lapses meant the societal
back-benches, or exile to the badlands of Bosnia-Herzegovina.

As final break-up approached during the first fifteen years of this century, the Sovereign absolutism crucial to multinational Austria whizzed round in accelerating circles like water nearing the plughole. Public relations, stylishness and great wheezes became its spiritual life-blood – a cultural reassurance of eternal life, as it were, though in truth it was the last curtain before oblivion.

Among such wizard ideas was the concept of a gigantic commemorative exhibition to stun the world. Its purpose would be to radiate the Great Idea to the rest of mankind – that is, Austria-Hungary's inimitable combination of Peace, true civilization and immaculate trendiness. When Musil was growing up there was a distinct feeling about that 'Austria' had lost some of its meaning and former prestige. Brilliant refurbishment was required. No Millenium was available for the purpose, but there was another anniversary coming up – Franz Josef's seventieth on the Hapsburg Imperial throne. This was due in 1918. The old boy had been around longer than almost everybody in Europe could remember. He stood for God, honour, loyalty, great whiskers, maidenhood, decent beer, and anything else which any decent chap could plausibly proclaim indispensable.

I had visited this age previously, when trying to consider the strange question of the British Monarchy, a still-surviving palimpsest with one foot in feudalism and the other in green politics and multiculturalism.[2] I recalled reading parts of Musil's satire *The Man Without Qualities* at the same time. But all that occurred in a previous age – the one when both Windsordom and Socialism were still alive as mentalities. Then followed a much briefer moment of what one can see in retrospect was really the onset of climatic extinction. The psychic mystiques of the British Crown-State and 'British Socialism' went down together, not altogether accidentally, and by 1998

both had become Heritage sites. During the twenty years following the publication of *The Break-up of Britain* in 1977, I had
unpardonably forgotten all too much about both forms of life.
That must be why the quality-less (but might one not say
equally, the 'post-modern'?) Man of late Hapsburg times had
been so deeply buried.

Aus Wien nach London: 'Trust Me!'

There are at this moment very likely dozens of people writing
novels and satires about the Millenium Project. They would be
well advised to turn first to *The Man Without Qualities*. Although
1180 pages long (Picador, 1996) it is every bit as funny as its
great contemporary, *Ulysses*. Musil gives an ironic and medita-
tive account of the preposterous preparations for the
Mega-Exhibition of eighty years ago. Its hero is a young sap
called Ulrich (his surname is never disclosed, to avoid embar-
rassing the family). The crafty Leinsdorf makes him into the
Secretary of the Organizing Committee before he knows what's
happening, and his life turns into an endless purgatory of meetings, corridor intrigue and crappy proposals. Every Viennese
café and lecture-theatre is busy churning out 'lightning
thought, ready to leap at the world's throat' and chew it into
submission. Technicism, Accelerationism, Cubism and
Photogenic Revisionism compete for pre-eminent place in the
great spectacle. Outradicalizing one's opponents comes to be
seen as the key tactic, the consequence being what another
character perceives (adapting his *fin-de-siècle* terminology
slightly) as 'so many contending think-tanks assembled blind-
fold in a polyhedron, each armed with a stick and ordered to go
straight ahead . . .'

Amidst the febrile hubbub, Diotima is constantly whispering

into his and everyone else's ear. She thinks things are getting out of control every minute of the day. And in a sense they are: in effect it is the whole strip-cartoon of a disintegrating and self-deluding social order which tramples over poor Ulrich's somewhat quality-less personality. He can't escape his fate through sex, and ends up a bit round the bend. The dark side of 'Kakania' (as Musil called the Austro-Hungarian Empire) comes to haunt him in the shape of the half-human serial killer, Moosbrugger. This beloved monster of the Vienna tabloids seems to stand for (in today's terms) a supposed underclass or conscience-less chaos – that is, the nightmare which many thought might follow the Monarchy's collapse in Central Europe. In a different timescale, he might have made an exemplary football hooligan.

'Trust me!' was the dying *Leitmotiv* of the Austro-Hungarian State, its useless message to eternity. Political news consisted almost entirely of gossip concerning the supposed deeper thoughts or feelings within the charmed circle of power. Nothing counted but knowing (or affecting to know) the intentions and relationships – frequently tormented or incestuous – among the higher servants of the Crown. This subjectivity was no accident. It was close to being the soul of Vienna, a social culture describable as 'dazzling', provided one remembers this term can also mean 'showy', 'pseudo', 'quick-fix' and insanely pretentious. Within its ambit (as Freud had already shown) everything meant something different from what appeared or was openly stated. Austria-Hungary's curious pseudo-democracy (universal suffrage plus powerlessness) was in truth the instrument of a State with just one remaining idea: to continue existing in grandeur.[3] Descended from the Holy Roman Empire, the Hapsburg multinational Union was (above all in the *mentalité* of her servants) no miserable republic or ghastly little folk-state. Impaled upon a ray of timeless sun-

light, it had become – at least for those in charge – the talisman
of humanity itself.

One reason analysts have failed to compare Ukania with its
predecessor in decay, 'Kakania', is simply an accidental time-
lapse. The idea persists of Austria-Hungary being truly old and
'feudal' while Great Britain is middle-aged and yet somehow
intrinsically 'modern'. In truth, the later Hapsburg imperium was
effectively only as old as Napoleon and Metternich – i.e. a good
deal more youthful than the empire of transplanted Hanover
(later 'Windsor'). Its predecessor, the Holy Roman Empire, had
indeed been a relic of mediaeval times; but Napoleon knocked
that down in his great campaigns of 1800 to 1802. From 1804 a
Heritage-Centre equivalent was set up to try and keep order
across Central Europe. Not surprisingly its management attached
great importance from the outset to the reinvention of traditions.
After 1848 (when it was briefly booted out of Vienna by another
revolution) the imperial nostalgia-industry became even more
central, and indeed something of a patent-mark.

Though effectively less 'immemorial' than Britain or the
United States, this régime devoted the kind of resources Musil
describes to appearing both timeless and talismanic. Its aristocracy sought to make the civilized management of
multinationalism into a substitute for democracy. The ambition may have been sympathetic enough. But the point to
observe here is that this was a modern (even a somewhat post-
modern) ambition. It was not 'traditional' at all. And it failed
because, even then, there was no substitute for democracy –
not because of overmuch old-fashionedness or a hopeless
addiction to 'feudalism'. Lasting for (and hence coming from)
all eternity was simply the religiously-flavoured dope of the
régime. It was meant to preserve hierarchy, and to cushion the
rending impact of urbanization and literacy upon the countryside of Central Europe.

Radicalism in *la société du spectacle*

What the State dope-peddlers of that time meant was that in the radiant fullness of time (as the Great Exhibition would demonstrate) things might – and indeed must – get awfully radical, but this was out of the question *now*. In the meantime, voters just had to, well . . . trust them (and the mummified old Monarch). For the time being (which might last quite a while, one could never tell) safety-first came both first and last, alongside the stability of the family and the *Krone*, keeping people like Moosbrugger off the streets, keeping up with the Germans, Russians, French, etc., keeping what was left of the Vienna Woods and (normally left to the last) keeping the Croats, Slovaks, Slovenes, Czechs, Ruthenes, Bosniacs, Hungarians, Rumanians, Jews, Kosovars, Italians, Poles and Gypsies in their places, and at least half-content with their fates.

However, eternity had become hard work by around 1900. Greatness demanded ever-increasing effort in the face of modernization – and above all, efforts at keeping up appearances. That was why one always had to be intending to change almost everything. The real object may have been to keep things unchanged in as gracious a manner as possible (including the old handmade wallpaper) – yet insincerity in a tediously petit-bourgeois sense had nothing to do with it, since Premiers and Ministers were talking the language of State, usually quite sincerely.

Vulgar souls called all this the 'prison-house of nationalities'. But its defenders have pointed out how cushy the jail had become since 1867 (when the central power had struck a new deal with the Hungarians). The most convincing expression of the new times was the great Austro-imperial Social-Democratic Party. It was New and loyal to the Empire; it regarded big as

better and more rational than small; and it was at the same
time devoted to the *appropriate* liberation of all the minorities
and restless nations – 'devolution' (as this would subsequently
be called). The ingenuity that went into this conjuring trick
was staggering. Vienna is famous as the forge of most 20th century idea-systems, but her achievements in this direction have
remained under-rated (no doubt because Paris, London and
Washington have for so long considered themselves immune
from national-identity gymnastics).

Social Democrat Otto Bauer's *Die Nationalitätenfrage* (The
Nationalities Question) was the principal theory of circle-
squaring, a great and humane if occasionally baffling work. A
century later it remains untranslated into English.[4]

The Russian Bolsheviks did acquire a sort of pock-marked
skinhead version of it, courtesy of the magpie Joseph Stalin.
Biographers record the latter's visit to Vienna in 1913, where he
is supposed to have composed the fatefully important *Marxism
and the National Question* in the cafés on Schönbrunner Schloss-
strasse. But somehow the grand idea fell to pieces in Russia, a
country where even capitalism cannot be made to work. The
result was Soviet Nationalities Policy, laid to final if uneasy
rest in the 1980s.

'Youthism', or Steaming in Circles

The 1918 Mega-Exhibition & Commemoration never happened, of course, since 1914 forestalled it (possibly the one
unqualifiedly good thing to be said of the World War I). Franz
Josef was dead by then also, his imperium shrunk down into a
folk-republic. But the spirit of *Kakanien* is not. Nor does it
endure solely in the weirdly contemporary pages of *The Man
Without Qualities*.

One other imperially-configured State would survive the 20th century mill-race, thanks to a combination of overseas resources, powerful allies, insular geography, good luck, élite adaptability and the same kind of masterly dottiness that Musil depicts with loving and yet despairing irony. That State also developed its Crown-Socialism. And to this successor would be granted, amid far more prolonged cadences of decline, a power which the Austro-Hungarian Social Democrats never experienced. In the Central European empire, universal suffrage was conceded only in 1907, and then suspended 'for the duration of the war' (which in a political sense would then last over thirty years). By 1916 Friedrich Adler, son of the Social-Democrat Leader Victor Adler, felt desperate enough about the obstacles to progress to shoot Prime Minister Count Stürgkh dead, instantly becoming a national (and indeed international) hero.

The United Kingdom Labour Party avoided such extremes (although many must have at least toyed with similar ideas during the latter years of Mrs Thatcher's Premiership). Thus towards the century's end it would be British Socialism, or the shade thereof, which had the honour of setting about a resolution of the British Question of Nationalities. It has done so within a psycho-political framework in some ways similar to that depicted in *The Man Without Qualities*. With one vital difference, however. Although a good deal older than Austria-Hungary in the sense of its authentic continuity, the United Kingdom had, as part of that continuity, made and consolidated earlier political advances. After revolt, disastrous civil war and successful invasion, it had arrived at a representative parliamentary form embodying the sovereignty of both the Crown and the victorious social élite. In comparative terms that was an early, and for long exemplary, achievement.

But this constitutional structure was then canonized as all-puissant 'tradition' – i.e. as the very Platonic archetype of 'democracy' rather than just a primitive transition towards it. Hence an initial advance was petrified into backwardness and, up until 1997 at least, permitted only piecemeal, marginal changes. Conservation stifled farther system-change, over many generations. Yet in the end democratization was to make its fatal comeback – as in Austria-Hungary – through the bias of nationalism.

'Youthism' is not a bad term for the resultant terminal condition: a strategy of decrepitude designed to show that youthfulness is irrepressible, in charge, and will be henceforth all-conquering. Its enactment demands resolute uniformity – indeed a virtual totalitarianism of approach and disposition, without which its absurdity would simply be too obvious. Everyone must conform to a prescribed glee and radicalism, and produce his or her quota of signifiers for the 'third way'. That is, for the notional forward passage in between the fuddy-duddy and the intolerably naff or crass – the exploded shards of old Right and Left, as it were, so ghastly that it becomes bad taste even to mention them. Since no such route is actually possible, the consequence is circular motion. Not by coincidence (as we Marxists used to love saying) this is precisely what the profounder instinct of a State approaching the end of its tether requires.

There are other important advantages which come with the baggage of Youthism. Going round in circles appeals strongly to two vital constituencies: the theorists and the capitalists. Increasingly important (and naturally, self-important) in periods of disorientation, the former enjoy nothing so much as standing boldly on the prow of the great ship, gazing forward to infinite horizons like the young couple on James Cameron's *Titanic*. Their job has become to relay encouraging messages backwards to crew and passengers – a heartening task, more glamorous than the often glum labours of social science.

Also, the risks of contradiction are small. Actually, nothing whatever is visible on the empty ocean ahead. Hence creative speculation can enjoy the unusual advantage of projecting pretty well what it likes there, without incurring the verdict of irresponsibility. But this is no longer idle fantasizing. It becomes responsible think-tankery – the laboratory synthesis of 'scenarios', game-plans and spiffing ideas, constantly fuelled by the dizzying sensation of guiding those up on the bridge.

As for the capitalists, circular political motion is close to their heart's desire. It keeps the game-rules the same for them and supplies a basically good conscience as well. The unceasing demolition of preceding society ceases to be their fault alone. Formerly called 'conservatism', mainly to distinguish it from Satanic vistas of Socialist upheaval, this process now gets much more matter-of-fact. Things melt obligingly and pretty calmly into the air of oblivion, as the people imbibe their governmentally-prescribed medication of bracing modernization. Thus a steady-as-she-goes, there-is-no-alternative course of affairs comes to be blessed by forgiveness: great industrialists are no longer swindlers, sleaze-bags and despoilers of the poor – just decent philistine citizens like anyone else. Is it surprising that they start actively to support the régime which looks like guaranteeing this prized status? That they line up and begin to embarrass politicians with their proffered contributions?

Some critics have tended to perceive conspiracy behind all this, Jack London's old iron fist of cigar-chomping cliques and City cabals. I doubt if such assumptions are necessary. Actual radicalism like the Poll Tax or the miners' strikes used to upset businessfolk dreadfully; virtual radicalism is by contrast a heavenly-seeming dispensation which combines edifying and endless Progress with the changeless ground-rules of profitability, as well as with the style of stodgy grandeur which most *nouveaux-riches* seem instinctively to prefer. Like the

House of Lords, the Buckingham Palace waxwork show would be best preserved – if only it could be given a more convincing semblance of life. And who better for that than young New Socialists and their 'Third Way'?[5] This show is worth paying for.

Faking it: Multinationalism on the Cheap

Had Bauer, Karl Renner and their comrades ever manoeuvred Austro-Marxism into power, it might have been more straight-forward to impose such a system. Where absolutism had endured so long, democratic traditions were feeble. That was not the case in 1997 Britain. Though rigid with disuse, early advances had not been abandoned. However, this tri-secular inheritance from the English and Scottish Revolutions did con-tain a deadly weakness in its very brain-stem, which now flowered into Blairism. Liberal traditions might be strong but (as we have seen) the constitution that should have long ago encoded them was non-existent. Regal Parliamentarism had substituted its own inherited customs for the standard forms of post-1776 world statehood, and with the passage of time these customs had themselves grown archaic. By Margaret Thatcher's time they had become a tribute paid for far too long by modernizers to an antique (and mainly imaginary) stability. Invented traditions are invariably the most rapidly fossilized, and the most difficult to change. They rapidly grow arthritic with success and self-congratulation – all the more so when they have become popular as a spectacle, like the schoolboy caperings of Westminster and the fairy-gilt coaches of post-Victorian Windsordom.

However decrepit its Parliamentarism really was, Britain none the less required an electoral endorsement for change –

even for 'virtual' or pseudo-redemptive change. In fact approaching this Holy of Holies with any kind of reforming intent needed a tidal-wave election victory, inherently difficult of attainment. That alone could foster the climate of phoney consensus inside which, briefly, a Leinsdorf-style Royal Socialism might flourish. This occurred only twice for Britain's Crown-Socialist Left, in 1945 and then (more emphatically) in 1997, in the shape of a massive 'out with the rascals' convulsion quite unthinkable in Austria-Hungary except as a general revolutionary movement.

Yet here too the similarities remain as striking as the differences. In the section entitled 'Pseudoreality Prevails', we find Leinsdorf sensing trouble brewing up connected with the nationalities. He thinks for a moment about having some demonstrators shot. This causes him to tug a bit at his trim little beard, until he feels 'his innate kindliness' breaking through. He sends Ulrich back to Diotima with a message that she should worry less about these troublemakers:

> The more of a case they have, the more quickly they adjust themselves to realities when given a chance. I don't know whether you've noticed this, but there has never yet been an opposition party that didn't cease to be in opposition once they took over the helm . . . This is, if I may say so, the basic reality, the touchstone, the continuity in politics . . .

But it is important to remember the Count was too complacent here, as the narrative proceeds to make clear. Had Vienna's Imperial Social Democrats actually been given their own chance of dealing with the Nationalities Question, one fatal obstacle would have remained in their way. However steadily the helm was held, there was an iceberg waiting which no think-tank could dispel.

This grim truth dawns on Ulrich when he finds himself caught up in a Viennese street mob. At first he rather enjoys the sensation, in his usual dazed, philosophizing way. Then he suddenly realizes this is a nationalist crowd, gathering to heave bricks through the windows of his friend and mentor, Leinsdorf himself. They are Germans who feel indignant that the régime has been doing far too much for the Slavs. It was all very well to grant this or that 'autonomy' to the peripheral peoples, particularly on the cultural side. A bit of poetry and folk-dance never harmed anybody. But then the peripherals had taken to demanding far too much, just one damned thing after another. And also, Germans could never be treated in the same way.

Numerically, the German population was only about one-third of the Empire, but its culture was dominant and its language prevailed from Silesia to Sarajevo. Though increasingly multicultural, Vienna remained an essentially German metropolis where popular identity was increasingly influenced by the Germanic ideologies of Prussia and the north. Hence a potential Great-German nation was counterposed to the Hapsburg 'mixture of races' (a sinister phrase the guttersnipe press was beginning to use, and people were beginning to believe). Old-timers like Leinsdorf (and Emperor Franz Josef) could still proclaim that 'the Germans will have to be won over by the non-Germans, whether it hurts or not', but fewer and fewer actual Germans were willing to be won over.

No, what they pined for was their own grandeur, not 'devolution' and boring equality with inferior breeds. In *The Man Without Qualities* this is expressed through the frightful worm Hans Sepp, a devotee of Physical Culture Clubs and the Federation of Arms-bearing Students, who thinks that the Great Commemoration Committee is 'an incredibly vicious scheme against all that's German in this country'. He is forever gabbling about the Gothic Ego and Teutonic spiritualism, and convinced there is something rather sub-Aryan about sex. His girl-friend Gerda (representing 'a fairly typical Viennese bourgeois family', in the words of one American commentator) is less carried away by this idea. She strongly fancies Ulrich. Yet when she at last gets him into bed it is only to have a fit of hysterics which ends the relationship, and returns her to her unspeakable anti-Semite.

Sepp is a figure of drawing-room fun. But there were of course many real and more malevolent creatures poised to exploit his daft ideas, in Vienna, Linz, Munich and other places. Beyond him (in terms of Musil's fable) stood the ghoulish threat of Moosbrugger, a psychopath immune to reason and eventually to human decency. Yet even these were not the root of the difficulty. The abiding problem was structural rather than personal. The dilemma was that all reform or modernization of the imperium had to proceed via a new deal for its component national parts – hence, via a new constitution bestowing something like equality on a dozen or more populations. But one of these, the German-speakers (who happened to be at the centre of things) were uninterested in, or positively hostile towards being equal. A second, the Hungarians, were also unenthusiastic about changes which might affect their own dominance over adjacent minorities like the Slovaks and the Croats.

So behind the new-start rhetoric both big partners in the Empire (who alone could carry out such reforms) were condemned to half-heartedness. Hence the need to fake it, and to uphold the great and ever-advancing Viennese confidence-trick by a general mechanics of spin-doctoring, including good-news professors, schmalzy circus-acts, wondrous uniforms and (had technology then permitted) Power-house Display Modules.

Stand-alone England

For the New Labour reformers of our later Empire, a multi-national reformation had also become indispensable by 1997. Decline had forced the State back at last upon the Socialists, albeit in dazzling New uniforms. Far too many of these blighters were Scots. But that too was unavoidable. Labour's Parliamentary basis was by then dependent upon support from the periphery, Scotland and Wales – and Labour supporters in both countries were now calling for autonomy as the price. They found themselves under mounting pressure from the nationalists in their respective communities. In addition there was Northern Ireland, the ulcer of the archipelago, a running sore from the past. The latter had been proved incurable by integration into either the Republic of Ireland or the United Kingdom. There also a devolutionary plan of some kind presented itself as the sole solution – making all-round decentralization a necessary agenda.

But did this not entail a new written constitution? Whether federal, confederal, hierarchical, egalitarian, consociational (or whatever) surely any radical new Britain would need a new all-round blueprint of the State? Banal calculations, indifferent to grandeur and eternal sunlight! Nothing of the sort would be needed *here*. Archetypes are for fine tuning and add-ons, not crass dismissal and replacement. Radical upgrades are one thing; substituting a new mother-board would be something else altogether – a revolution, and potentially very bad for business.

British Socialism had abandoned its Socialism, in other words, but not its Britishness. Of course the supposed triumph of Globalization – to which most United Kingdom Accelerationists now subscribed – did imply a certain contraction at the ideological level. Great Britain could no longer plausibly claim to lead the world just by casually throwing together an alternative model of human society. Chest-beating had subsided into chest-swelling. No, the oldest State in the 2000 AD world would have to settle for being a national variant of the liberal capitalism now deemed omnipresent and irresistible. However, there was at least the hope of being 'at the heart of Europe': a sort of better-than-nothing, wooden-spoon prize.

One can only willingly contract so far. The 'national' now so prominent in Tony Blair's orations had to continue to mean 'British' at least. There is a residual and yet still quite comforting non-smallness about this term. The nearer one draws to the end of the road, the more significant such residues and compensations are liable to feel. They mean that the end is not yet – that is, one is not yet like 'Russian' after Soviet, 'Turkish' after Ottoman, or miserably 'Serb' after the expansiveness of Yugoslavia. Clinging to what was left of greatness therefore entailed a cautious and less ostentatious conservation of the Centre, in order to balance the radicalization on the periphery.

In any case, the underlying configuration of the United Kingdom is unique. Its majority nationality enjoys a dominance which has since the Middle Ages been overwhelming rather than contestatory. Whereas the Germans had to fight for their control over the Hapsburg domains, the English have tended to take hegemony over their archipelago for granted. Germans and Hungarians together were still less than half of the Hapsburg domains – which was why there was no escape for them in any democratization process in Central Europe. But the English represent over 80%, even making allowance for new minorities who these days might prefer 'British' to English.

This latter preference is instinctive, and perfectly logical. 'England' and 'Britain' may seem much the same thing to the

English, and to distant observers. They never do, to immigrants or other archipelago dwellers. Like other minorities
before them, new immigrants feel the difference. In spite of its
Royal and other absurdities, it is possible to think that one
breathes more easily in a non-ethnic 'Britain' than one would
upon the narrower ground of England. As long as that more
restricted terrain remains constitutionally undefined the
incomer is bound to sense that it could be defined in other
ways: ethnically (or even racially), along the lines so emphatically prospected by Powellism in the 1960s. But long before
that an uncomfortable sense of relapse had haunted the native
imagination. One of the earliest of science-fiction fantasies,
Richard Jefferies's *After London*, is cited at the top of this chapter. In 1885 he already imagined a post-apocalyptic England
where the great metropolis had turned into a colossal smelly
swamp, surrounded by woods full of 'wild men', gypsies and
the invading Welsh. Almost nothing is known there of the
Scots, a distant tribe which keeps itself to itself.

Nor (one should recall) is this dominance of England merely
statistical. In the archipelago its economy has always enjoyed
an equivalent or even greater hegemony, and in the 20th century its south-eastern metropolitan centre has grown still more
important. Such prolonged and genuinely overwhelming predominance has given English identity an imprint entirely
different from that of the Teutons and Magyars in 'Kakania'.
The fact is that since the 18th century little significance has
been attached to Englishness as separate from 'British' or (for
about a century) British-Imperial. 'Taken for granted' does not
imply that English identity disappeared; but it did become
indwelling, and now reposes upon a deeper level.

After all, there had been a formidable weight of development and culture behind it before the Parliamentary formation
of a British-Union State between 1688 and 1707. Also, much of

that weight was borne forward into the era of modern unionism. As the Scots never ceased for three centuries to complain, the so-called British Parliament was from its first meeting little but the former English Parliament – and not even in serious disguise. However, Scotland represented a mere 9% of the UK total, Wales 4% and the rest still less; so it is not surprising that the popular-national self-image of the majority was rarely perturbed by protests or representations from such distant satellites. It settled down into Anglo-British ambiguity quite easily. From the 1760s up until the 1960s, this was also encouraged by the effects of overseas colonialism and commerce, processes in which the peripheral nationalities all played a part – sometimes a part out of proportion to their place inside the UK homeland.

One result of the low salience of Englishness was that the 'Hans Sepps' of English culture had in past times stood comparatively little chance. During the 1900–14 period described in *The Man Without Qualities* most chest-beating remained strongly British, albeit with a rising quotient of Englishry. Archipelagic alignment was also taken for granted. Even if the Sergeant-Major was assumed to be English, by and large the peripheral troops kept in line and did not contradict him until the Irish Easter Rising of 1916.

And even after that, there had seemed little need for the specific assertion of a narrower or stand-alone English variant. At the same time the Labour Party, now the leading opposition, became just as Britishized as the Conservatives and Liberals had been. This fidelity would remain unshaken until the 1960s. The subsequent half-century of imperial retreat and economic decline suggests in fact that only when the minor parts of the British-Irish archipelago come or act in some way together is there an impact sufficient to provoke stand-alone Englishness. By 1997, however, that condition was close to being realized.

The New Labour régime inherited a situation where all-round political initiative on the English periphery was no longer post-ponable. Such moves contained within them the threat of peripheral coalitions of interest, and of alliances outside the archipelago – and hence of an English counter-assertiveness.

Return of the Half-Repressed?

At the same time the renewed question of European Union integration was being posed, with the approach of the Euro-currency. During the concluding two years of the Conservative government (1995–97), a supposed threat to British identity and values was constantly invoked by the Euro-sceptic wing of the ruling party, and often diagnosed as a potential form of England-centred nationalism. Intermingled with this was the moral collapse of the Monarchy, which over the preceding cen-tury had been a dominant vehicle of the broader, Anglo-British imperium. Although lacking the executive power of its Hapsburg predecessor, the Windsor dynasty had compensated for this by much greater symbolic authority and popular charisma. From the 1850s until the 1990s, every successive government had colluded with its presumption and defended it from Republican attack. However 'invented', this kind of con-trived sacral appeal and pageantry were undoubtedly important in 'holding people together' (as they now began to notice, when the symbolism started to feel hollow).

In the 1990s the glamour abruptly waned, leaving Englishness that much more exposed. Intimations of United Kingdom mortality were by now crowding together: the formal end of Empire, stirrings of Republicanism, an Anglo-Irish agreement based on Britain's recognition that it no longer had to stay in control of Ulster, Welsh and Scottish dissent, a campaign for regional representation in the North-East of England, and an articulate and serious programme for reform of the British Constitution itself (Charter 88), to which some New Labour leaders had frequently paid lip-service.

And yet this confluence of impulses was still assembled around a relatively inactive centre. Whether interpreted as 'stability', inertia, backwardness or simply indifference, English identity itself appeared relatively unaffected by them. This was the same ambiguity which had in the past made Sepp-style chauvinism ineffective; but now it was also inhibiting mobilization in other directions as well. The English had too small a collective stake in drastic constitutional change. They remained comfortable in the contrived instincts of the British realm – the old and purposive Anglo-British ambivalence, basically unconcerned with (indeed hostile to) State-level reforms. Hence the main motor for a genuinely radical shift at the British or multinational level was simply inoperative.

Constitutional alterations normally require an alteration of the communal will: that is, a national or nationalist identity motion of some kind, whether of resentment, ascendancy, defeat or rebirth. Such a will might be stimulated and led 'from above' (as it had to be in Austria-Hungary). However, this entails the existence of a dissentient ruling élite which thinks in constitutional terms, and puts State reform resolutely ahead of social reform and economic policy. But such an order of priorities was quite alien to the modern United Kingdom ruling class – indeed nothing had been more alien to it. Constitutionalism had been familiar enough to its early-modern predecessors of the period 1640–1707. But the State constructed at that time was then reconfigured primarily through contests *against* what appeared as the more aggressive modernity shown in the revolutions of 1776 and 1789 – that is, the modern constitutionalism out of which today's nation-state world has mainly arisen. In those contests (as I noted earlier) the pioneer itself had become tradition-minded and custom-bound – 'empirical' in its philosophy and pragmatic in its political attitudes. British parliamentarism grew perfectly inseparable from such attitudes, and Blair's New Labour victory of 1997 was still far more an expression of them than a repudiation.

Without that more decisive break – a rupture on the level of grammar, as it were, rather than rhetoric – New Labour's political renaissance could only be undertaken 'the wrong way round'. It was fated by its own history to move periphery-first. Authority had to be conceded outwards without the prior establishment of a new central framework capable of encompassing all the new energies and demands. In France, when General de Gaulle decided it was time France 'married its own century', he set up a new Republican Constitution to consummate the wedding. In Germany and Italy, new federal or regional patterns of government were imposed after Fascism, in order to modulate and confine the unitary state. In Spain the post-Franco democracy designed and enabled the Catalan, Basque and other autonomous governments, by first of all erecting a radically novel political and juridical mainframe.

But in the United Kingdom the mainframe itself has remained sacrosanct. Behind a firework-display of fizzling rhetoric about change and modernization, it has simply been carried forward, and trusted to go on 'evolving'. Trust it, and therefore us: things will settle down and generally sort themselves out, while in the meantime (which could mean a lifetime) things can go on in the comfortable, circular kind of way people (i.e. England's people) are used to, albeit with some changes round the edges.

In France and Spain new State constitutions were seen as the necessary condition of a political break with the past. But after Thatcher, only a new *politics* was demanded, not a new framework for political living – and that in order to redeem and continue the past, not to break with it. Recent episodes of UK history may have come to be despised and rejected; but not the longer perspective of Britishness, within which success and world-leadership had been for so long celebrated. Only on the periphery had 'radical' changes become unavoidable, in the more European sense of ruptures or definite new departures. For 'Middle England' itself, these were reckoned to be superfluous – or at least indefinitely postponable.

There were in fact interesting poll and survey indications in the later 1990s that English opinion may have been a lot more open to new departures than party political leaders assumed. Unfortunately, it was the assumptions of the latter which counted. They continued to believe that dramatic departures of style and communication accompanied by minimal, adaptive changes to the constitution were most in accord with the subjacent mood. Hence some departure from the stick-insect rigidity of Thatcherism were in order – but not of such a kind as to frighten the horses. Socialism had been exorcised in accordance with the same supposed mood. After which, it would have seemed damnably un-British to start imposing an Hispanic-style revolution up top: surely some modernization-touches would do instead? Enhanced (only cynics would say 'disguised') by brilliant new ideas? Might not some thoroughly intelligent *bricolage*, plus a strong dose of Accelerationism, Technicism (etc.) restore the basis of Anglo-British statehood for long enough? And keep the restorers in governmental business for long enough too?

Thus Vienna prevailed, as it were, and post-1789 Europe was once more kept in its place: over there. Prince Charles was a dismal substitute for Franz Josef, perhaps. But then, making the best of 'the given' had long been a feature of British Empiricism, in politics as well as in philosophy. Thus Burke,

Smith, Hume and the other peripheral idea-factories of the
Empire had not laboured in vain, and their epigones now
showed they still had a swan-song or two in them.

The Vectors of Archaism

The past does not simply 'survive'. To be reproduced effectively within modernity it requires vehicles, social devices and
intentions. Through these what would otherwise be fossils
become allied to new interests and passions, acquiring the style
(even the fashionability) demanded by what the Situationists
originally called *la société du spectacle*. One of the key vectors for
this is economics.

It is still a common error to believe that Robert Musil's old
Empire was economically hopeless or doomed. In fact it did
fairly well until killed off by war and defeat. David Good and
other historians have shown how notably it was advancing by
1914, after a period in which Austria-Hungary had indeed
lagged behind industrially. Society there may have been unvi-
able, and particularly the contradiction-riven State – but this
was not for reasons rooted in economic development alone.
Like other deplorable truisms of the time to come, 'It's the
economy, stupid!' was quite familiar in Vienna.

'Was the Hapsburg Empire an economic failure in the sense
that it could not engineer modern economic growth prior to its
collapse?' asks Good. His answer is 'an unequivocal "no"'. The
Empire grew at a significantly faster rate than the United
Kingdom over the period between 1870 and 1914, and its GNP
per capita was by then equivalent to that of France. Of course
it straddled the ancient socio-economic gap between West and
East, and hence contained within its own borders a steep
'development gradient'. Yet the latter, Good points out, was

less steep than the one between the North and the South of the United States. The latter's 'impeccable credentials' as a model of successful capitalist evolution have been largely the result of backward projection from post-1945. Although it had not caught up with Belgium, the English Midlands or the Ruhr, Leinsdorf's Empire stood comparison with Mediterranean and peripheral Western Europe (which meant, with most of it).

The implication is plain, if disagreeable to economics-worshippers: there was no straightforward relationship between development and political success or stability. 'Modernization' never fails to create contradictions and stir things up. It provided Vienna (today, London) with greater resources to buy off opposition, dangle bribes, and be terribly broad-minded; but at the same time, it made the unbribable, the resentful and the contrary far more aware of their unequal, left-behind status. Not everyone can be bought off equally. Any measure of success – like the arrival of a railway, the opening of the first supermarket, sudden access to High School or College education – generates an irascible appetite for more, and more quickly. The broad-minded (blueprint in hand) then perceive this as unreasonable: impatient narrowness, egotism, jumping the queue. Thus a grander, encompassing, controlling sort of identity comes to oppose more particular, self-assertive, 'I'm-as-good-as-you' identities. The sharper the impact of socio-economic change, the more this clash turns towards nationalism – the sense that life-or-death may be at stake here, unless control of development is made to lie where it should (with us, not them).

Success in statistical tables and growth-leagues does not automatically favour a grateful, conserving philosophy of even-song, egotism and familial values. The British Conservatives discovered this in the late eighties, not long before they fell helplessly through the floor. Neither does stagnation and the sense of retreat or confinement encourage either revolution or nationalism (except among tiny minorities who know in the abstract that what people tolerate is actually 'intolerable', and inform them of this). There may have been some formative periods of industrialization when such combinations were possible – times when modernity existed only in pockets, as the privileged accident of one nation or another. But its generalization has swept this away. Along with the debris has gone what Emmanuel Todd has recently baptized as *L'Illusion économique* – the notion that economic development itself is the sufficient condition of any specific political or state pattern, or of the triumph of any particular ideology. The universal necessary condition of all advance ceases to be the special explanation of any one forward movement.

Modernity required – and in its later evolution goes on requiring – certain new economic and social circumstances. It does not follow that these circumstances determine modernity in the concrete sense of its lived and acculturized evolution. However one-sided, the socio-economic renaissance of Thatcherism had more strongly undermined the class basis of a traditionalist State than anything before it. Its deregulation and attacks on corporatism corroded the familial sense of a societal order which – like that of the Hapsburgs – had evolved over time an arm's length rapprochement with an earlier phase of capitalism. After the demolition of this structure, Nation and State no longer retained their long-established fit. Yet at the same time Thatcherism worshipped and propped up the State. On that level it was utterly philistine. Exaggerated loyalism and hysteria over timelessness became a kind of compensation for the régime's self-conscious economic radicalism – as if only endorsement of Monarchic and other rituals, and of the State's untouchable unity, could prevent *everything* that was solid from melting into the air.

Much did melt, of course. But by no means everything. It was probably the successful – or half-successful – side of Conservative economic regeneration which helped to carry forward the archaisms of Britishness into a new age. Although at a heavy cost, that aspect of it furnished a comparative advantage and stability which the 1997 change of political régime then inherited and exploited. In striking contrast to all previous Labour governments, Blair was able to undertake his devolutionary measures against the background of an over-strong currency and significant business support. His pro-European stance and agreement (albeit mainly 'in principle') to the common currency ensured a new level of City and big-business tolerance – or even approval – reflected in the climate of a famously Moosbruggerish British press.

Yet that same good fortune was bound also to rehabilitate some of the anachronism carried forward with it. A half-revolution must constantly insure itself against whatever has not been destroyed – against the past still there and in arms, as it were, against an identity discountenanced, even humiliated, yet not really broken up and cast into the tail-race of history. Huge New Labour efforts had gone into presenting this insurance policy between 1995 and 1997. It seemed the only way to win the kind of electoral victory which the British system prescribed. Over-adaptation to the economics of Thatcherism and deregulated liberalism, extreme canniness over all matters fiscal and financial, and a convert-like disavowal of Socialist money-throwing antics: these now became the surprising preconditions of renewal and change.

And yet, it would obviously be quite hard to avoid a general or blatant conservatism from arising around foundations like these. Hence the absolute necessity for an ostentatious, perfectly sincere and fireproof form of 'radicalism' to balance that tendency. The Tories had counterposed a mummified Statism against their radical economic upheavals. The Labourites now had to offset their mummified economics with an ostentatious display of verbosely political radicalism. We have seen something of what this meant – 'youthism', high-technicism, millennial and style-mania, and the accumulation of think-tanks and divining rods in appropriate official, quasi-official and entirely spontaneous polyhedrons.

Rather than from plutocratic plotting and self-interest, it is important to observe how this arose out of an objective dilemma. It derives from the structural fate of a decrepit multinational polity whose inherited nature renders it incapable of either solving its problems or dissolving them. It can only pretend to do both, with a kind of mounting insouciance and *braggadocio*. Ultra-prudent and custodial economics could not help favouring an equivalent conservation of the State – and so the prolongation of 1688–1707 anachronism. But at the same time, real changes of State had become unavoidable on the periphery, as had a distinctly un-conservative style of ideas and public policy. Thus the Scots were given back their Parliament, the Welsh were awarded a political voice, and the Northern Irish were reconciled to a new and only half-British Protectorate – all amid a clamorous fanfare of radicalism suggesting these were but early instalments of a gathering revolution.

At the Centre of affairs, however, the 'revolution' was meant from the start to be far more decorous, indeed not revolutionary at all. Some changes to Europe's most grotesque political relic, the House of Lords; a mild form of proportional representation (if approved by referendum); a half-Freedom of Information Act; an upgraded style of Monarchy affected (but not carried away) by Princess Diana's example; a proper place at Europe's heart (when economics permit, again via referendum) – all these decorous shifts were to occur within a comfortably indeterminate time frame, implying farther long cadences of stable British existence. From its first day in office, Blairism has planned to last longer than Thatcherism did. Thus what counts most in the 'gathering revolution' is clearly the gathering part; execution will come later, as and when opportunity allows (or quite possibly, fails to allow). And what if it gathers only to clear away again, or to be politely refused in referenda? Well, the deep assumption remains that Britain and 'Middle England' – the imaginary repository of the national life-force, nowadays usually assigned to southern suburbia – will survive that. Deeper down, in the central processing unit (or as would once have been said, the controlling instinct) of Britishness, this continuity is what matters most. Survival: in whatever grandeur remains possible.

A Prophecy of End-Time

About the contradictions of Blairism one thing will never be said: 'they could not have known'. In fact the *responsables* of the New Order were told, and it is already revealing to see how clearly they were told, that this time survival, continuity and grandeur would no longer be enough, however ably modulated and publicized. Political revolution was required. Only six months after Blair's electoral triumph, a study appeared with precisely that title: Anthony Barnett's *This Time: Our Constitutional Revolution* (Vintage Books, December 1997). It had a cover picture showing the Union Jack at half mast over Buckingham Palace, in a nostalgic September light. This was appropriate, for the book's story is like Musil's, only much more amazing: the foundering of a Crown-State recounted day by day, sometimes word by word, in contrast to the long ironic retrospect of *The Man Without Qualities*.

The British flag had only been raised over the Royal London residence by popular demand. Previously the Royal standard had only ever flown there when the Monarch was physically present, a demonstration that regality was of greater importance than mere nationality. Kingdom was the important half of 'United Kingdom', even if Parliament had made inroads on the rest of it. However, the bare flagpole now looked offensive to the huge crowds mourning the death of the Princess of Wales. Its indifferent nakedness seemed to accuse their grief, and their caring – as if Queen Elizabeth and her household (then on their annual holiday at Balmoral) were also indifferent. Did they not care – or might they even be pleased – about the loss of their outcast daughter? In death the latter had acquired a title: 'the People's Princess'. Prime Minister Blair confirmed this after the fatal crash in Paris, in what was immediately seen as a stroke of public-relations genius. It was as if he scented from extremely far off the odour of a revolution from below.

There was a lot of gooey sentiment and romanticism mixed up with the resentment, of course, as both left- and right-wing critics of the mood insisted. But what did they expect? A century and a half of patient effort had gone into the formation of romantic-popular Monarchism. It was a broader élite project pursued by governments of both left and right, which had long since cast national identity into this specific mould. That mould had been a form of control. Yet now, briefly, the same force was out of control and in the streets, as a mass idolization of somebody both 'inappropriate' and dead. Yet there were both Socialists and Reactionaries who found nothing to say but: 'This is a bit much!'

In truth nothing could have indicated more clearly the Viennese malaise of the electorate which had voted so resoundingly for radical change four months previously. Barnett was surely right to devote so much space to analysing the incident. It showed the availability of public opinion for a sort of change previously unthinkable. For all its sentimentality, he observes, the Diana cult none the less 'expressed a form of the contemporary that connects to the landslide of May 1st', and implied the possible 'normalization' of British political life. Under Thatcherism society had in an almost literal sense become 'divorced' from the old State, including its petrified Monarchy. In the September days of 1997 the divorce had been spontaneously completed, in –

> . . . a vast movement of people who by their very existence demonstrated that the premise of the 300-year-old British Constitution had been swept away. The people are now independent-minded and capable . . . The question now is whether the political élite will allow the constitutional transformation to proceed.

His argument is of course that the renovated élite must not just allow but compel it to proceed: '*This Time*' is the only time likely to be available for a widely popular reconstruction of the State, a genuine revolution from above. Hence the urgency of tone in the book, and its sometimes hectoring manner. Behind it lies the sense (also the fear) of there being no other time coming. Even if launched from above, a revolution can only be 'genuine' when it meets and is modified by some positive response from below. The moments when such conjunction is possible are rare. To let one go would be folly.

There was only one way of realizing that moment – the route described in some detail over a number of years by Charter 88, the vigorous reform group which Barnett helped to found in the 1980s, and for some time led in the '90s. It is not as if *This Time* were a lonely or eccentric cry from somewhere beneath the stones. The message came right out of the most significant non-party campaign of the '90s, and many Labour Party leaders had professed warm sympathy with its aims. Since the some-what miserable 300th anniversary commemorations of 1688's original revolutionary imposition, the Charter had pleaded passionately that enough was enough – even a standard UNO-issue off-the-shelf Constitution would (some now thought) be better than William and Mary's quaint palimpsest of cod-feudal shards, early-modern scratchings and bipartisan 'traditions' reinvented so often that no one had the slightest idea what purpose they originally served. And surely, with some imagination and national pride, wouldn't the unthinkable become possible? A new British Constitution meriting its capital letter, inspired by the approaching century rather than the one before the one before last?

Barnett's indictment of the *ancien régime* takes up all the first part of his book ('The Meaning of 1997') and overflows constantly into the second ('Voicing the Constitution'). The reader is left by it in a kind of trance, like the suspension of belief that used to attack Ethiopian intellectuals of the 1970s when they returned home from studying abroad to confront the court of Lion-King Haile Selassie: *how is all this still possible?* At the end of the 20th century? With the democratization of the globe in full spate, and Nelson Mandela running South Africa? *How dare it endure one day longer on earth?*

The least that could be expected after May 1997 was surely a statement of some exit plans, and a sketch of the replacement. This need not be a *pronunciamiento* accompanied by a detailed blueprint: instead, what the author recommended was something like Anthony Giddens's 'Utopian realism':

> That means articulating clear, principled goals and then setting about them with practical measures that are given the space necessary to be assessed in a context of consent . . . (p. 273)

But on the other hand such a programme does have to be uttered. With all the respect due to Karl Popper and George Soros (both suitably endorsed in *This Time*) even a pragmatic, anti-grand-theory prospectus must at least be adumbrated, since without that ' . . . the country has no clear idea what "the greatest constitutional change for a century" means and where it is supposed to lead'.

By the end of the year Blair took office, however, there was still no such idea in place. As Barnett worriedly pointed out in December 1997, the statement had been promised before the election, and then simply never delivered. Now, the democratic revival which had been so strongly in the air of both 1 May and early September needed its momentum to be kept going. The practical measures undertaken (like devolution) demanded 'a sense of larger purpose . . . In terms of the constitution, a clear statement of principles and purpose. The sooner the better.'

Methodone Kingdom

Alas, 'the sooner the better' implies the later the worse. As winter turned into spring, the government's first anniversary was celebrated, and Mr Blair's first Cabinet 'reshuffle' of July 1998 ensconced New Labour's authority more firmly, it became steadily clearer that the first instalment might well be the last. The maximal and daring might already have collapsed into the minimal and safeguarding. No statement of grand constitutional renewal was ever to come. Instead, there would be another long-lived 'régime' of decline-management – a generational reign, as it were, comparable to that of Mrs Thatcher in 1979–97. Once more, 'radicalism' would boil down to staying afloat, albeit in an interestingly different way.

As with the early concessions to Scotland, Wales and Ireland, some constitutional changes were still needed to secure that way. One was a form of proportionality in political elections, to qualify the desperate lurches and 'landslide' turn-arounds of the past. The second was some change to Great Britain's revising chamber. Alongside the 'modernized Monarchy' rendered critical by the Diana affair, a more 'acceptable' House of Lords was also needed. These vectors of continuity had themselves to be upgraded, simply to pursue the time-honoured rôle assigned them. They certainly represented overdue episodes of modernization. But in the hardening context of Blair's 2000 régime they could also be stability-reforms. Thus the 'radical' would be a realignment of the archaic, rather than the straightforward replacement which Charter 88 and *This Time* pleaded for.

Electoral change was the more important of the two. The fantastic lurches of 1979 and 1997 had become too dangerous for an antique creaking across the threshold of the Third Millenium. In a Europe and (soon) an archipelago regulated by proportional electoralism, the boxing-ring pantomine of 'first-past-the-post' was no longer easily sustainable. True, Blair's party had benefited from the old mechanisms in May 1997. But only in the wake of prolonged adversity, during which both the Left and the centre of UK politics had been under-represented for nearly two decades. If the system was left intact, nothing could be surer than an eventual surge in the other direction. The instinct of Labourism (even the New sort) was that in Britain, and particularly in England, this reversal action would happen sooner rather than later, and was more liable to affect the Left than the Right.

The ancient theory had been that knock-outs ensured 'strong government'. This might have been all very well when the British Empire possessed a fundamentally strong ruling class – the old patriciate, culturally at one although ruling via different parties. But things had altered fundamentally. The combination of decline and Mrs Thatcher had ruined that élite. She started off her reign with a Cabinet of grandees and great acreage, and ended with one of journalists, estate-agents and sleaze-merchants. These put her out of business in 1990, then revealed themselves as incapable of setting up on their own account. So 'the system' now came to mean nothing but inebriate parliamentary majorities based on a minority of the votes cast, generating machismo-power, think-tank mania, mediaeval staggering fits like the Poll Tax, unrestrained *petty-bourgeois* opportunism, and Sovereignty-delusions which the rest of the world now sniggered at.

New Labour was second-born into this post-patrician world. Which meant that its 1997 majority bore the wounds of four successive KOs, and the scars from a prolonged agony of internal modernization. Was it not due some compensation? That meant not just obtaining but staying in office. On his first day in power, Tony Blair launched an electoral campaign for the post-millennium ballots of 2002 and 2007. What was most 'new' about reformed Labourism was this hardened and re-oriented will – the determination to construct not merely a stand-in government, but a different and more stably-based British élite order.

Rapid Assemblage of New Ruling Class

This meant in turn that New Labourism, unlike the Thatcherites, was directly confronting what one must call the sociological problem of Great Britain *in extremis*. That is, how to replace the former ruling class by a plausible substitute. 'Britain', the Empire's rump-state, can only be kept going by some new regulating and stabilizing cadre, one really capable of taking over

from the gentlemen. Hostile critics claimed from the outset that
Blairite 'radicalism' is mere conservatism; but actually it is more
like *conservationism*. One should not judge it solely in terms of
the former Left-Right spectrum. Seen rather in terms of cura-
torship, as a form of State survival-kit, it becomes more
comprehensible. The Conservative first-born ('natural party of
government', etc.) had been smashed into pitiful wreckage by
the farce of Thatcher's last days and the May 1997 landslide. It
would be in a life-raft for years to come. To the second-in-line
now fell the spoils, but also the onerous duty, of preserving and
renewing one of history's outstanding polities – the oldest existing State in the world with any claim to modernity.

From 1997 onwards, much effort would be expended around
a single question. Just what *is* Tony Blair's project? – asked
many sceptical minds, particularly on the Left. The replies
have been curiously sparse and unconvincing. But that may be
because these inquirers have generally been searching for a
Socialism-substitute – some novel formula for social-policy
redemption and advance. Accompanying this quest went a perfectly logical idea: the new government may as yet be
professing no such formula, but at least some Cabinet craniums
(preferably those in charge) must surely have one? Surely they
must know what they're doing, if only they would tell us (and
meanwhile, listen to our advice, engage in dialogue, etc.).

However, what if the logic itself were erroneous, in the sense
of misdirected? If (i.e.) there is neither a 'project' of that kind, nor
the smallest chance of one being concealed in private rumina-
tions anywhere round the Cabinet table? Would it not then
follow that the only effective 'project' of end-Britain is *diminuendo*
survival – transition from the management of decline into the
management of disintegration, leading eventually to a suitable
testament and funeral arrangements? Both countering economic
decline ('Thatcherism') and re-engineering the political control-

system ('Blairism') have naturally presented their aims as 'radical modernization'. But both these words have become terms of bluster, especially 'radical'. After the eighteen years of Mrs Thatcher and Blair's 1997 election campaign, it has come to signify little more than 'Have a nice day!' in the United States.

The problems addressed may indeed be 'radical' (basic, through-and-through, fundamental, etc.) but the available or short-term answers are really of a theme-park nature. There is no conceivable radical solution, in the sense so much bruited about by Mr Blair's thinkies and cultural gospellers. The unwritten goal of Youthism is death, even though – as in Mexican ritual commemorations – its processions and exhibitions may be filled with exuberant, even hysterical, life. The stage-management and scripting of the interval can (naturally) only be the work of the party in power. But the existential dilemma structuring its parade means that the party must be (or anyway try to be) the Party. That is, it must be a class-substitute – a permanent-seeming élite which makes the end-time bearable. New Labour had to justify its '-ism' by both being and showing that it was much more than a 'movement' in Tony Benn's or Michael Foot's sense – an ethical crusade occasionally permitted into office. It had now mutated into a replacement patriciate, the armature of a farther phase of British statehood, indelibly Great in both name and nature. While manoeuvring towards election-worthiness in the years 1994–97 it had been in reality transforming itself into such a cadre – an élite-surrogate. So, State-worthiness turned out to be the wingèd creature inside the dull chrysalis of Old Labour, still so fatally encrusted by Clause 4 and the Socialist old-stagers of the historic Left.

As it showed at once, even before the liberation of 1 May, this creature flies by different rules from the mouldy night-moth of the 1970s and '80s. Having lost its officer-class, the drifting multinational ship of State needed a new discipline and direction. The administration of these demanded an equivalent discipline and brio from the replacements. Their movement was assuming nothing less than the task of being Britain. Promotion to long-range heritage-governance was sustainable only via ostentatious rigidity and uniformity – through 'discipline' in an enhanced and visibly enforced mode, much greater than that usually associated with political parties (except in the former Communist countries). The result was that 'totalitarianism' of public relations and the predominance of censors and message-watchers which has been so much satirized by critics. Sometimes such Blairite symptoms have been explained in terms of malevolence, or the sheer egotism of a new Machiavellian Prince. But to some extent, surely, they can be seen as arising from quite objective constraints. Are they not also a response to the prolonged withdrawal symptoms of collapsing Britishness?

It is simply not possible to grow a new political élite overnight, or even in a few years. Revolution alone could accomplish that. Blairism is not revolutionary, and not even a Revolution from above. It is the cautious avoidance of revolution-from-above by a whipped-on evolution-from-above (interspersed, of course, with colourful appeals to the populace). Under the conditions of United Kingdom decay, evolutionary stability and sang-froid are demanded even of the undertakers. 'Trust us!' remains the law of surrogacy as it was that of Empire – in some ways possibly even more so than during the preceding history of the British élite.

New Ruling Class Considers Options

The simulation of caste-power is a miserable affair, whose hollowness can only be concealed by a lordly affectation of utter unity and inflexible will. For some years Mrs Thatcher had provided a personal version of this, until it became insupportable to both her own party and the system. She had demonstrated both the force and the limitations of personal charisma as a compensation for decline. Hence a more systemic approach was now needed, which the corporate traditions of Labourism naturally strove to furnish (once Socialism had been purged). The traditional corpus of Labour offered a more collective ethos and organization to build on, in conjunction with the personal *rayonnement* of Blair.

However, that combination needed ideological reinforcement of the developing cadre-structure – 'discipline', daily ideal methodone, unremitting morale-boosting, etc. – plus a minimal political plan for permanence. On this side, Thatcher had banked simply on prayer-book endorsement of the old Ukanian apparatus. Blair's intuition saw the folly of this, above all in the light of New Labour's inescapable commitments to the periphery. The sole advance-route possible was one of 'adaptation' to the new-old dilemma, through minimal remodelling of the Westminster machinery.

In the House of Commons, this implied a coalition policy – the replacement (or modification) of simple-majority aberrancy via the construction of a more sustainable centre ground. The material was present, in the shape of the traditional centre-ground movement, the Liberal Democrats. The latter had been a permanent minority since the 1920s, but one with strong regional foundations as well as a powerful historical presence going back to the 1688 foundation of Britain. Traumatized like the Labour Party by the Thatcher-Major decades, the Liberal Democrats were also now more aligned with post-Socialist Labourism in ideological terms. This provided the conditions for a more enduring power-alliance – but only if the electoral system was reformed to give the Liberal Democrats a more reasonable representation in the Commons. For half a century they had been protesting against the unfairness of two-partyism, a system which had condemned them to representative limbo.

Thus an empirical way forward presented itself to New Labour: minimal changes to the unwritten Constitution which would simultaneously avoid the perils of Charter 88's projected shake-up and confirm them in power as a long-term élite of redemption. Would they not eventually seem 'the natural party of government', the conservatives of a century to come? In the first year of Blair a Commission was set up to recommend the new election system, headed by former Labour Minister Roy Jenkins (now a Liberal Democrat, as well as a Lord). There was little doubt from the day of its inception that his committee's recommendation would be for a minimally proportional voting system. Nor that the New Labour majority would, after the humphing and haaa . . . ing time demanded by abandonment of any tri-secular ritual, endorse the changes. Then the public relations bravura associated with Blairism would surely win a referendum on the proposal?

Or would it? In the summer of 1998 some doubt must have developed over even these modest proposals. Lord Jenkins's suggestions would certainly be reasonable. But would they be Project-worthy, and safe? How else may one understand the strange affair of 'The Constitutional Declaration', and its even stranger aftermath? Dated 11 June, the full title of this statement was: '*Constitutional Declaration* Agreed by the Government and the Liberal Democrat Party at a Meeting of the Joint Consultative Committee'. That committee was founded before the 1997 election, to discuss and coordinate Labour and Liberal Democratic policy on reforming government. After an age of total immobility on this plane, it had been felt that the main opposition parties should combine on a broader platform, and help win popular support (probably by referendum) for changes to the sacred device.

But its fifth meeting was to be more than simple reaffirmation of previous joint-party aims. It was a declaration, presumably to the people, and presumably intended to affect them in some way. Also it was 'launched', not just put out: 'Blair and Ashdown Launch Constitutional Declaration'. As it happened, I was at around that time called on to present evidence to a House of Commons Select Committee, the one on Scottish Affairs. It was investigating future relations between Westminster and the new Edinburgh Parliament, and the new pronouncement seemed likely to have some bearing on its deliberations. I tried to get a copy.

This sounds simple. And so it should, surely, for the citizens to whom (in Declaration-speak) power is being brought day by day closer, and whose rights to Information (etc.) are now so regularly endorsed. In the week after 11 June I made three calls to the No. 10 Downing Street Press Office. The first surprise was how difficult it proved to identify just which Declaration/Appeal/Statement was being requested. On each occasion the assumption at the other end was that callers would want copies of Chancellor Gordon Brown's announcement about privatization – 'launched' at the same moment. 'Constitutional declaration? Ah . . . just a minute please' was each time followed by a pause, and on one occasion by: 'Oh . . . you mean the *Party* declaration . . . *got you*, right!' There followed the standard name-and-address ritual, plus assurance it would be in the post. But a week later, nothing had come in the post.

In one of the few press comments on the Constitutional Declaration, Matthew d'Ancona suggested in the *Sunday Telegraph* that its timing was no accident:

On an ordinary day, the long-planned Blair-Ashdown statement – a poorly-written pledge to 'put power closer to the
people' – would have been subjected to much sterner
scrutiny. In practice, it was all but forgotten in the excitement surrounding the Chancellor's auction of state assets . . .
(14 June)

'The last thing we want at the moment is a big debate about
the constitution', one Minister had told him. The Declaration
was in truth a consoling gesture towards the Liberal Democrats,
who had begun to suffer from growing suspicion about the government's reforming intentions. It was the sort of thing which
would once have crept out of 'smoke-filled rooms', rather than
been launched – a party stand-off, as it were, curiously disguised as a ringing *pronunciamiento* to the farthest corners of the
land.

Still, D'Ancona's comments made me still more anxious to
see the document. I phoned again, carefully repressing any
hint of outraged citizenship. The Select Committee was meeting the next day, so time was short. Would it not be possible for
Downing Street to deliver a copy of the Declaration to the
Houses of Parliament, where I could pick it up by hand? 'Ah,
well, I suppose so . . .' came the answer, '. . . but I don't think
that's a good idea. No. Things just tend to get lost down there.
Wait a minute . . .' Out-of-earshot confabulation followed, and
then: '. . . Tell you what. Just go to the police box at the
Downing Street gates tomorrow morning on your way to the
Commons. We'll make sure it's waiting for you.'

And so it came about that on a fine June morning, strolling
down Whitehall to my seat of government, I turned into
Downing Street for guidance. Two iconic policemen were
indeed there, in shirtsleeves, and carefully inscribed the
request in a large notebook. But they had no Declaration. 'Just

hang on there, Sir!' said one of the officers, picking up the phone. Ten minutes went by. And then at last a lady secretary emerged out of the famous glossy black door carrying a large brown envelope. She hastened up to the police cabin. The Constitutional Declaration was mine. Ten minutes remained to read it before the Committee was due to convene.

They were more than enough. Even allowing for the five-minute walk to Parliament Square, seconds sufficed for a three-page document of such nerve-stunning banality. D'Ancona had been exaggerating: the pledge was not 'written' at all, but ground out of a word-processor programmed entirely with exhumed clichés and rubber-stamp exhortations. At the end came the 'Declaration': 'We ask for the support of the British people in putting power where it belongs, in their hands'. But what the declaration meant was something like this: the gladsome torrent of constitutional modernization has subsided into a stagnant puddle in which, none the less, appearances have to be kept up.

Options have to be kept open; but only just. Lord Jenkins's Report was always likely to be 'accepted'; but once accepted, it was also at once perceived as likely to benefit from some farther years of contemplation and reconsideration. 'Years' – or even Parliamentary Sessions? Two months later it was repeatedly rumoured that the changes, and the referendum, would be put off until after the next General Election (i.e. after 2001 or 2002).

By September, we find Matthew d'Ancona noting how opposition has mounted to the reform within Blair's own party, while the experience of power has simultaneously diminished the enthusiasm of its modernizers. Hence the most probable compromise may 'postpone the changes until, at the earliest, the election after next' (i.e. 2006 or 2007). He may have been exaggerating again. The likely timetables cited after publica-tion of the Jenkins document were that it might be realizable *in eight years or so.* On the other hand, one never knew. All things considered (Boundary Commission changes, elections, etc.) eleven years might be a more realistic prospect. Thus old-fashioned reform had been triumphantly replaced by virtual reform, a mantle for inertia and will-lessness. Robert Musil would have been delighted by such ingenious procrastination, the gymnastics of sincere deceit. He never invented anything half as Byzantine.

Another of the truisms in the 11 June Declaration does admit: 'Constitutional change requires the widest possible consensus, and that will take time to deliver in full . . .' But more significant (especially for Liberal Democrats) was the fact that it was not *against* anything. It was not (for instance) opposed to time-wasting, unnecessary delay, or futile postponement in the hope that the issue itself would somehow vanish from human ken. No, for collaborators of the new régime the only real enemy loitering out there is separatism. As Peter Macmahon pointed out in *The Scotsman*, one finds the document's solitary tooth on page 1. It turns out to be sunk into Plaid Cymru and the SNP – those wreckers, out to destroy the old thing, even before it has a chance to get itself modernized. Years or even decades are fine for reforming (or perhaps after all, not reforming) things British. But what counts *now* is to stop the separatist scoundrels in their tracks. Among all the other bromides, a faint whiff of Third Way chloroform also arises from this text: 'This is the new politics: between an old-fashioned centralized state, and disintegration . . .'

The Fate of Lordship

Secondly there is the problem of aristocracy. Reform of the UK's second chamber was needed to underwrite the new class's tenser and more focused authority. When Blair came into office he and his nation were still confronting a genuinely astonishing possibility: that the globe's 'oldest democracy', 'Mother of Parliaments' (etc.) might soon be embarking upon the Third Millenium AD with a still-functioning hereditary system. In the 19th century Radicals had sometimes made tactical pacts with the nobility, usually against what are now called 'market forces'. But in the 21st century? Reborn as Youthism, could House of Commons 'Radicalism' really cut some unprecedented deal with bloodline voting and genetic entitlement? Under Thatcher's economistic version of the radical credo, Lordship had counted for little. Her political philistinism occluded the anomaly, assisted by the crude bloodline fact that most Lords were Conservatives, and did whatever the government told them between 1979 and 1997.

Clearly this would change. But there was also the question of status and ideal appearance – much more significant for a régime forced forward on to a terrain of political salience and constitutional adjustments. It would simply be ridiculous for any new-style hegemony to try and co-exist with the world's outstanding reliquary of feudalism. The national theme-park implications would be intolerable. However – as with the electoral reform quandary – certain features of the ancient régime's prodigious accumulation of bric-à-brac helped in the formulation of a 'compromise'.

In the course of the previous half-century pseudo-Lordship had been added on to the real bedline product. Each Honours List (New Year and Midsummer) now announces a number of 'Life Peers' – non-hereditary baronages granted solely for the individual's lifespan. These are like non-elective Senatorships, terminable only by decease. Nomination is via a committee system concerned both with 'proper' party representation (mostly rewarding veteran MPs) and with supposed civic or

social merit – 'outstanding achievement', preferably in some
politically harmless arena. Life Peerages carry the same voting
rights as those inherited from the Norman Conquest, but are
still far fewer in number. The rise in sinecure and patronage
since Harold Wilson's (subsequently Lord Wilson's) period of
office has not sufficiently outpaced the breeding power of
lineage.

The House of Lords is these days restricted to censure and
recommendations on the legislation passed by the 'Lower
Chamber' (as it is still called). Since the latter has now appropriated United Kingdom Sovereignty, or Crown-power, a
convention had since World War I ensured that the Upper
Chamber would never finally refuse to pass Commons laws.
However, they could still delay legislation as well as query it,
and sometimes spoke of disregarding the gentleman's convention and reverting to pre-World War I practice. One such
episode had left a particularly deep mark on the consciousness
of both the Labour Party and the general public.

In 1988 the Life Peers who mostly attend to the business of
today's House of Lords had become alarmed by Mrs Thatcher's
Poll Tax. Even time-serving has-beens could sense the likelihood of mutiny over this. Thus an alliance of pseudo-feudal
off-scourings with popular resentment was briefly threatened,
which might have rejected the infamous law. It was to prevent
this that the true-Brit Peerage was called forth from its hinter-
lands to ensure passage of the measure.

What ensued was unforgettable. Even a Man quite Without
Qualities could not have failed to be impressed. It was a fully
Ethiopian spectacle worthy of some Benjamin Disraeli novel.
Bentleys and ambulances laden with Thatcher-worshippers
converged upon St Stephen's Palace from every decayed estate
in the Kingdom, so that the undead might vote through the
century's most unspeakably stupid legislation. A kind of hole

was burned into the climate of opinion by the event, which still left strong traces a decade later. That episode alone (one might have thought) should have been enough to guarantee straight-forward and instant abolition of this institution by any government with the faintest claim to being 'radical' in any older and more honourable sense.

Not, however, by a government whose pretensions were to virtual radicalism alone. Or (more precisely) to virtuality fused with profound caution and a mounting sense of Stately duty. The Blairites decided to abolish hereditary-right voting, while retaining the institution. Instead of moving over to an elected Senate in the classical pattern, the Life-Peer principle was to be evolved farther. These Lords-for-a-day would become, in effect, like a working extension of the Monarchy – a ceremonial political guard-room, permitted to tut-tut about legislation and counsel to their heart's content, but without even vestigial powers of interference.

Governments would in this way retain the valuable authority of seniority-reward and status-endowment, plus that sense of stable continuity which even grotesque traditions are keen to foster – the feeling of social life going on, unanxious and 'time-honoured'. 'Time-honoured' is an important concept – not on any account to be confused with 'time-worn', 'exhausted' or 'as-good-as-dead'. Nor should the uniforms, furniture and wigs be overlooked. While absurd in themselves, they have never functioned 'in themselves': they exist invariably in an intimate alliance with quite interesting and gossip-worthy matters – like who gets what, why, in recompense for which favour or in com-pensation for which injury or failure? This sort of thing is less awesome than descent from Normans and Plantagenets, but also more interesting and more appropriate to a pot-noodle régime seeking (against obvious odds) to evolve a new courtly style of its own.

In late July 1998, one of the most 'sparkling' representatives
of Labour Newness was appointed to superintend Lords
reform, Baroness Jay. I cite the term 'sparkling' simply because
it was employed in all newspaper accounts of the event. The
Independent on Sunday (for example) described her promotion
under the headline: 'How Labour aristocrat Jay walked effortlessly to the top' (2 August, p. 3). Margaret Jay happens to be
the daughter of ex-Premier James (now Lord) Callaghan, and
was formerly married to journalist and one-time diplomat Peter
Jay, son of another Labour Ministerial eminence, Douglas Jay.
The Baroness had 'perfect credentials for the job', and was
'known for her formidable talent for networking . . . as a key
member of the Prime Minister's trusted inner circle'. Another
Baroness is quoted as declaring – 'Margaret Jay is the ideal
person to quell any discord in the House of Lords over Labour
reform . . . She is a discreet gossip, and not in the least bit
pompous'. Much of the rest of the Article is devoted to ampli-
fying this point. As was invariably said in the past of all genuine
blue-bloods (including Queen Elizabeth II) Mrs Jay turns out
to be full of human warmth, has a sense of humour, and will
have time left over to cook for you even when terribly busy.
The new Life-Peer ruling class is surprisingly like the old.

I merely quote this account without elaboration, lest any
reader should think that elements of misplaced irony may have
intruded upon some of my earlier arguments. The *Independent*
story was accompanied, incidentally, by a preposterous diagram
of the new élite 'network' around Mrs Jay, which apparently
extends from Chérie Blair to Meryl Streep, via the BBC's John
Birt, Rabbi Julia Neuberger, the Seventh Duke of
Marlborough, Barry Humphries, Anna Ford and Sir Stephen
Spender – 'Poet, now deceased'. In the contemplation of
Blairism, no irony can be misplaced and satire grows daily more
redundant. A Musil of today's United Kingdom would have to

pit himself against a self-satire now routinely built into the system, and unavoidably replicated in even the most straight-forward or pedestrian accounts of it.

Following abolition of the shameful body, a farther logical move might have been to replace Lordship with regional or national representation – that is, with a second chamber on German or Spanish lines, in which the different populations and territories of the UK could voice distinct opinions and interests. After the Devolution of power one might have thought in fact the case for such a body was stronger. The very existence of assemblies in Wales, Scotland and Ulster will in any case generate demand for some new representation at the centre. Would it not be better to give such voices formal status within the renewed framework of State?

But of course this cannot be, for reasons already noted. Such logic would still be suicidal for Britain, and no smooth talk of fed-eralism, or even of asymmetrical pseudo- or semi-federalism, will make any difference to this fact. The English would have to find representation in such a body, surely. And there is no obvi-ous way that could happen without their being automatically over-represented. The potential conflicts of a non-unitary state, unregulated by a new Constitution, could not really be arranged by a crypto-Lordly surrogate for such a statute and law.

Far safer, therefore, to stick to pseudo-nobility and Mrs Jay's 'networking'. The termination of mere Inheritance is now required in order to safeguard and rebuild Heritage. It is time bloodline gave way to focus group. Fibreglass Lords and Ladies (suitably extended in terms of recruitment) will provide a stronger buttress for the still-crystallizing new élite. The latter's interests now require that Middle England be appeased and comforted on this important level of the old imagined commu-nity – not stirred up and worried by new and quite needless challenges.

A Prophet Ignored

Barnett's *This Time* had the misfortune to be proposing the non-available answer: revolution. Its whole tone was damnably and deliberately un-British, even though – as the author patiently explains a number of times – he is actually trying to save Britain in a more serious sense, by acting pre-emptively against threats of secessionist or exclusionary nationalism. Such a noble wish still leaves out something indispensable. To be recast in 21st century constitutional mode, Britain must first be saved from the British. Unfortunately, Blairism is at bottom last-ditch Britishness, and this turning was rapidly defining itself during the very months when Barnett's clarion-call was making its way through the presses. By the time it was published, the current of renovation had already clearly gone into contraflow.

During the decades of the Right, when Charter 88 got going, radicalizing Britain had seemed to mean saving Ukania from demented economists, fake Americanizers and astrological mis-readings of Adam Smith. After May 1997, its sense abruptly shifted: Britain had now to be saved by the Left. But no longer by the stalwart old Left, still vaguely comparable to the Austrian Social Democrats – patrician to the heart, liberal-imperial, Protestant, morality-encrusted. Such had been the party of Attlee, Stafford Cripps, Lord Callaghan and (ultimately) of John Smith. But that lay now in the grave alongside these gentlemen.

In its place there stood general disorientation in search of legitimacy. The new Blairite 'Left' remained so by historic descent and affiliation, and yet had cast aside almost everything related to previous British left-wing ideology, in order to gain power. There was no successor ideology to 'British Socialism'. No one could have accomplished such a feat in the short time following John Smith's death in 1994 – least of all in a world where State Socialism was still in accelerating and general retreat. Thus the idea-free inheritor could only be a vanguard of hungry but somewhat empty 'modernizers' . . . still in search of their own blueprint of modernity. It stood condemned to compose such 'modernity' on the hoof, in other words. Many of its policies were simply appropriated from the earlier, popular phase of Thatcherism – lessons wisely if ungratefully learnt, and accompanied by the firm intention of never returning to Old-Left corporatism and dependency. But this alone would never a New Age make. A stronger display-identity was needed: hence the 'virtual revolution', and the cacophony of polyhedrons and post-modern circus-acts – the unconscious mimicry of Britain's great Central-European predecessor.

Even in decline, however, a social and State fabric remains far stronger than those who would change it by incantation. It is likely to reimpose itself, or most of itself. This is exactly what Anthony Barnett sensed might happen, if the will faltered, and what he was publishing his eloquent sermon against. The one guarantee against such underlying continuity (he maintained) was a new State, based upon a new Constitution; which entailed, for a time, an absolute priority of constitutional over other issues; which implied a government that would assert this priority over the economic and social-policy questions customarily central to British politics; which demanded that reform be made the sort of popular-national cause which Charter 88 had fought for over the previous decade.

These imperatives hang together. But if they failed to hang together, he could see they might all be defeated separately. And in such a defeat, even the positive piecemeal reforms applauded in the pages of *This Time* – devolution, Ireland, electoral reform, the opening to Europe, the Lords – would end up as survival-rafts rather than new departures. The British 'constitutional revolution' had to cohere; the trouble is that the *ancien régime* coheres as well, even after the battering it took during the 1980s, even so close to its quietus.

The collapse of party-political Conservatism in 1997 meant there was little for it to cling to but the new, raw, would-be élite. Which meant that in a quite novel sense (as we have seen) the way was open for New Labourism to at least temporarily become 'Britain' – that is, a replacement for the ruling class broken and demoralized by the grim abrasion and failures of the two decades since the late seventies. Much in the regimentation and rigidity of New Labour may have from the start responded to this challenge. Was its famous mobilization of the post-'94 period just to win an election? Or was it (as I have argued) about power in a much profounder, more salvationist sense – the stiffening of a now struggling collective instinct to keep the British polity going? Would 'modernization' come to mean basic survival, rather than the creative choice of futures which so much future-oriented rhetoric suggests?

The subsequent fate of Barnett's polemic surely supports a gloomier interpretation of events. His book fell straight into a black hole of indifference bordering on hostility. Its assumption had been a continuing, even a rising, tide of support for planned central change – for constitutionalism as the coherent and determined *raison d'être* of the new power. But what the book's reception showed was the almost total absence of such a tide. Far from captaining the onward momentum, Charter 88 was marginalized into a vaguely supporting rôle, a gadfly to the Left. Critics on the conventional Left denounced the government's failure or capitulation on social or economic matters, and particularly on welfare. But their emphasis was already the contrary of Barnett's. Governmental faltering over constitutional issues came to be perceived as secondary – even forgiveable. What was a written Constitution, after all, compared to the past achievements of Liberal-Left Britain? And compared to the grim necessities of welfare shrinkage and an underclass being attacked from above?

Thus in the early-Blairite cultural atmosphere there was a deadly mixture of toxic influences, all already hostile to plain Painite radicalism. On one hand a wing of nostalgics, voicing elegiac regret for past Socialist achievement, which they considered betrayed by the new administration. But their factional answer was self-evidently useless: resuscitation of the world now lost, or else invention of a new-model doctrine which (at least initially) could hardly help smelling and feeling awfully like the old one. Or on the other hand there was public-relations post-modernism: smart devices and conceptual ways around 'outmoded' problems or attitudes. The latter could, all too easily, be made to include dreary old nation-state constitutionalism. If everything solid is melting into the air in that sense, why bother trying to pin it down again into an old-fangled Constitution?

The prophetic admonition of *This Time* fell exactly between these current streams of thought. It clearly despised the tomb-cults of nostalgic Leftism, yet insisted that real novelty depended upon pushing through a few plain-talking, 'old-fashioned' reforms – the sort eschewed historically by the Britishness of both Left and Right. As if by slide-rule design, therefore, Barnett managed to utter what almost nobody at that moment of time wanted to hear. The most significant political diagnosis of Ukania's *fin-de-siècle* passed practically unnoticed amid the court gossip, the hand-wringing of defunct Socialism, and the deranged séance-mentality of William Hague's refugee Toryism.

One gets the sense from reading *This Time* that it will be small consolation to the author to have been right. While exhorting a new régime to get it right, he could not help cataloguing the ways it could go wrong. As he was writing, those ways piled up around him. By December 1997, when the book appeared, they loomed over him: the spectre of a less-than-half revolution, already contracting into its own compromises and conceits. Thatcher also had brought about a less-than-half redemption, which had ruined both her and her party. But this was even more serious. If as I have argued 'Blairism' is really a last-ditch attempt at maintaining the United Kingdom by the formation of a pot-noodle ruling class, then nothing much can be visible beyond it. In different ways the nations of the old composite State are likely to end by throwing it off; and afterwards, they will evolve into differing selves – the identities for so long occluded by the superimposition of Britishness. The fall from such an apotheosis can only be into depths as yet unplumbed. Whether or not the great renewal prospected in *This Time* was possible, its failure must leave us 'after Britain', in a genuinely post-imperial condition.

'Corporate Populism'

In the summer of 1998 Blair's government submitted an 'Annual Report' to the people. The business-style title was deliberate. It began with a 'ten-point contract', and a full page portrait of the Leader in his board-room (the Cabinet Room at 10 Downing Street). 'Changing a government is like sweeping away the entire senior management of a company', he announced. In spite of critics saying 'this Government is more concerned with style than substance', he insisted it had made a good start. To underline Board-room confidence the *Annual Report* was full of full-colour illustrations of customers, with improbable messages scrawled over them in white lettering – for example, a girl sitting in front of the Bank of England saying: 'I am pleased with changes that have been made and am looking forward to the improvements in the transport system.'

Barnett followed up *This Time* with an incisive account of the Report's assumptions. Unable to implement a new conception of the state, Blairism had defaulted to the model of a business company. Great Britain had in all earnest become what journalists had so often dubbed it in the past – Great Britain plc, 'the image of agency provided by big companies'. So Socialism had lapsed finally into 'corporate populism'. This is neither ancient subjecthood nor modern constitutional citizenship. It is more like a weak identity-hybrid, at a curious tangent to both. Voters are seen as customers (like the girl at the Bank of England), while the Party-Executive –

> . . . manages party, cabinet and civil service as if they were parts of a single giant company whose aim is to persuade voters that they are happy customers who want to return Labour to office.

This is certainly better than mere deference. After all, customers are expected to object and criticize a bit (even if most don't, most of the time). But then, by taking their protests into account, the management normally expects to reinforce its own market share. It is 'the modernization of subjecthood', rather than a replacement for it. The Sovereign Crown gives way to the Managing Director and his unanimous executive Board, devoted at once to profitability and (again in *Annual Report* language) to Britain 'regaining its pride and ambition, at home and abroad' and telling the right story at all times: 'we are a great nation, filled with creative, innovative, compassionate people' (pp. 8–9). A great nation, but much more emphatically a capitalist one. Where the Poll Tax had failed, an *Annual Report* now appeared to be signalling success.

So here was the economic vector of archaism, seriously at work. Mrs Thatcher's 'economic revolution' was still advancing, and no longer beneath the level of the state. Thanks to the English economy's traditional strength – the global force of the City of London and finance-capital – economic modernization was still possible, and still comparatively effective. Manufacturing modernization was far less attainable, and in fact had been largely abandoned under Thatcher. But the remainder was capable of taking over the ideological garb of statehood at least for a time – a 'business' nation if no longer an industrial one, appealing to a business-minded folk. Cost-effective-conscious to the core, New-Labour Britishers no longer needed *un plebiscite de tous les jours*, Ernest Renan's 19th century formula for civic nationalism – daily reaffirmation of the French, American or other dream through moments of pride and aspiration. Now, a daily visit to the supermarket would do just as well, coupled with daily reminders of Sterling's strength and the foreign conquests of British 'world-class' business. Blair was right: style is substance, it sells things in the global super-market and guarantees cybernetic prosperity. This is also why the Millenium Dome is identified with the national interest.

'Corporate populism' is absolute philistinism. Another reason for the business class to support New Labour, of course, but one which seems inseparable from a frightful risk. Its apparatus of consumers and 'stakeholders' mimics democracy, substituting brand-loyalty and ordinariness for hope and glory. This can seem possible, even attractive, *while things go well* in the narrowly economic terms to which the creed awards priority. Even then there may be a resentful underclass that has no stake, and public sector or non-commercial enterprises which fall behind; but rapid growth for the majority cushions and con-ceals these downsides. When the growth-momentum ceases, however, such compensatory effects are likely to vanish totally.

People will then have to fall back on the non-corporate, less than cost-effective nation – on a national community and state as Renan (and so many others) have perceived them. That is, on communal faith and justice, the extended family of egalitarian dreams. Everyone knows that a corporation will not 'support' customers in any comparable sense, beyond the limits of profitability; but everyone feels that is exactly what a nation should do. Brand-loyalty is precisely *not* 'belonging' in the more visceral sense associated with national identity. Indeed it easily becomes the opposite of belonging: sell-out, Devil take the hindmost, moving on (or out) to maintain profitability. Since the national factor cannot really be costed, it is easily caricatured as a question of soulful romanticism or delusion. However, such common sense is itself philistine. It fails to recognize something crucial. When Marks & Spencer betrays its customers the result is an annoyance; for a nation-state to let its citizens down can be a question of life or death, and not in wartime alone.

Peoples have not 'imagined' such communities by chance, or out of irrational impulsions from the soul. 'Identities' are not aesthetic choices but ways of existing, or of trying to exist better. This is the 'nation' which has counted in modern, nationalist times, and it is not very like the portraits in Blair's *Annual Report*. The national-popular has generally been not-so-great, hard done by, struggling, threatened, at war, filled with not always 'creative' and sometimes angry people who think they can't afford so much compassion, and look around for redemptive leadership. They turn to the nation of war memorials, oaths, poetry, sacrifice and mythic blood. It is the coiner of the phrase 'imagined community', Benedict Anderson, who has himself underlined the contrast between these two worlds in a recent essay, 'The Goodness of Nations'. Democracies must feel themselves more than the data of Annual Reports, even euphoric ones. He uses an odd selection of things to make the point – the war memorial at New Haven, Connecticut, an episode of The Simpsons, the North Indian 'celibacy movement' – but since he wrote post-1997 Britain may already have supplied a more telling one.

It is given by the contrast mentioned earlier, between the popular reaction to the death of the Princess of Wales and New Labour's response – the reaction typified, about a year later, by this *Annual Report*. In late-August to September 1997 the living (in Anderson's terminology) were in the streets and trying, however sentimentally and confusedly, to 'secure the Rightness of the country' and reorient it away from the shame of a rotten decade. A year later, they had become ridiculous illustrations in a kind of annual *Sales Report*. Populism had already been recuperated and rendered respectable, and also given this small-minded and neo-liberal cast. Somehow, business as usual had resumed, and Normalcy been enhanced as never before, carrying forward much of Mrs Thatcher's *Geist* but with the added panache and excitement of a new sales drive. 'Britain' was buzzing once more, but the sound was a reassuring one: safety-first *redressement* rather than the unsettling music of republican constitutionalism.

'England and . . .'

Just how safe the *Annual Report* country is meant to become was convincingly shown in early 1999. Although Scotland is the biggest problem for Blairland, Wales remains its closest neighbour. As well as the physical intimacy of a long north-south marchland, the two countries were historically united by early conquest and absorption. In the modern era that union of unequals has normally been awarded a strange name of its own, which appears in all legal documents where it is necessary to

treat Scotland, Northern Ireland or other dependencies separately: 'England-and-Wales'. The term conveys a bare
modicum of recognition with an associated stress on functional
unity. Whatever gestures may be needed elsewhere, here we
have two who are truly as one.

The post-imperial return of Wales has therefore been very
distinct from that of Scotland. It has resembled much more
closely the typical ethno-linguistic trajectory of repressed
nationhood – cultural mobilization directed towards nation-
building and the eventual formation of a state. After Blair's
electoral victory of 1997 a first Welsh Parliament was part of the
pay-off. This was conceived quite differently from the
Edinburgh one – as a 'first-instalment', non-legislative body
with executive control over the existing Welsh Office budget
but otherwise limited to debating and offering advice. When it
came to power, the Cardiff 'National Assembly' members were
to be consumers indeed. In the Year 2000 *Annual Report* they
will no doubt have their own colour-spread and appropriate
pseudo-critique, most likely along the lines of – 'So far so good
in Wales, but give us more . . .' (something or other . . . roads,
language facilities, Life Peers).

But six months before the National Assembly met, the
New England-and-Wales was already in trouble. The
Assembly was conceived as a voice. But the trouble with
allowing a national voice to speak up is that it may say something. Alas, speech can indeed be a form of action. It may
even say (do) something disagreeable or (as in this case) something vexingly Welsh. Blair's reading of the old Austro-Marxist
runes made cultural Welshness a blessing, naturally. But only
provided it did not impinge upon the profounder peace signalled by the 'and' of England-and-Wales, whereby England
will go on conducting the orchestra to which choir and harp
would continue to make their traditional contribution.

In 1997 and early 1998 the Welsh Assembly plan was guided by the Welsh Secretary of State (and leader of the Welsh Labour Party) Ron Davies. He led the successful cross-party campaign for a 'Yes' vote which reversed the decision of a previous referendum in 1979. Critics commented on the narrowness of the victory, compared to Scotland, but usually overlooked the huge shift in opinion it represented. Mr Davies himself never made this mistake. He frequently emphasized the continuing trend, as distinct from the arrangements of any one moment. 'Devolution is a process, not an event' was his way of putting this.

Such an attitude might in time have boded ill for London, but we shall never know, for Davies was prematurely struck down in the summer of 1998. It was not a London omnibus or a fatal illness that did for him, but scandal. The after-effects of an ill-understood fracas on Clapham Common forced his resignation as Government Minister, party leader – and almost certainly first Prime Minister of the new Assembly in 1999. A successor had unexpectedly to be elected. And this accident of history cast a revealing light on how Devolution was now regarded at Westminster.

For Blair and his Cabinet, Devolution is emphatically an event, not a process. Nothing could have been done about Ron Davies. He came with the territory and had been responsible for the referendum success. But after his disgrace they were determined no other process-merchant would take his place: only the safest and most pliable of Leaders would do – preferably someone impeccably British, and 'not too keen' on the whole autonomy project. They had had to change the British Constitution in Northern Ireland for the sake of a Peace 'process', and were extremely disinclined to do so again to placate a new form of local government in England's oldest internal colony. A line had now to be drawn.

Once more, the actual phenomenon of Blairism at work pre-empts any conceivable satire. Suppose a hostile Tory commentator had written something like this, for example: 'Power-freak Blair, like the tin-pot dictator he actually is, has chosen the most notoriously supine, cardboard figure in the Welsh Party to do his bidding, using every rotten trick in the old Party rule-book to get his own way while continuing to rant about reform and third-way democracy – just the way Eastern Europe used to be!' He would, alas, only have been saying in tabloid-speak what every other journalist was then to write in his or her own fashion. In *The Times* William Rees-Mogg put it this way:

Wales has been insulted . . . by the way in which the choice of Leader for the Assembly has been manipulated. When Tony Blair was chosen as Leader of the Labour Party, the trade union section of the electoral college operated 'one man, one vote'. When Alun Michael was chosen Labour Leader for Wales, the majority of the trade unions returned to the old block vote principle. Three trade union leaders were sufficient to cast the votes which gave Alun Michael his victory . . .

Thus in the end a resounding majority of actual Welsh members voted for Rhodri Morgan, a well-educated dissident with trouble written all over him; and Mr Michael was wheeled on to centre-stage by traditional Old Corruption, amid a tropical downpour of Radical and New-Life protestations. As Rees-Mogg concluded, a great number of those whose vote was scorned in this way were likely to think '. . . devolution to Wales is a sham, a cover for the maintenance of English supremacy, enforced by the Blairite rigging of the leadership election', and turn to Plaid Cymru. Six months later, at the first elections, they did so turn.

It was not as if the government's attitude was confined to Wales. Although less crassly, analogous pressures were being applied in Scotland as well, and also in London around the selection of Labour's candidate for the new Mayor. At the same time a BBC *Panorama* documentary was broadcast on just this wider theme, and gave a convincing picture of a régime back-pedalling furiously to undo, or at least restrain, some of the awkward political consequences of Devolution. A general counter-revolution was under way designed to preserve 'England and . . .' everywhere else too, in approximately their traditional rôles within the mystery-play of Britishness. Too many voters had been taken in, concluded Rees-Mogg. They had thought the rhetoric was authentic and 'believed that the three "D" words – Devolution, Diversity and Democracy – meant something, were more than mere slogans . . . Neither in Wales, Scotland nor in London does that now appear to be true.' Peter Preston arrived at a similar verdict in the same day's *Guardian*:

> The troubles that begin to flow in irksome abundance – resurgent Scots Nationalists, roaring Rhodri, taunting Ken – are not, it is becoming clear, isolated events. They are part of a structure. They won't go away . . .'

England's England

The 'structure' Preston complains of is 'Britain' or, more accurately, England's Britain. Unshed save in emptily radical terms, this armature of fate was bound to reassert itself after the shocks of 1997. There are now too many examples of it even to list, and some of them will appear later in this book. The core of the problem is that behind England's Britain there lies

England's England, the country which has not merely 'not spoken yet' but, in effect, refrained from speaking because a British-imperial class and ethos have been in possession for so long of its vocal cords. A class has spoken for it. This is the evident sense in which England has been *even more* affected and deformed by imperial globalization than other parts of the archipelago.

I referred earlier to Richard Jefferies's strange vision of the wilderness that might come 'after London'. Stranger still is the fantasy which recently took the same path one hundred and ten years later, Julian Barnes's *England, England.* This imagines the former culture not simply emigrating or disappearing as in Jefferies's case, but being transplanted in theme-park form to the Isle of Wight. Sir Jack Pitman, a business and media tycoon reminiscent of Robert Maxwell, 'reconstructs' Englishness on the island, complete with a downsized Westminster, Windsor, Manchester United, White Cliffs, Imperialism, Harrods, whingeing, etc. Invented tradition is everywhere, like 'the old English custom of downing a pint of Old Skullsplitter with a twiglet up each nostril'. 'We are not talking heritage centre', he rumbles, 'we are offering *the thing itself . . .*' This project is disastrously successful, and declares independence as a microstate of truly corporate populism. Meanwhile, the real 'real England', a mainland thus deprived of its essence, sinks slowly backwards into time. 'Anglia' takes over from Britain. 'Quaintness, diminution, failure' create a different landscape, possessed by a new-old innocence and goodness:

> Chemicals drained from the land, the colours grew gentler, and the light untainted; the moon, with less competition, now rose more dominantly. In the enlarged countryside, wildlife bred freely. Hares multiplied; deer and boar were released into the woods from game farms; the urban fox

returned to a healthier diet of bloodied, pulsing flesh. Common land was re-established; fields and farms grew smaller; hedgerows were replanted . . .

Martha Cochrane, who has abandoned Isle-of-Wight England for this arcadia, asks herself 'if a nation could reverse its course and its habits', but of course the answer is her own life in this country isolated from Europe and the world, in which items are again 'sold by the hundredweight, stone and pound for amounts expressed in pounds, shillings and pence', where 'four-lane motorways peter out into woodland, with a gypsy caravan titupping over the lurched, volcanic tarmac', and thunder has regained its divinity.

In *This Time* Anthony Barnett acknowledged the necessity of English reaffirmation as part of the new constitutional process. It has to be more than the rebranding advocated by Mark Leonard's Demos pamphlet *BritainTM* (1997), which would amount to acquiescing in Jack Pitman's futurescape. Such 'modernization of the theme park' won't do, even given the *rayonnement* of the Millenium Dome. Nor is 'mongrelization' a solution – that is, a self-conscious embracing of multicultural diversity in preference to ethnic majority nativism. That was argued for in Philip Dodd's *The Battle Over Britain* (1996), where ethnic minorities and regional identities capture the dissolved essence of the nation and remanifest it as an inherently variegated democracy. But such a 'preference' has to be *expressed*. How can it be shown, without a constitutional mode of expression, and a prior redefinition of Sovereignty? Democracy is not popular instinct or the simple prevalence of a majority: it is a constitution, or nothing. If this is not put first, then it will come last – and quite possibly too late.

In *The Times* of 12 February (coinciding with the devolutionary débâcle in Wales) Political Editor Philip Webster announced something else. It was like a cloud the size of a man's hand, in a diminutive box on page 10. But behind it lies a great storm, gathering below the horizon: 'Beckett to give England a Voice'. Mrs Beckett's Ministerial plan is to 'give England a distinct voice in Parliament after Scottish and Welsh devolution' by setting up a committee of English MPs. Although humbly named the 'Standing Committee on Regional Affairs' there is no one in Scotland, Wales or Ireland who will be deceived for a second by this: it would be the *de facto* English Parliament, convened on its own for the first time since 1546 (when Wales was formally incorporated). Since no provision was made for the majority in Blair's radical project, it will be forced to make its own, erupting bit by bit, using disguise and alias, proceeding through an obstacle course of tactical accidents and afterthoughts. The Government's 'Modernisation Select Committee' was supposed to agree Mrs Beckett's scheme and (the report concluded) 'will almost certainly back the idea'.

Whether it does or not, evolution in that sense is unavoidable. On that plane, Tam Dalyell's old 'West Lothian Question' was certainly not mistaken, even if he himself drew so many mistaken conclusions from it. The impact of Scottish and Welsh self-government upon the former constitution of the United Kingdom is bound to be significant. The Parliamentary élite will be disrupted in its business, even if the majority of voters remains indifferent. A disruption of the Establishment will be translated into a concern, even a scandal, for the masses. All issues will be seen as aggravated, if not provoked, by ill-considered changes on the periphery. Since these cannot be undone, the centre itself will have to act, and affirm its own rights. The Standing Committee of English Members will be called upon to speak, and not in a hushed Select-Committee monotone. It will speak for England, the people and nation, and its very informality – its air of having arisen from the regional ranks – may bestow upon the body a spontaneous, even revolutionary appearance: 'It's time someone spoke out!'– and stopped 'them' having things all their own way.

Populism like this finds its own way to nationalism, and there is nothing new or inherently harmful in that. However, it would have been better to plan for it, by putting a coherent, overall constitutional change *first*, rather than leaving it in this way to the uncertain and possibly uncontrollable last. An intelligible *Grundgesetz* would at least have paved part of the way towards equality of representation and treatment. In Austria-Hungary the Germans may not have wanted such equality, but at least they had the choice: nobody pretended they were not there, or 'took them for granted' in that curious sense which has dogged Englishness throughout the long decline of Britain.

It is from this occlusion that the dominant scenarios of English futurity seem to have come. On one hand the idea of reversion to an irrecoverable rurality – the natural wilderness or village condition of a post-British culture. On the other, the more advanced (but also more negative) longing for a virtual dissolution of identity into multiculturalism or 'Europe' – meaning here a broader identity-format within which nations somehow disperse or painlessly cease to matter.

There is no available formula for a post-British England: the issue has simply been avoided in these ways. It would have been better tackled straightforwardly, as Charter 88 demanded – and yet this was impossible, because of the very nature of the old system to which the Charterites were forced to appeal. Hence it can only be done in a crabwise, half-avowed and belated fashion. Blair's Project makes it likely that England will return on the street corner, rather than via a maternity room with appropriate care and facilities. Croaking tabloids, saloon-bar resentment and back-bench populism are likely to

attend the birth and to have their say. Democracy is constitutional or nothing. Without a systematic form, its ugly cousins
will be tempted to move in and demand their rights – *their*
nation, the one always sat upon and then at last betrayed by an
élite of faint-hearts, half-breeds and alien interests.

In the Spring of 1999 war conditions gave some renewed
vitality to the Project, as they had done to Mrs Thatcher's in
1982. The true history of the Kosovo conflict has hardly been
started at the time of writing, so no informed judgement on
Britain's (and Blair's) rôle is yet possible. But what has happened so far suggests a great amplification of leadership
charisma – far beyond what the Tory crusade gained from their
government's actual defeat of Argentina seventeen years ago.
New Labour acted only as part of an alliance, and Blair as the
most flamboyant and pugnacious part of its 'war party'. When
asked on a Channel 4 news programme whether the Serbian
withdrawal had 'gone to his head' Mr Blair replied in his usual
diffident, boyish manner that he didn't think so, and that experience had shown him how 'what goes up must come down'.

The previous evening's New Labour election broadcast (for
the Euro-elections taking place the same week) had been
entirely focused on his function as Great Leader, with a *vox pop*
gallery of adulation accompanied by scenes of cheering crowds
and admiring foreign statesmen. Although her rapport with
Ronald Reagan had in some way prefigured Blair's to Clinton,
Mrs Thatcher never came near this level of straightforward
star-worship. The suggestion was that Blair has become Leader
of both the West and Europe, as well as reconciler of Ireland
and liberator of Wales and Scotland. An Empire restored
indeed: in 1982 it took Thatcher another year to win a general
election on the wave of her bellicose popularity, but by that
time the war had already won two contests for New Labour –
the first Scottish election, and the new election to Strasbourg.

But a more extensive analysis of this process is impossible here, where I must focus on what is likely to be its main polarizing contrast: the return of Scotland after 1999, from its own peculiar sort of invisibility. The Union from which England too must fall was a complex phenomenon, involving a variety of formal and customary relationships with the Irish of both South and North, the Welsh, the Cornish, and the inhabitants of the Channel Islands, Man and the Northern Isles. However, it has also rested since 1707 upon one crucial armature, the Treaty of Union with the Scots. In the Hapsburg imperium there was no one link as important and as long-preserved as this one – or at least, not until the 1867 settlement with Hungary, which itself became a precursor of the state's downfall. For Britain, on the contrary, the Union Treaty was a precondition of imperial success and expansion over two and a half centuries. Yet (I will argue) nothing now appears more certain than its imminent end.

CHAPTER TWO

The Return of Scotland

Nomad, pity's statistic,
He journeyed into back-time, a ditch-lord's
Anachronism. Time turned into place.
Society gave up its ghost,
Geography its nationhood;
He put on hodden grey and climbed
Into resistant solitude.

Douglas Dunn, 'Moorlander' in
Dante's Drum-kit (1993)

In The Time Before

It's a great honour to be with you today, for this collective celebration.* Seventy years represents a conventional lifetime, what used to be considered ripe old age. But things have changed, and are continuing to change under our feet. For the Scottish National Party, three-score-and-ten represents a new beginning. It comes just before the realization of the party's historic aim, or at least of the main part of it – a self-rule quite capable of becoming independence, if that is what most of the nation turns out to want.

As the well-kent ballad demands, one has to think again.

* An address given in Edinburgh on 16 January 1999, at a party for the seventieth anniversary of the founding of the Scottish National Party in 1928. I am grateful to George Reid and William Wolfe for their invitation to the event, and for agreeing to the publication of the address here.

What this moment imposes is nothing less than a different sense of history. Seventy years is a long time in individual terms but also a fairly short one within the three-hundred-year span which, simultaneously, cannot help coming into view here – that is, from 1707 to the present. This span of time is already beginning to look like a single episode. It is turning into the long moment during which, exceptionally, Scotland did *not* have its own parliament and state.

A very short time ago it took a great effort of will and imagination to see our history that way. Now, suddenly, everyone can do it, and is doing it, practically effortlessly. A day-ticket to the new Museum of Scotland is enough. Twenty minutes or so over there will show what independence – and indeed 'independence in Europe' – once meant, within a building whose very existence and architectural sense do far more than reverently contain a national past. I know much of the timing of the Museum's appearance has been coincidence. None the less, its strange mixture of feudal keep and spaceship somehow fits exactly the moment we are in.

Gordon Benson's great tower of the past stands where Chambers Street joins 'George IV Bridge'. Why does this latter name so suddenly feel odd, even comic? Because Walter Scott's favoured Dynasty is now struggling to survive a time that neither of them could imagine? This is a tower which invites one into more than history – and so warmly and confidently. The interior which one then enters is also an unfolding one – the theatre of a new time which I don't think will be so quickly outmoded, either architecturally or politically.

As the end of the British Union nears, everything in it already starts to look different. Rather than looking at the history of this Party, therefore – too many people here know infinitely more about that than I ever will – I have been looking at the longer term. Looking (in fact) at the bizarre history of the Scottish state, how it 'went into recess' nearly three centuries ago, and how it is returning from limbo today. It went into hibernation under Queen Anne, and is gradually coming round again under Queen Elizabeth I and II – more important, into the falling world of the latter's chief servant, Anthony Blair. I've been looking at the accounts given by some of the protagonists – like Sir John Clerk of Penicuik and George Lockhart of Carnwath – as well as those of later historians like Walter Scott, David Daiches, Christopher Harvie and Michael Lynch.

The Moral Fable of Union

Not much is now likely to be uncovered about the facts of the Union; but what counts most today is surely just how different – even utterly different – the story now feels. It's true that a familiar sort of moral rage remains inseparable from any re-reading of it. I at least find I still can't help applauding the patriots and hissing the villains. Even Unionist scholars have usually been affected by the sheer concentration of what must be called (in today's terms, the lingo of imploding Union) 'sleaze and cronyism', in the Scottish Parliaments of 1703 to 1707. The two-faced Duke of Hamilton, the nostalgic hypocrisy of Lord Seafield's 'auld sang', Andrew Fletcher's staunch but futile defence of (as it were) Lib-Dem federalism, the antics of the '*squadrone volante*' (the semi-organized turncoats, or 'cross-benchers' as they would say at Westminster), and in the background the sound of Joe's drum up and down Edinburgh High Street, calling futilely for popular protest against élite betrayal. There will always be something irresistible about this folk-tale of conspiracy and sell-out.

But all the same, something has evaporated from it today – as if one didn't need to blame and hiss the villains quite so much.

In the longer arc of time, they have been proved wrong, and are already retreating behind a veil of real distance. In 1707 it was intended that the Scottish nation retreat into history in that way. Instead, it is the agents of its subordination who have ended up in aspic, beyond the glass of living resentment or condemnation. Not (it's still important to say) in ignominy or oblivion. That would be misplaced. Most of them were never just 'traitors' (not even those who suddenly paid off their debts after 1707). By and large they thought it was for the best; and they have only proved wrong in terms which extended far beyond their own lifetimes, into the last phase of the British imperium.

The Union is normally dated from May 1707, when the official celebrations were held. However, the decisive date was the Second Reading in the Scottish Parliament. That took place on – yes – 16 January, two hundred and ninety-two years ago today. On that day one of the Members, George Lockhart, absented himself from Parliament Hall. He knew this would be the final vote, 'the last day Scotland was Scotland', and he could not bear to be there. This determined Lanarkshire Jacobite and Episcopalian has suffered from a rather bad press over the whole Union period, and often been dismissed (even by writers like David Daiches) as 'intemperate' or as an incurable 'romantic'.

Well . . . I don't know – it's true he never changed his mind about the last day, or about the Stuart cause, and undeniably Lockhart suffered from (let's say) a rather exaggerated aversion to the Presbyterian clergy. But Ministers apart, there is not much in the *Memoirs* which will strike a contemporary reader as over-romantic or fanatical. Lockhart was re-elected as Member for the 'shire of Edinburgh' to the first Great-British Parliament after the Treaty, and spent much of his time down in London attempting to do what the SNP members there are still doing today – that is, trying to get out of it. It is worth quoting his own account of the

motion for the Dissolution of the Union which he aired in a letter
to the other Scottish representatives in the year 1712.

Five years on from the Union he reminded the others that
real equality of treatment was not obtainable within the newly
united Kingdom, hence 'If matters stood long on such a foot-
ing, the ruine and misery of Scotland was unavoidable . . .
(and) . . . there was consequently no way under the sun to prevent future misery but by breaking of these shackles and
redeeming ourselves out of this state of bondage'. It was time
to 'look forwards not backwards' and for every man to put his
helping hand to 'draw us out of the ditch we were fallen into,
which alone could be accomplished by dissolving the Union'.
How was this to be accomplished? 'I submit myself to the
judgement of others' (he continues) –

> . . . but in my opinion it ought first to be demanded and
> attempted by the same method it was establisht, I mean by
> a legal parliamentary way; and that the Parliament of Great
> Britain could dissolve its united constitution by restoring the
> two kingdoms to their former distinct states, as well as these
> two states had dissolved their several constitutions by con-
> joining and incorporating them into one and the same, was
> by parity of reason undeniable . . .

Although his motion was supported by most Scottish members (including by some who had enjoyed sudden post-1707
prosperity) Lockhart knew quite well there was little chance of
getting it accepted then and there. But he went on to add,
movingly, that –

> . . . as I make no question but, some time or other, the Scots
> nation would assert and, I hope, recover their liberties, it
> becomes us to show them a good example, and I reckon it a

good step towards dissolving the Union, if it was once fairly
tabled and sett agoing . . .

It cheers one up to read this sort of thing, and see a forgotten
remark out of a distant archive becoming tomorrow's news.
But at the same time one can't help feeling a new mixture of
sadness and anger, something rather different from the retrospective morality-play of the 1707 heroes and villains. The
Laird of Carnwath could not know that it would take two hundred and eighty-five years to set his project properly a-going.
And this was to be partly because by then something else had
started up, also unknowable – or at least, unknowable in its
implications – by him or by any of the other protagonists.

The River of Loss

On that damnable 16 January in 1707 when the Treaty was
approved, it was as if an underground stream had welled up. At
first a trickle in Parliament Hall, it swelled before long into a
dark river of doubt, incertitude and helpless postponement.
Today one realizes with a start how familiar this is, only five
years later, at the time we find Lockhart planning his motion.
The waters of an equivocal, half-resentful and yet inescapable
dependency were even then above the knees of him and his
fellow-resisters, and still rising. We were already into a threatened eternity of half-life, as it were, what turned into the limbo
beyond Scotland's 'last day'.
	Scotland was a society which by 1707 had been a state for far
too long – about half a millennium – to cease being one. And
yet (of course) it had to, after the fateful decision, at least in the
primary sense proclaimed by the Parliamentary Treaty. This
made the new Union government responsible for 'high

politics', in the sense of all dignified or important matters like war and peace, taxation, and foreign relations. Other things were left to the Scottish institutions – legal and local administration, property, schooling, and so on.

Mind you, it can't be said that everything left in national hands was 'low' or less dignified, since 1707's 'Devolution' included the care of souls. The Church of Scotland was established at the same time (to Lockhart's annoyance) as principal curator of the people's inner being, thus guaranteeing a national stamp upon the heavens as well as on the parish pump. That enabled Unionists to argue, then as now, that 'what really counts' remains our own: the hearth and the hereafter. I suppose the only real change is that 'souls' are today viewed somewhat differently. Salvation has been to some extent replaced by the idea of 'culture'. At that time the de-statified Scots were urged to be content with true piety and the afterlife; now they are encouraged to keep out of trouble by indulging in the secular cultivation of literature and the arts. When it comes to commendable self-expression, Godliness has given way to the Booker Prize, Scottish Television and Runrig.

But however one judges such particular consequences, they amounted to a permanent and institutionalized division of both corporate and individual *identity*. Nobody in the 18th century used the latter term, which is of recent coinage. The fact long preceded the word, however, and we can see it operating more clearly in retrospect. As a collective identity or 'community', a nation is in fact defined by a complex skein of relationships between 'high' and 'low', and in the case of a small and ancient nation such relationships were close.[1] Their permanent dislocation could not fail to produce an analogous disruption of outlook and judgement, a sundered mentality which henceforth had to function on two levels.

This was the metaphorical wound out of which the

underground stream had surged, as from a structural and now inescapable disablement. In the longer reach of time it is what appears as the river of loss: corrosive, numbing, and seeping relentlessly through the foundations of every Scottish generation since then.[2] Though unmentioned in the words of the Treaty, it was the true mortgage paid for entry into its new House of Westminster. And it was to be paid 'for all time coming', the unredeemable pledge of a subordinate and half-recognized existence. Walter Scott called it Scotland's 'quiet way' – a side or dependent way into modernity, as it were, bargain-price progress without the stresses of statehood. 'Quiet': as per the regulations of secular quietism – ancillary, auxiliary, lieutenant-like, Boswellish, first-secretarial, taken-care-of, sound under fire and in the engine-room. There have been worse fates, as nostalgic Unionists constantly remind us.

Yes – and better ones too. I think the main (and so often unacknowledged) fact to recall here is that an equivalently unredeemable resentment was always inseparable from such a deal. This is not for one minute to ignore or discount the advantages – and notably the economic advantages – which the Scots in the long run obtained from being joined up with the English in the British Empire. These were in fact far greater than the most enthusiastic original protagonists of Union could have dreamt. It is simply to point out that they have consistently been obtained at a certain cost, and with certain associated disadvantages which – in the still longer run – have outlasted and at last eclipsed material prosperity. The maimed state-nation of the Scots has outlasted the Empire. As it comes to itself once more, I think it is the view back over that over-long half-life which brings one to the different, retrospective anger I mentioned earlier. For goodness' sake, the time for all *that* is surely over.

This has – once and for all, and I think it can now be said

with a certain impatience – nothing to do with 'ethnicity', or with aversion to English people as individuals, still less to suppurating nonsense about blood and descent. The resentment inseparable from it has been hatred of a collective situation, which has always embodied an unhealthy measure of self-hatred too – since of course our own ancestors helped to create the situation, and for long collaborated eagerly with it. But it's over. Isn't that what this National Party stands for? Recognizing that it's over, and long past time to act on the knowledge? To the new Scottish Parliament will fall the first burden of that shift; but the burden seems to me actually a great honour. We are lucky enough to live in the moment of Scotland's return – the day when (in Douglas Dunn's metaphor) the moorlander comes down at last from his surly back-time solitude, the internal exile accompanying the brassy assertion of Britishness.

The petty counter-resentments of the moment don't matter. Some of these do merit contempt; and I'm all for letting them have what they deserve – but I don't want to plunge back into that today. There has been too much point-scoring acrimony over the last thirty years, most in this room will be tired of it, I know I am.

Misunderstanding Identity

One of the features of New Labour's campaign against independence has been a consistent denigration of 'identity'. The Chancellor of the Exchequer, for instance, accused this Party of attaching far too much importance to it, rather than to the substantial issues of social and economic policy which Holyrood ought to focus upon. What the Scots need, he argued recently, is more money spent on education and health, not the mere appearances of 'the old nation state':

The real battle next May will be between those who put
the politics of social justice first, and those who practise the
politics of national identity above anything else . . .[3]

The implication here is of course that social justice and social
policy deal with 'real' problems while the politics of identity is
about posturing and irrelevant display – having ambassadors
and an army, being 'recognized' elsewhere, and so forth.

Chancellor Brown's contraposition of broad-minded 'realism' and narrow or fanatical 'delusions' is the oldest item in the
Unionist book. Regrettably I must point out it is itself based
upon a philistine illusion. Based, that is, on the conviction that
the economic or budgetary problems of the moment are self-
evidently far more significant than long-term considerations of
power and persistent collective consciousness. Actually, they
never are. 'Identity' is about just these persistent factors
which – to put it mildly – have proved far more enduring than
the economic waves of the British Union.

Previous generations were informed in the same self-
important tones – the Chamber-speak of Westminster – that
Imperial Free Trade and colonization were the crushingly significant and material matters which made self-rule irrelevant.
Then it was the turn of Scottish heavy industry and mining. Oh
yes, how well one recalls the absolute necessity of preserving
these, something achievable only by first Liberal then Labour
loyalty. Unswerving Britishness was always the serious, practical
answer. No more of that romantic, backward-looking dreaming
and literary dithering: as all the world knows, the Scots are a
hard-headed, bread-and-butter race too sensible for nationalism.

It was not so. Today we can see that as a matter of the merest
historical fact it was the practical concerns that were the narrow
illusions of a day. They came, and they went – dressed to kill
(as Dunn has also put it) in the thunderous identity-modes of

Britannic supremacism, Royalty and self-regard. And we can be sure that New Labour's equivalent – the comparatively puny array of bribes and enticements outlined in the Chancellor's pamphlet – will come and go much sooner than they did.

What has persisted through and underneath all these, however, is the underlying structure of the dismembered nation – the ruined or deconstructed polity of 1707, as it were – and the mentality of division or incompletion which has always accompanied it. This is what I meant earlier by loss: the corrosive and disabling stream that has coursed through Scottish society – and in a sense through the veins of every individual – since that time. I know talk of this kind is liable to evoke Freud, or even Jung and W.B. Yeats: the mythology of a national unconscious. But actually no great excursions into that cloudy realm are required: we have all endured this familiar all our lives and know him only too well. He is none other than the Scots' most famous and unshakable drinking companion: 'lack of self-confidence'. This is Douglas Dunn's 'Moorlander', the anachronism crouched miserably in the collective mentality of modern Scotland, running like the 'black water' of absent chronicles and unresolved transactions.

Everyone has lamented this crapulous, cringing swine each day of my own time, and for damned good reason. It will take more than a few platitudes to save him now. Absence of self-confidence is only the natural condition of a social formation whose collective or historical 'self' has been partly lobotomized and partly placed in cold storage. That is, the inveterate state of a nation never destroyed but permitted half-life within relatively unalterable parameters – low-pressure or 'low-political' autonomy founded on good behaviour at home, around the hearth, and then amply rewarded by the external (imperial) life-support system, the sustaining outward *habitus* of Britishness.

Everyone here knows this toad on our backs, and also his historical and psychological quirks. Obliged to follow rather than lead, he has been smartly servile on one hand but often, by a sort of compensation, wildly aggressive and chest-beating on the other. Different generations have manifested this inherited dilemma and its famously 'split personality' in many different ways, and I will not (you will be glad to hear) try to recount their history again today – through the Enlightenment, 19th century Empire-building and emigration, militarism and so on.[4] But I can't resist singling out one consistent and fairly central current within the stream, which has been less noticed: *shame*.

Shame is by its nature drawn to concealment and circuitous or reluctant expression. It tends to be betrayed rather than voiced or honestly commented upon. Salman Rushdie's great story with this name, *Shame*, is a wonderful depiction of its machinery and effects in the Indian Subcontinent. It is part of the explanation of why the Scots have often understood themselves so badly – and at the same time made it difficult for outsiders to understand them. Some things just can't be tolerated, and so have to be pretended away, grinningly made light of or kept out of view. The 'Moorlander' is like a shadow on the map in Dunn's poem, a truth fearful in part because occluded –

That fast corner of darkness
That was on the edge of the headlamps.

It was one thing to be wiped off the map politically by force, like the Incas, the Zulus and innumerable others; another altogether to have *willingly* half-withdrawn from it into the category of semi-oblivion. Shame appertains mainly to will and responsibility – hence to the gnawing awareness that, in a collective sense, one *could* help being dependent, second-rate, also-ran and ultimately negligable.

The comparative study of nationalism has shown how one-sided it can be to dwell exclusively on the positive sentiments linked to collective identity: items like 'belonging', 'community', 'roots', patriotic inclusiveness (and so on). Actually negative, even profoundly negative, emotions have been as important in generating nationalism. Not so much 'love of country', in fact, as detestation of it, sheer inability to stand it as it is, in the fallen state of subjection and impotence. At the limit such attitudes amount I suppose to what one has to call national nihilism, the conviction of the irredeemable hopelessness attaching to what is most intimately one's own. That too is 'identity' (unnoticed by many who skate on the thin ice of the term). Such despair entails the hopelessness of the personal *self*, since the latter is partly configured by 'belonging' to a particular society. Roots can strangle as well as sustain. Thus 'belonging' can turn into a kind of curse, from which one must escape at all costs, by flight, emigration or pretending to be somebody else.

While *most people* don't succumb to the shame of inexistence, *some* do. These have tended in Scotland to be a sub-class of the educated, the stratum later labelled as 'intellectuals'. Those who (for many different reasons) avoided conscription as cadres of institutional quietism have been particularly susceptible to the shameful furies, and reacted against them in various ways. For long the most common was what might be called departure-lounge internationalism, an outward-bound complex of attitudes forever recoiling from the unspeakable parochialism and psychic cramps of home. Though not always complaisant about Great Britain, these emigrants did tend to benefit from it – obviously, imperium and metropolis could deliver at least a broader *Heimat*, and one arguably more compatible with Socialism, Liberalism and other formulae of the moment. Most migration has more modest aims, like a better

job and future for the children. Moral and spiritual transformation may or may not occur as well, depending on circumstances.
But for this more specialist and intellectual movement such
factors often loomed far larger: becoming someone else, as it
were, adopting and displaying a superior *persona*.

In my personal case this outward-bound neurosis led to
frankly nihilistic excesses about strangling Kirk Ministers and
mowing down be-kilted landowners with a Marxist machine-
gun. The point is that such attitudes were just part of that
structural dislocation of identity I have been referring to. They
were the obverse of douce conformism and being the good
boys of Britishness. Naturally, they also made it difficult to be
a nationalist. Sectarian, rigid and cranky, the patriot faith of
those days could not help being rather like some conspiracy to
reproduce the contents of Hugh MacDiarmid's 'living tomb',
rather than leap out of it. As we *are* leaping out at last it is
important to mention this; but there is no particular point in
hand-wringing repentance, thank God. Younger minds are
bored by it. The point is that both our *intéllos* and earlier
Scottish nationalism itself were victims of a common fate. They
have just had to recover jointly from their interrelated shames.
They managed to do so in the 1980s, with some help from Mrs
Thatcher.

Farther *à propos* identity in the time of darkness, I vividly
recall the one thing that did make a difference in the otherwise
unspeakable 1950s.[5] There was a single episode then which
affected a despairing eighteen-year-old and even shook up the
whole departure-lounge. It was a gesture of *pure* 'identity-politics', almost a joke. I'm referring, of course, to the stealing of
the Stone of Destiny from Westminster Abbey by a small band
of romantic, irresponsible student ne'er-do-wells (on the film
archive some of them look disconcertingly like today's
Chancellor of the Exchequer in *his* younger days). *This* was

what stirred the quiescent Scotland of 1950–51 – not the plans
for the coal industry, Stafford Cripps's budget or Ernest Bevin's
Cold War foreign policy. Today, all these momentous and terribly British issues might as well have taken place on Mars, as far
as popular or political memory is concerned. The effects of the
'prank' would be far more enduring. What else lay behind
Secretary of State Michael Forsyth's ill-judged return of the
relic in 1996, and the truly magnificent display of ingratitude
which he and the Duke of York encountered in Edinburgh
High Street?[6]

The Rising River

How is this cankered past to be altered and undone? Over the
past year, more or less since the implications of the referendum
vote sank in, all observers have been struck by a curious and at
first sight inexplicable sense of inevitability about the course of
events. From being unthinkable by most Scots, independence
has become quite calmly acceptable to most, and indeed – as
several surveys have shown – actually expected by them. They
mostly believe that Scotland will become independent within
a foreseeable time frame, like ten or fifteen years. This is man-
ifestly a deep or underground shift in opinion and feeling,
which has attained its most striking expression so far in the
new support for independence among the Catholic electorate
of Glasgow and the central belt.

But what has caused it? The most preposterous diagnoses
and verdicts have been appearing in the *Scotsman* and *Herald*
newspapers recently, and no doubt readers will have to endure
many more of these. They amount to accusing the chattering
élite, and especially the Labour Party élite – even Donald
Dewar – of moral flabbiness and backsliding. More backbone,

therefore, a more stern and convincing defence of Unionism is required in order to forestall the final triumph of the Damned. The argument in defence of Union *has* to be made more convincingly, so that Devolution will be given a chance of working. Without more 'Nat-bashing' (as this is also revealingly called) the pernicious post-referendum slide may continue, until a deluded public is cast into separation before it quite understands the awful fate being imposed on it.[7]

One way of assessing this odd sort of vengeful hopelessness is (again) simply to look backwards, at the origins of it all. Then too there was inevitability at work, accompanied by moral appeals and denunciations, and much wringing of hands. But it was all the other way round. Indeed there was one particular meeting which can be seen as casting a sharp and still relevant light upon today – and also, I suppose, upon meetings likely to be held tomorrow, in the first years of the coming century. The Commissioners appointed by the Scottish Parliament to negotiate the treaty sometimes met outside the Royal Palace of Westminster, in the house of the Scottish Secretary of State.[8] This was then the Earl of Mar, later the leader of the 1715 Rebellion but a decade earlier (in the words of Sir John Clerk of Penicuik) 'very forward for the Union and the settlement of the succession in the Protestant family of Hannover'. On 16 April 1706 (Clerk goes on) –

> The Commissioners met there amongst themselves, the first general point debated . . . was whether they should propose to the English a Federal union between the two nations, or an incorporating union. The first was most favoured by the people of Scotland, but all the Scots Commissioners, to a Man, considered it impracticable, for that in all Federal unions there behoved to be a supreme power lodged somewhere, and wherever this was lodged it henceforth became

the States General, or, in our way of speaking, the Parliament
of Great Britain, under the same royal power and authority as
the two nations are at present . . .

In contemporary terms one might say the Commissioners were
stressing the problem of 'Sovereignty', or the ultimate location
of authority within the proposed Union. This was inevitable
because –

In things of the greatest consequence to the two nations, as
in Councils relating to peace and war and subsidies, *it was
impossible that the Representatives or their suffrages in both nations
could be equal*, but must be regulated in proportion to the
power and richness of the several publick burdens or taxa-
tions that could affect them; in a word, the Scots
Commissioners saw that no Union could subsist between
the two nations but an incorporating perpetual one . . .[9] (my
italics)

There we have it: the authentic logic of (in Paul Henderson
Scott's phrase) getting into bed with a Sovereign elephant.
Forget about federation and looser arrangements by gentle-
manly agreement. Not long before this Mar himself had written
to William Carstares, the Principal of Edinburgh University
(like John Clerk, another strong Unionist) to say that down in
London serious opinion would concede nothing unless
Scotland agreed to 'an entire union'. If the Scottish
Commissioners went for anything less, then –

. . . they will never meet with us, for they think all the
notions about federal unions and forms a mere jest or
chimera . . .'

So, Andrew Fletcher of Saltoun might go on boring the breeches off anyone he could corner for long enough with his visions of a Dutch-style or decentralized solution (like David Martin, MEP, and many Lib Dems today). Such ideas might be quite splendid in themselves; but they just weren't on.

The point was not simply that the English Parliament demanded incorporation, but that it was right to do so. *This* is what the Commissioners were really recognizing, against the will of many or even most of them. Any lesser or more conditional union between two such hopelessly unequal polities could never work out, at least in what Clerk calls 'things of the greatest consequence' – which were naturally what the whole deal turned on. At bottom Union was about finally separating Scotland from France, and being able to go on unimpeded to contest French hegemony in the wider world.[10]

In those circumstances, the logic of aggregation – of putting two countries together – was indeed 'entire union' and monolithic sovereignty. Any attempt at realization of the intermediate 'jests or chimeras' would have produced instability, and a constant uncertainty of response from Edinburgh over vital issues like whether or not to go to war over Spain, or in the Americas, or how to share out and dispose of 'subsidies' (public expenditure). Had the countries been something like equal in demography or wealth then I suppose London would indeed have had to put up with this. But that was the nub: both Parliamentary delegations knew that they did not. A generation before, Oliver Cromwell's Protectorate had conquered and partly assimilated Scotland. It could be done again. For Union to 'subsist' in a stable fashion – or, to 'bed down' and become 'workable', as Donald Dewar says about today's Devolution – it had inevitably to be governed by the dominant partner, take it or leave it (and really, there was no leaving it).

Does this logic still exist? Yes, of course the 'Sovereignty' of the Anglo-British state continues, and so does its *modus operandi*. We still cohabit within the 1688 state, which still has the House of Lords and the Monarchy (and intends to keep both going). That power still has the 'Mace' on the House of Commons table, as a symbol of Absolute or 'imperial' authority, it still retains a nuclear deterrent and its Permanent member's seat on the Security Council (and intends to keep the lot). Indeed for all her reforming contortions, Mrs Thatcher's rule greatly reinforced its centralism and unitary character. Nor has this central redoubt been affected by Blair's changes, other than rhetorically – he still hopes Devolution will strengthen the all-British realm, rather than dislocating it.

So what is it that has changed? The logic of Anglo-British statehood may still be there, however, *it is now working in reverse*. It seems to me that one inevitability has in the end been replaced by another. Compelled at last to retreat in practice from out-and-out Sovereignty, the United Kingdom is now struggling *not* to go all the way. But on this matter at least, Tam Dalyell's West Lothian scarecrow was croaking out the truth: *that* kind of Unitarism qualified will be that kind of Unitarism lost. For the UK state, power devolved is emphatically *not* power retained. The United Kingdom is indeed being 'hoist on its own petard', particularly in Scotland (but probably soon in Wales as well). In other words, the very same factors which three hundred years ago rendered 'incorporation' inevitable are probably now working to make its contrary, separation, just as unavoidable. But if this is the underlying situation, may it not be also the true dilemma which the Scottish mood of inevitabilism is already instinctively registering?

It does so as it registers the feebleness of New Labour's whole approach to 'Devolution'. There is an atmosphere, an ill-concealed feeling here which I suspect most people register more clearly than all the fatherly platitudes and Blairite chest-beating.

What the latter are manifesting (as well as concealing) may be simply the untenability of the force-field behind the show of the Devolutionary theatre. We should remember here that the message is being picked up by very sensitive antennae. If there is one thing which post-1707 Scotland is qualified to know from a hundred miles off, it is lack of conviction. And since the referendum, we have been treated to this every day on the government and Labour Party side: 'Have your nation back, fine, but . . . hey, just stay in line, not your *state* please!'

'Nationalism' here is plainly identified with the wilful undoing of subordinate statehood – and almost nothing else. Hence national identity is splendid (self-respect, culture, etc.) but *state* identity remains proscribed, if not a form of crime. Since the latter happens to be the one thing which really counts, in the odd Scottish dilemma, public sentiment picks up the contradiction instantly. Since the proscription is no longer enforceable by Cromwellian means, it will have to be upheld by consent – by the long-dormant collective will in Scotland, the people's sovereignty which was rediscovered and affirmed in the 1980s and early '90s. So the appeal implicit in the Devolution laws is to the post-1999 political generation and can only be: 'you *will* stay British won't you?'

But practically in the same breath, the Labour legislators have also been telling people that Devolution is 'a process' – i.e. something ongoing, whose meaning will have to be worked out over time. Again, 'worked out' appears to entail consent and cooperation. Doesn't this mean input from both parties – that is, from Holyrood and Westminster together? And will that not have to be on a presumption of equality – that is, to contain real negotiation rather than just 'consultation'? There is in fact only one mode of equality possible here: that between equally self-governing states. The Devolutionary demand to stay in line is (as it were) a demand for permanently self-curtailed and non-disturbing input. Having been reconstituted, the Nation must agree ('for all time coming', in the 1707 phrase) never to do anything peremptory, unsettling, different or likely to upset big business or the Queen.

In September 1997, however, the electorate was surely voting for 'the process', rather than for the precise stipulations of the Devolution White Paper. It was endorsing a direction of affairs, not the traffic lights and road-markings along the route. And at the same time, what that endorsement was doing was – here I revert to the metaphor used earlier – to bring the underground river up to the surface. That is, the 'identity-river' or undermining stream of abnegation, self-suppression and doubt, what had been (until then) the sustaining junior-partner negativism of modern Scotland. For the first time since 1707 – since 'the last day Scotland was Scotland' – the black waters reached the open air again, and began to flow something like normally.

This is why next day everything was quietly yet finally different. This process was largely invisible to outsiders, and no one should blame them for that. After all, National Liberation has more customarily meant the release of prisoners, guerrillas being welcomed from the hills, mass flag-raising and revenge upon collaborators. But because none of this took place here, it is erroneous to conclude that nothing happened. An earth-shift did occur, once and for all, and it will never be undone. It simply took a different form, one subjectively plain to most inhabitants though (naturally) occluded by philistines, Scottish government Ministers, and newspaper editorialists and intellectuals who dread above all things the end of their cherished ambiguity.[11] Scotland was – or at any rate had started to be – a nation again. Looking backwards in the longer optic evoked here, one could also say that the state of Scotland had begun to emerge from post-1707 cold storage and move towards resuming its authority and legitimacy.

Hugh MacDiarmid always thought Scotland needed an 'upswelling of the incalculable' to put things right – and this is indeed what has taken place. But the 'incalculable' does not mean 'the irrational' or the surfacing of atavistic impulses. A wider comparative view shows how all developments in modern national identity have involved something analogous – a 'conversion process', as it were, whereby relatively suddenly large numbers shift from one identity-perspective to another. Such translations never happen *only* incrementally or individually (though naturally this takes place too, and it may be a necessary condition of the communal change). What made English, Scottish and Irish colonists become 'American' in the 18th century, or turned Tuscans, Venetians and *Sardi* into 'Italians' in the 19th century was neither discrete calculation nor 'instinct'. It is more like a collective (and to some extent infectious) impulse arising from quite a complex spectrum of circumstances, some modern and others inherited (or at least, anterior). Its impact causes one identity-formula to acquire authority or – relatively suddenly – to appear natural.

It may be objected that this is placing too much importance on the single moment of the referendum. But I think that's wrong too. It fails to acknowledge something fundamental about identity politics. However long it may take to get to a given threshold, what makes it a threshold is being crossed; and the crossing itself is a symbolic matter – a profound signal of transition, as it were.

In the case of September 1997 it had indeed taken at least thirty years to get there, from Winifred Ewing's Hamilton by-election victory in 1967, via the rise and fall of the 70s, the defeat of 1979, the campaigns for a Scottish Parliament, the Constitutional Convention and Claim of Right, the sense of unity shown during the referendum campaign itself – and so on. However, those thirty years had *also* to be summed up,

embodied in a recognizable and mobilizing gesture. As soon
that was made, the effects were fundamental, and by their very
nature cumulative and ongoing. The profound relief felt at the
result was not simply at having avoided another 1979. It was
more like relief at a now incontrovertible existence and presence – the return of Scotland, as it were, from her long,
enforced self-exile in the nether regions of British Union and
Empire.

In the Wind of Change

If this historical analysis is right, then certain things must
follow, about the present political situation. Labourites and
other Unionists are still persisting in a basic mistake. They
want to believe that factors like these I have highlighted – self-
confidence, collective optimism, the felt wind of change – can
somehow be measured out and limited or apportioned, like
health or education budgets, or the rate of income tax. Their
notion of identity-politics is limited to Embassies, flags, chest-
beating and imposed ethnicity. In the referendum (they insist)
you voted for just so much, the Devolution pint-measure – and
that's that. 'Look son', they say, ' . . . see the mark on the glass,
eh? Well, that's *it*! . . .'

No one will be entitled to a dram extra, and in fact to
demand it would be downright undemocratic. All good-
behaviour Scots must now settle down and 'draw breath',
grateful (like their forebears) for what they've got, and
renouncing all farther tumult and upheaval. Thus we live still
within the epoch of 'all time coming', and at present *Scotsman*
and *Herald* both rub this dreary point in several times a week.
Labour and the Lib Dems alike claim that any 'process' must
remain gey canny. They seem to think instinctively of a

seamlessly British, pragmatic, piecemeal kind of 'process', the sort devoid of identity-tantrums and unhealthy forms of national display or protest. Resurrection has been permitted – but only provided the resurrectees agree to remain within the Kirkyard and go on minding their own parochial-sepulchral business.

The Collapsing House

A Liberal Democrat was putting this point to me in a pub around New Year time, and at one point she used the phrase 'too far, too fast'. This rang a bell, in relation to those things I had been looking up in the library, though I couldn't at once recall just what it was. I had to go back for another search, but after a while it came back to me. It too was in Lockhart's diary, and not far from the section I quoted earlier. While trying to promote his dissolution motion in the Commons, he went to see Robert Harley, the Earl of Oxford. Harley was the Tory leader, a favourite of Queen Anne's, and kept up a clandestine relationship with the Stuart court in exile (which of course made him sympathetic to Lockhart). He was also Chancellor of the Exchequer, and at that time much – nay, incessantly – pre-occupied with problems of nepotism and sexual scandal in both Party and government. When Lockhart raised the matter of ending the Union, he apparently answered 'somewhat briskly' (which at that time seems to have meant something like 'with extreme irritation'):

> You are driving too far and too fast, Lockhart, you will bring down an old house about our ears, and the Queen will highly resent your conduct . . .

Note the presence of the 'old house' in all this. Almost three centuries ago the Constitution was already perceived as a crumbling old dump liable to be damaged by insubordination. Actually, the *British* Constitution was at that point just five years old, while the Glorious & Bloodless Revolution of 1688 lay only twenty-four years in the past. But of course what Harley meant was the old house that counted, the one belonging to England (Anglo-Saxon freedom, Norman Yoke, mists of time etc.). This was *the* Constitution, the one which had achieved incorporation rather than been incorporated. Nor would it have occurred to him that the state which Lockhart was trying to reprieve was equally old (and equally in need of repair). Now as then, the plea emerging out of such arguments is – 'slow down', don't be carried away, give intermediate solutions a chance, whether as stable Devolution or (the Liberal Democrats' preference) as 'federalism' – classical or 'assymetrical' – Euro-regionalism, or some variety of consociationalism.

In the early 1700s, I noted before that such jests and chimeras stood no chance. Today (if the argument is pursued) they stand just as little. This is for reasons quite unconnected with their cleverness, or even their desirability as blueprints or prospectuses. In 1707 they were distractions because London thought they were. That is, they were diversions or impediments to the coherent, unanimous and radical deployment of power alone worthy of a great and coolly Sovereign state. In 2000 they will still remain chimeras, for substantially the same reasons – the basically unaltering motives of the Elephant.

Even in decline, the latter has no intention whatever of letting its Greatness-conservation campaign be unduly precipitated, interfered with or diverted from whatever most suits 'Middle England'. It would much rather talk about all that for a century or so. Lockhart understood in 1712 that the answer was to get out of the bed, rather than work out fantasy-schemes for new protocols of cohabitation. As he pointed out, these space-sharing formulae would in any case prove of greatest benefit to whoever (as in this case) takes up about 85% of the space.

If this is right then something is bound to follow in party and Parliamentary terms also. Far from it being terribly risky, irresponsible and juvenile to move towards getting out of the Union bed, it may well be dangerous, and indeed positively childish, to hang around in it for the sake of a misunderstood 'auld lang syne' – a wish not to offend and upset our neighbours, after such a prolonged period of connubial interaction. What this would actually entail is sticking with the Union querulously, ungratefully and naggingly, via daily or weekly quarrels about just how much or how little, who has the right to do or to have what, in comparison with whom, and without the Queen being too resentful. That, surely, is the most depressing prospect of all, and also the one most likely in the end to exasperate the Elephant and imperil decent or civic relations.[12]

On the other hand, just facing up to getting out – which I suspect people are already doing instinctively – would imply recognition of the need for a new, *agreed* relationship. 'Agreed' here would have to mean genuinely agreed, as between equals; which in turn would imply junking the Treaty of Union and replacing it with something better – not smuggling it back into the readjusted status quo (which is precisely what the Scotland Bill has done).[13]

But if that's so, then as a matter of tactics it might be unfortunate for the SNP (or the Liberal Democrats) to get involved in any sort of cohabitation or coalition deal in the new Parliament, where the price of office became an agreement to be good. Good, that is, in the sense of *not* trying to get out of the Union too quickly, or too upsettingly. This might entail postponing any farther plebiscite for (say) the duration of a Parliamentary session. Of course nobody can know in advance when the 'right' moment will be. That is bound to depend upon the quite unforeseeable circumstances of some future conjuncture, and to involve events far outside Scotland. On the other hand, no one can know that such a moment will *not* present itself either, in the context (say) of a London Labour régime tumbling out of popular favour, losing a referendum on Europe, or otherwise disgracing itself. So it would surely be vital to keep the door open for that possibility.

The point is, this is no longer about jests and academic chimeras. The wind is actually blowing, and pushing the returned stream along. A machinery has started up, and already generated quite unforeseen consequences. The world of non-confidence, stagnation and eternal black holes has vanished. On the level that counts most, Scotland is already in the post-Cold War domain of restored nationhood, democracy and 'globalization'. Whereas previously Scots could never 'do it for themselves', now they have difficulty in understanding just why someone else should go on doing it for them. This was vividly demonstrated, for instance, in the controversy over the BBC's proposed 'Scottish evening news' programme at the end of 1998. Although sabotaged by pressures from government in the end, one feature of the campaign for a 'Scottish Six' was that almost *everyone* in Scotland now supported it – including resolute supporters of nothing-but Devolution.

Hyper-fundamentalism

At this point I do have to say something about the history and internal divisions of the SNP, albeit with a good deal of trepidation. But it has become too important to leave out. For the

first forty years of its existence this party was unavoidably a tiny
sect. Now suddenly it has turned into a determinant of national
existence, the artificer of statehood. Everyone can see how
under Alex Salmond's leadership things have changed. But
have they had a chance to change enough?

The party's rise may have been linked to the decline and fall
of British grandeur; but from the 1920s until the 1960s that
prestige remained considerable. Not only was the weight of
'Britishness' crushing, nearly all organized politics was unavoidably set in its terms. Mass representation had arisen under the
conditions of the Union, via English-dominated parties, and –
as I noted earlier – most of the intellectuals linked to the political stratum were in any case 'outward-bound' in a cultural
sense. Nor was there a folk tradition based on peasant small-
holding and land struggles, except in parts of Highland
Scotland and (by the 20th century) directly concerning very
few people. Nor did 'the nation' have to be constructed in the
usual institutional sense, since the Treaty of Union had left
that in place. By the 1950s these structures may have been in a
dismal and stultified condition, but nobody could claim the
Scots were without institutions 'of their own'.

All these factors made an extraordinarily heavy boulder to
push up the hill. There is nothing surprising about the distort-
ing effects of such efforts, or the way in which a sect-mentality
is formed. It is a common aspect of modern political life – on
both the far Left and the extreme Right, for example, as well as
among small or minority religious groups. But what is unusual
is to find such traits so pronounced and persistent in a *national*
movement.

Sects have to be 'fundamental' since they are by definition
against heavy odds: high-profile purism and strident ideological clamour are parts of their normal baggage. So are paranoia
and the nourishing pleasures of denunciation. A definition of

oneself in such terms entails the categorization of others as either ignorant (untouched by the true light) or as 'traitors' (touched by it and yet refusing its Grace, for motives which can only be disreputable). The supreme joy of fundamentalism is castigation of the unworthy, above all when apparently close to the pure-in-heart, *and* in charge: an Elect unmasked, and overdue for come-uppance. It is also important to keep in mind how unimportant *defeat* is for authentic sectarianism. Indeed, defeat is itself always a kind of triumph: farther evidence of Satan's power, endorsement of 'I told you so!', and reinforcement of the will to (ultimately) prevail.[14]

National movements tend to be afflicted by fundamentalism while on the rise, and then lose it when they succeed. Now within reach of power and influence, the SNP ought to be shedding some of the purist baggage. It seems to have discarded a lot of it, but it's not so easy for an observer to be sure. This very long story of minority – almost underground – development may have bequeathed a harder carapace, one which takes correspondingly longer to diminish or demobilize. It may have passed down some capacity for what could be called 'hyper-fundamentalism', a rigidity so militant and indurate that still more time and experience might be required for the normal embodiment and display of power – the trouble being, as anyone can see, that there is no longer much time for mutations of that sort. Things are moving too fast, and certain to accelerate again after the summer of 1999. We're in the rapids right now. The stream has come up to the surface only to rush straight into the mill-race. In six months the SNP will certainly be helping to turn the wheel; and it may be the main force behind it.

'We're all fundamentalists now' is the way George Reid has put the resultant situation. Devolution is now the status quo, and no longer dismissable as a snare and delusion: there *is* only one way forward, so it would be daft not to be reasonably united on it. That way appears also to be opened by public opinion, by the structural shifts in Scottish voting patterns, and by British New Labour's probable fall from grace. The tentative emergence of an English Parliament or assembly also seem likely to give more incentives to state-building at Holyrood. But all this success may be a bit much for what Douglas Dunn has called 'the stern mountain preacher' in his (or her) coat of Biblical night.[15] What they wanted was a party and a people that would heed *their* call – not be given its opportunity through compromise and the 'half-way house' of Home Rule. That the irredeemably corrupt Labour Party should provide this chance was the worst insult of all – a virtual guarantee of sell-out and infamy. So the temptation to carry on denouncing must still be strong.

I would rephrase Reid's paradox this way. We can't all be *fundamentalists*, of course, since moderate fundamentalism is a contradiction in terms. But in the new situation, we should all be focusing on the fundamental aim, independence, though with less assistance from the '-ism'. Patent-right purism has become a distraction – or, looked at in another way, it may now have served its historical purpose. That purpose was not just an eccentric delusion. On the contrary, from the 1920s to the 1970s it kept something alive: an undoubted and unappeasable recalcitrance, a refusal to go down in that black river – to drown for good in the chasms of self-doubt and indifference. That deserves to be honoured in recollection today – even as we recognize that its time is really over. The element of truth in nationalist fundamentalism lay in its rooted opposition to the hegemony of a fundamental power which for an interminable age seemed impenetrable – the Sovereignty of England's Westminster, and of its imperial Crown.

But as the latter have become shadows, so (surely) has the

need for that kind of resistance to them. The dark old trench-war is giving way to a different style of civic warfare in constant movement and development. The Holyrood Parliament will become a forum for this more normal politics, in which neither Members nor voters want or require constant reminders of Biblical night, or the austere delights of righteous abstention. The seventy years have been worth it. But surely to goodness it's time the different wings of this movement agreed more cordially on that much, and got down to making the Parliament work in the way they want.

In a Civic Style

But I can't end on a note of dubiety, even if things are getting better there too. The positive temper generated by the referendum now feeds off itself, and generates the wish and expectation for more. Back in 1712 Lockhart was unable to call upon this kind of organized popular mood. It was too soon for such a national-popular identity to take political shape. He lived in the late period of absolutist rule and assumptions, when nationalism was still nascent and monarchical-style Sovereignty remained the norm – even in post-revolutionary England and Scotland. Also, it is worth insisting again how Scotland itself had been a state long before turning into a nation in that modern sense. It was (as it remains today) a state-nation, not the other way round. This is probably why he and many others placed what seems to us such an inordinate emphasis upon the Stuart dynasty. A native royal state seemed at that time the only way back, in spite of the train of disappointments left behind by the 17th century incumbents to the throne.

Today I think he would be a straightforward Republican. I

know some in the SNP would prefer to maintain the constitutional monarchy, at least for a transitional period; but few doubt
that the new constitution Scotland now needs will really be a
Republican one. It rests upon a restored nation, but one which is
much more than rediscovered or 'freed from bondage' in the
normal sense. The clichés just don't fit. The Scottish *state* is of an
antiquity comparable to England's and that of the Isle of Man;
but it resigned many of its crucial functions before a modern
national society could develop within it. Because contemporary
urban-industrial society then evolved with a British bias and
organization, a more distinct nationality is actually in formation
now, today (and I don't just mean in the trite sense of peoples
forever changing, and so on). That too was part of the significance of September 1997. The river of loss not only surged up
from the underworld, it entered a new landscape altogether –
and found itself at once changed in composition and direction
from what had for so long been running in estranged darkness.

So it is not an exaggeration to speak of a genuinely 'new
nation' here: this is the first moment at which national society
and state will be in anything like a modern conjunction in
Scotland. The SNP has helped to create this situation, and in
turn been re-created by it – as have other political formations,
even the Scottish Labour Party. It is simply not the case that
any kind of pre-formed or ethnically-configured nationality-
Geist 'erupted' in the eighties and nineties. There are fantasists
who find it convenient to believe something like this, but I
won't take up more time discussing them today. The state and
political factors have been as dominant in Scotland's restoration
as they were in its eclipse, and they are surely likely to remain
so in the coming era of self-rule. The fatal Treaty has already
been renounced in people's minds. It will soon be revoked in
law, by negotiation and (as Lockhart wanted so long ago) 'in a
parliamentary way'.

This is why a civic style of nationalism is at home here. That's what is really being commemorated and celebrated this afternoon. 'We should not disfigure ourselves with villany of hatred', in Henderson's great words of 1943 – he was speaking of the Germans, in the depths of the war. Nor do we need to. I don't think anyone here thinks in terms of giving lessons to the English, or anybody else. It is sometimes thought that our sort of 'civic nationalism' is a kind of artifice, something superimposed and secondary to the 'real thing'. The latter – genuine community, unthinking togetherness, the fate of descent and pre-conscious or 'ethnic' union – is still all too often depicted by a mistaken theory as the essence of contemporary nationality, and hence of post-Cold War politics.

It is not.

That much I do think we have learned in Scotland, and I am confident that the knowledge will sustain the new Parliament through the trials ahead.

CHAPTER THREE

The Last Days of Sovereignty

I desire a perfect Union of Lawes and persons, and such a Naturalizing as may make one body of both Kingdomes under mee your King. That I and my posteritie (if it so please God) may rule over you to the world's ende; Such an Union as was of the Scots and Pictes in Scotland, and of the Heptarchie here in England. And for Scotland I avow such an Union, as if you had got it by Conquest, but such a Conquest as may be cemented by love, the only sure bond of subjection or friendship.

King James VI and I, Speech to Both Houses of Parliament at Whitehall, 31 March 1607

The Landscape of Sovereignty

The week before the 1 May General Election Robert Harris wrote in his *Sunday Times* column that the interminable electoral campaign had probably been a waste of time for the outgoing government. It had made no difference to voting intentions because 'the tectonic plates had shifted' already to determine the outcome. I think this was more than just a striking phrase. Deeper pressures had indeed asserted themselves, and are continuing to do so. The fault-lines are still widening, and we are still trying to work out just what they are.

Theorists of nationality-politics have invented the term 'ethnoscape' to describe certain aspects of traditional national identity. By analogy, what we are dealing with here might be called the 'sovereigntyscape' of the United Kingdom – the deeper configuration of central authority inherited and taken for granted, and in practice grafted on to most ideas (including popular ideas) of the nation, of 'what it means' to be British or English. I think it is in this zone that the tectonic shifts are occurring. The two outstanding manifestations so far have been the precipitous decline of the Monarchy since around 1990, and 1997's electoral earthquake – 'the Labour landslide' as most comment called it (appropriately enough in the context of Harris's metaphor).

But there is another old-fashioned metaphor which might be applied too. It could equally be said that 'a crisis of the State' is going on. Marxists used to be fond of this idea, which implied that social forces (notably economic ones) were outpacing and undermining the existing power-structures, and hence bringing about an inevitable 'collapse' (with any luck, a revolution) from which Progress would emerge victorious, guided of course by the Marxists. A crisis of the State is by definition a crisis of Sovereignty.

Sovereignty is the ultimate or last-resort power of decision over a given population and territory. The question is a fundamental one, but I don't propose to tackle its philosophical side directly here. Everyone knows that in Great Britain a peculiar mysticism attaches to the notion, reflecting the metempsychosis of the late-feudal Crown into a representative Parliament, after the Revolutions between 1640 and 1688. Given the aristocratic or patrician nature of the resultant English representation, an extraordinarily centralized and élitist apparatus of power and administration was created. It was voiced literally by James VI and I in the above quotation, at the moment of birth of the British Union. Then the Crown-in-Parliament became the sovereignty-mode of what Liah

Greenfeld has called 'God's first-born' – the early-modern or
primitive template of the nation-state. This lasted three centuries, plenty of time to acquire delusions of immemoriality.
Round about its 300th birthday in 1988, however, in the thirty-
fifth year of the reign of Elizabeth II and I (and the ninth of
Counter-Sovereign Margaret), it began to exhibit serious symptoms.

As if stricken by a premonitory curse, the Crown began
abruptly to de-metempsychose into a tacky Heritage sideshow.
Parliament was left as sole manager of the national team-identity.
But the theatre of Westminster was insufficiently equipped for
the rôle. No one now took the House of Lords seriously either.
More important, the House of Commons had declined as well:
the forum of the nation was now more mocked than reverenced.
It was another unforeseen effect of Thatcherism, for which
debate and collegial criticism had been merely impediments to
radicalism. Televizing it was regarded at the time as an audacious
masterstroke. Few were those who thought that transmitting it
unchanged might make things worse. But in fact the slide was to
continue unchanged, and under Blair (as indicated earlier) it has
attained new levels of irrelevance and contempt.

So the Deposition of Margaret in 1990 consigned Britain to
a sort of Hades, John Major's nether kingdom of dinge, sleaze,
rigor mortis constitutionalism, tread-water triumphalism and
anti-European xenophobia. It is tempting but erroneous to
speak of the old régime as having 'scraped the bottom of the
barrel' here. That would imply that there had been something
else in the barrel – previous stratagems or reforming devices
attempted and found wanting until, *in extremis*, the political
class just had to go for the bilgewater. Of course this was not so.
Mother-of-Parliament-land had no requirement for such stratagems and devices: historic-exemplary status implies that
nationalist status-anxiety is for wimp-lands alone. Where first-

born nationhood is threatened, therefore, there *is* only the barrel-bottom: it can never be our fault, so *they* must be to blame. Hence identity may legitimately be redefined by the crudest means to hand: in this case a spluttering concoction of warm beer, bicycling clerics, filthy abattoirs, plotting foreigners and Sir James Goldsmith.

Beneath the rotting barrel lies the sand, fortunately: a 'sovereignty' which is both conditioning and outlasting the fall of Britain. But the banks of sovereignty are now themselves shifting rapidly in new tides. The *locus* of debate has at last shifted decisively from the economy to the state. It always used to be said (usually by apologists of Old Corruption) that the people 'had no interest in constitutional questions'. Well, they seem to be acquiring one fast. That was in any case always a piece of Westminster dullardry. Ah for the days of such pseudo-shrewdness, such unflinching self-admiration! Naturally there could be little popular concern with reforming a Constitution which everyone had been taught to revere alongside the State Opening and Vera Lynn.

But all that meant is that people used to behave themselves. In the 1980s they stopped behaving themselves. This was partly Thatcher's doing, and probably the most forgiveable part of her show. Britishness had been a kind of synthetic Middle Ages where people herded themselves into the appropriate classes, with a degree of Monarchical regulation. Alas, when rebellion against it began in the 1960s, it proved uncontrollable. The Royal Family and the Tory Party stopped behaving themselves too. And finally even the Labour Party, the last hope of the old-fashioned, embarked upon a noisy and compromising (though possibly brief) *affaire* with democracy. About the same time as the National Lottery, identity-Angst crept at last into the British soul and led it to query 'the way we're governed' – which means Sovereignty.

Occluded Multinationalism

Thus did 1989's End of History (etc.) reach the shores of Ukania. Hegel disembarked a century and a half late, but with devastating consequences. One effect of Communism's collapse had been a great expansion of the view, as historians realized that the fateful eternity of the Cold War had been but one dismal chapter in a longer and far more interesting story. Similarly, in archipelagic terms, we ought now to try and perceive Archaic-British Sovereignty as an episode now approaching its end. It started with the late-feudal assimilation of Wales and ended (morally speaking, at least) amid the strident hysteria of Tory no-surrender Unionism between 1992 and 1997.

The United Kingdom state was neither a standard-issue nation-state nor an *ancien régime* comparable to the Hapsburg and other empires. It escaped from the latter by stopping James's posteritie well short of the world's ende (although retaining certain similarities to them); and so far it has never made it as the former. However, the important thing is to recall that it never *had* to make it in that way. This was probably because of its *sui generis* location within modernity.

Location explains most things for students of nationalism, as it is reputed to do for estate agents. The prime mover would not itself be directly configured by the developmental process to which it gave rise. Nor (with the exception of Ireland) would that process recoil directly upon it and compel such shifts, until very late in the day. Here is part of the reason why, right down to the present, the dominant British-Isles *ethnos* has remained so studiedly vague and indefinite about being English. On that fundamental level, the plane of sovereignty, today's 'Englishness' can be seen as a long-term locational effect rather than a natural or ethno-genetic one.

Remaining an early-modern state-nation within what became the nation-state world presented certain problems. One of these was dealing with the other archipelago *ethnies*. A crucial part of the evolution of 'Britain' and the Britons lay within the formative interim of 1688 to 1789 – that is, in circumstances that were clearly post-feudal, but still pre-nationalist. The incorporation of Wales had been attempted by crass pre-modern methods well before this moment – but after 1688 these were no longer usable. From 1650 to 1660 Cromwell's proto-Jacobin experiments with terror and assimilation had also proved futile – in Ireland, in the long run, much worse than futile. In order to align them with the new dominant-state project of overseas mercantile conquest and colonization, different techniques of subordination or co-option were required. Such methods eventually failed with the Irish, but they succeeded for much longer with the Scots. And it is the breakdown of that longer-lasting success which provides the context of the Blair government's 'devolution', and today's political problem.

So today's crisis returns us logically to another, that accompanying the establishment of the Williamite régime of 1688 to 1702. Before the Prince of Orange's great *coup d'état* in 1688 the Stuarts had certainly done their best with Perfect Union. James launched it with great enthusiasm and determination. I mentioned him to begin with because he deserves greater recognition: 'The wisest fool in Christendom' he may have been, but he also invented 'Great Britain', and tried extraordinarily hard to make it work. It was an eerie experience re-reading his addresses to the English Parliament earlier this year, at the same time as John Major was perched on his campaign soapbox groaning about saving the Union.

In the good old days before 1989, when a decade felt like a long time everywhere, and an eternity in Britain, 1603 had felt

extremely remote. It appeared coeval with the British Ark.
Then in the mid-nineties the truth abruptly dawned, more
forcibly in Scotland than elsewhere. It had been, so to speak,
yesterday evening, and we were still enduring the hangover.
That 'primal posteritie' may have mostly departed, but much
of its vessel was left behind. Indeed we were still aboard the
damned thing, it was sinking, and the lifeboats would almost
certainly turn out to be leaking.

Abrupt psychic reversals can occur at such moments. Was it
something like what mattered most about past life, flashing
before the drowning person's eyes? It suddenly it became clear
how 'too long ago to matter' had been itself a perfectly crass
ideology – an injection of wilfully timeless statehood, as it
were. Under its spell the same Prime Minister found it possible
to blather in a curiously matter-of-fact manner about Britain's
'thousand years of history'. There was some amusement, thank
God; but nobody dialled 999 for help. The Problem was turned
upside down too. It ceased being, 'how can such an immemorial polity ever end?', and became, 'how on earth does it keep
going at all?' – and under *this* management?

One vital element in that survival has been what one could
call 'occluded' nationalism.[1] 'Occlusion', in this metaphorical
sense, means shutting off from the centre of vision or concern –
taking for granted, tolerable marginalization rather than exci-
sion. This was how the formative crisis of what would become
'Britain', the contemporary polity, was ultimately resolved after
1707. The crisis around the Treaty of Union itself derived from
the failure of Absolute Monarchy. Had Jacobean Mark I
Sovereignty lasted longer, then the English unitary state would
presumably have expanded more straightforwardly, like the
French one. Whether as Royal despotism or as a successor
Republic, it would have sought to repeat the earlier Welsh and
Cromwellian experiences in Scotland and Ireland. We can be

reasonably sure today that such a state would not have 'solved' the national questions of the British Isles; but it might have installed a more ordinary pattern of nationality-politics. Albion might then (for example) have ended up seeming less perfidious to the French, and the latter less damnably 'continental' to the British.

Instead, English Absolutism was struck down by a mixture of decapitation, socio-religious revolt and military invasion, and gave way to the formidable élite authority mentioned before, that of an English-style *parlement* which then incorporated itself as collective Sovereign. This Leviathan then retained the actual (personal) monarch as a dependent or (ultimately) as a national-popular mascot – an emblem of conservative (indeed eternal) nationhood. The odd entity was theorized from the margins, by Enlightenment characters like Edmund Burke, David Hume and Adam Smith. They used their eccentric origins to theorize what was essentially the new world of the centre, England.

This basic shift in the centre of gravity was confirmed by the 1689 Declaration of Rights which greeted and allowed William III's accession to the throne. Perfect union by Royal Sovereignty had failed in practice but (more important) had now become impossible in principle. This was the heart of the formative crisis. Any new approach had to be parliament-centred, and had therefore to involve complex negotiations and a written treaty with the parliament of Scotland. That treaty would also become the written part of William's new instrument of reign, the head of the Leviathan which was to create such massive shock-waves around the globe over the following two centuries: the Great-British constitution.

But these were mainly uncharted waters in 1700 Europe. Such a non-regal union of states (but not of nations) implied an original configuration of sovereign power: an élite-civic supranational identity, as it were, which either disregarded nationality and religious faith or treated them as quite separate (and subordinate) issues. Both parliamentary élites had interests in striking such a deal, summarized by Brian Levack as follows:

> The two parliaments were reduced to one, and Scots and Englishmen were given complete freedom of trade in either kingdom, but the administration of the two countries was never fully unified, and their laws and churches were kept separate. This arrangement. which lacks any parallel in Europe, has been described as quasi-federalism. Whatever one may call it, it has been responsible for maintaining Scotland as a 'satellite' of England . . .

The 'occluded' bit of this bargain is indicated by the last sentence. For the resultant multinational character would remain of great importance to the 'satellite' (or weaker partner), and yet – in the longer term – be largely hidden from the dominant one. The 'quasi' part of 'quasi-federalism' has the same meaning. Federation in a more modern sense rests upon constitutional agreement among at least notionally equal governments, who retain some separate representation and voice – a guaranteed if circumscribed sovereignty. Whereas here the whole point was to *remove* such representation and voice – without the trouble of transforming or removing the nation behind them. The Jameses, the Charleses and Oliver Cromwell had all tried that and failed. The formula now to be employed was an 'incorporation' of states which left sub-state institutions alone to support nationhood in the component countries, through their respective local landed élites and churches. The latter were still the 'nations' which counted – not *le menu peuple*, the underlings, field or trade people, and under them again, the indecipherable rabble or mob.

But of course this 'occlusion' or setting-aside of nations meant different things in each case. 'The Treaty established a British state', concludes Professor Levack, '. . . nothing more and nothing less'. Scotland, Ireland and Wales could indeed be set aside for most practical aims of the novel state-form; *England* really could not. The latter's natural predominance meant that a new overarching constitution served mainly its purposes, and would be perceived as its own. What was limitation to the periphery was a kind of expansion for the heartland – the consolidation rather than the cession of hegemony. The disregard of 'occlusion' worked in two ways, therefore. Formally speaking all nationalities set aside mere nationhood for the grander statehood; but *informally* – always the decisive level in old Britain – this implied suppression (or in the case of Scotland, self-suppression) for minorities and a sort of comfortable expansion for the majority.

Irreformable Unitarism?

The underlying demography and economics of the archipelago – with England representing today more than three-quarters of the whole – meant that such a state could then behave pretty well 'as if' it was a unitary polity. The predominance of the English was not so great in the early 18th century, admittedly. But it was sufficient to build out from, in pre-democratic times. In practice, the English Parliament simply turned into the United Kingdom Parliament and got its own way with a name-change. Later on, such pragmatic unitarism was buttressed by a 19th century reconstruction of the Monarchy. Transformed into a popular ideology-code, this worked as a state-ordained nationalism-substitute until the great collapse of the 1990s. Approaching the year 2000 we are still living in 'as if' land. Originally the Irish were the largest minority, but in the 19th century they were overtaken by the Scots, who were still too few, too far off, ill-organized and (in European terms) 'unconnected' to interfere with such a *de facto* English interpretation of Britishness.

This old interpretation is still the British atmosphere we breathe. But it is ceasing to prevail so easily, because of the new crisis of sovereignty created by a combination of British decline, the European Union, and the advance of non-élite (or anti-élite) democracy. As a result the crisis of dis-formation of Crown-in-Parliament absolutism is now seriously upon us. 1997's electoral lurch was another symptom of this (whether or not it indicates any deeper will to escape). And one of its victims now seems certain to be the style of multinational sovereignty whose origins we have been looking at. The 'quasi' in quasi-federalism rested upon a set of early-modern assumptions which have at last become openly archaic – but the prefix cannot simply be dropped, either, thus leaving straightforward 'federalism' in place.

'Occluded multinationalism' depended completely upon the absence of political voice in its 'satellites'. 'In things of the greatest consequence to the two nations, as in Councils relating to peace and war and subsidies' (as Sir John Clerk put it in 1706, see Chapter Two, above) their voices were deemed solidary. The mechanism for this was the mounting socio-cultural solidarity of the landed and patrician classes over the archipelago. The fusion-process at this level was paramount, and led to an exaltation of class over nation. Under Marxist influence, the category of 'class' was to become for a time pre-eminent in British 20th century sociology and social history – as if (for example) the 'making of the English working class' was a focal point in development.[2] But from the angle of nationalism the same phenomenon appears quite differently.

It was the formation of a transnational state-oriented stratum – virtually a caste-structure – which rendered stratification of such great functional importance, and in turn bestowed an equivalent rigidity (and multinational character) upon proletarian opposition. Both sociologists and socialist-minded historians have sought the origins of this 'class structure' in economics, rather than in the broader, multidisciplinary approach linked to nation theory.

That was the single most important meaning of 'incorporation' in the old 1707 sense. More exactly, it was that meaning *for the majority*. But the point has never been taken in quite the same way by the satellites themselves. As Harris pointed out in the 1997 article quoted before, not much was said of any importance during the longest election campaign in history. Among the important statements, however, were some made at its outset by Conrad Russell on the Constitution. Re-reading the Treaty of Union, he underlined how it had been in fact 'an international treaty between two equal sovereign states . . . (which) may be thought by some to be capable of renegotiation', and also recognized 'a residual Scottish sovereignty'. This may be a museum-piece in England, but lives on in the satellite:

> What the Scots have wanted ever since 1603 is recognition as equal partners in a union with England. This the English, because of their unitary theory of sovereignty, have consistently denied them.

In other words, when Scots have talked about 'being British', staying in the Union (etc.) most of them have never meant what the English – and especially English political leaders – thought they meant by these apparently harmless phrases. What Russell's own class thought it signified was 'being like us'; while their Scottish equivalents thought of it as 'being *like them*' – for the most part willingly, sometimes enthusiastically, yet always with a sense of unplaceable alternatives (Douglas Dunn's 'moorlander' *Geist* of no fixed abode, the errant displaced person in the dark). Such misunderstandings are vital to an unwritten constitution. Anti-nationalist polemicists have sometimes said 'nations' are constituted by how much history they misinterpret, forge or forget. Yes – and so are multi-national states.

Though less blatantly obvious than in the case of Northern Ireland, Scottish and Welsh *mésententes* are just as profound, and just as reflective of the present crisis. Hence (Russell goes on) –

> For Scots the point of devolution is to destroy this uncon-
> scious English supremacism . . . Something like two-thirds of
> Scots want to preserve the Union with England, but they do
> not want, and have never wanted, to preserve it on exclu-
> sively English terms.[3]

Some other conclusions seem to me to follow from his acute observations. For London, 'Devolution' has always been precisely that: 'power retained', or a way of preserving the old terms, while affecting the more democratic or liberal approach made obligatory by the post-'89 climate. Lady Thatcher's version lay in pretending to devolve power to 'the individual' (entrepreneurs, families, etc.). Blair, on the other hand, in the phrase which the election campaign made sadly famous (though naturally more in Scotland than in England), would much rather give nothing of significance away to a northerly 'parish council'. Since his Scottish Party had become fixated (for good reason) on the idea of *something* happening, he had no option about going ahead. But like nearly everyone in England he interprets the result as simply a more democratic form of administration, a benign modernization-move in no way affecting the existing structure of sovereignty. It will function on the plane of local government (broadly interpreted). The Scots by contrast (including many in the Labour Party, and some Conservatives) will welcome the reconstituted parliament as a reappearance (albeit one-legged) of sovereignty among them – something more like equality, therefore, 'their due' in the sense of what the Treaty should have meant, and so on. Could misunderstanding be deeper, or more total?

In sovereignty questions, voice is all, or at least the source of all. This did not seem to be true for long enough, granted. But that was possible, and endured so long, because a kind of compensated anaesthesis was held in place. The vocal cords were not excised by 1707, but they were re-routed via the class structure to the Westminster modem, and translated into Unitarist-speak. A Scoto-British idiom emerged out of the process – that odd tongue which the Labour Party in Scotland is still struggling to rediscover and articulate. In that sense, 1707 'incorporation' was a form of semi-strangulation, for long justified in the name of British progress. Notoriously, Scots of all classes had for long a strong interest in British and Imperial progress: hence their silence was compensated, and half-bearable during the decades of empire and a centrally-administered welfare state. Although even then it never really signified to them submergence in a Perfect Union or (as James fantasized it later on in the same speech) 'Golden conquest cymented with Love'.

West-Lothianitis

Decline leaves the main body with two constitutional ways of tackling its satellite-problem. One was the obdurate rigidity of the stick-insect (Thatcher and Major). The other is a display of Lampedusan zeal for as much of the New as can be counted on not to disturb the Old too much (Blair). The euphoria of the 1997 moment has not yet vanished as I write, and I realize anyone making such a glum suggestion is liable to be condemned as a curmudgeon. After twenty years of constitutional catatonia someone appears to actually change something, and what do you do – sneer, and look for faults!

But I have already defended a more sober stance on the 'New Everything' mood, in the first chapter of this book. In general terms, there is likely to be less ground for the negotiation of novelty into the system than appears at first sight – *particularly* in a period of euphoric expectation. A state in steepening long-term decline will tend to consolidate or fall back upon its essence, even while it searches (avidly, as at present) for new survival-formulae. The New Labour government inherits easily the most dense, refractory and metropole-centred power-system in Europe. That historical unitarism was borne to a new level altogether by the reforming passion of Baroness Thatcher, who in some respects remains Blair's heroine and model. He wants to move in a different direction, but also to do 'as she did' in the sense of rapidly, popularly and decisively (even ruthlessly). Farthermore, he has something she which didn't have: a new party. The new Premier's authority enjoys the crucial vehicle of a 'modernized' party where greater individual democracy has been counter-balanced by intensified central domination. To regain office, in other words, Kinnock, Smith and he were forced to transform Labourism along parameters which were (immediately) those of 'Thatcherism' but (more profoundly) could not help also being those of an ultra-centralist polity approaching the end of its tether.

They made Labour a party of power rather than protest; but

'power' is not an abstraction. A party reconfigured in these circumstances becomes, however unwittingly, the prime bearer of *actual* 'sovereignty'. For all Britannic subjects power still has the defined form of Crown-in-Parliament, the airless Courtroom-Chamber by the Thames, the wondrously flexible Constitution (and all the rest of it). Also, we know how the object was attained: through the kind of absurd tip-over inherent in the ancient electoral system – too great a victory, in other words, and one owed to the mechanism of élite representation rather than democracy. It would seem to follow that the 'Presidentialism' so many commentators have depicted is not a passing or merely personal phenomenon. It is most probably (in the terms I recommended earlier) a farther phase in the crisis of the state: from Monarch-substitute to pretend-President.

Yes, 'it could be all be different *if* . . .' – but I have dealt earlier with aspects of the subjectivity and 'real intentions' of the new régime. The point is that the sovereignty-problem is structural, and not personal. And also that most of it seems inscribed in the original historic solution found for what was actually to be the impermanent transformation or extension of England into 'Britain'. This solution was a by-product of early-Enlightenment civism: by definition it avoided the perils and tumults of the nationalism which subsequently informed such alterations of the map. However, it took place well before democracy too; and hence was never sanctioned by popular will or what Ernest Renan would later call the 'daily plebiscite' of wider representation. The absence of farther revolutions of the state, so consistently lauded by worshippers of the system, meant also that this primitive-civic nationalism had to be preserved in the aspic of its time. The price of non-revolution was a palimpsest nature, in other words, later re-coded by Edmund Burke as 'evolutionary', 'gradual' and hence superior to all the rest of the post-1789 world.[4]

One aspect of the palimpsest was 1707's treaty-preservation of an institutional national society and of a strong national consciousness, albeit exiled to 'satellite' limbo. Nationalism (in what would become the standard ethno-linguistic sense of the 19th and 20th centuries) was slow to evolve there for a perfectly obvious reason: in Scotland, there was no 'nation' to be built, redeemed, 'imagined' (etc.) by means of the usual formulae. The nation was there already. It had never gone away, or been repressed, liquidated or assimilated. These fates had overtaken the state part of it alone. Also, the rest had been around as long as England, and (whatever the long-run faults of the Union) was not subsequently to become *under*-developed. Lowland Scotland would undergo an agrarian and then an industrial revolution comparable to those in the South. Such 'incorporation' was nothing like colonization, even if it meant a good deal of (so to speak) self-colonization.

In the lecture referred to previously (Chapter Two, note 12) Michael Ignatieff has warned both Scots and the *québecois* against overplaying the posture of victimization in their current dilemmas. He's right, and it follows that their national liberation will not be much like decolonization either. On the other hand, it does not follow either that statehood, whether resumed or new, ought *not* to be a part of such liberation. 'Disincorporation' would be a more accurate phrase for the latter – so far, a relatively low-key process in Scotland marked by successive attempts at reconstituting a broadly-based civic-political (rather than an ethnic) identity. The reacquisition of voice has been as odd as the way it was lost three centuries ago.

'It is no accident that . . .': another fine old Marxist phrase. It gives me great pleasure to contribute to its revival, by pointing out that by no accident is Conrad Russell an authority on the 17th century foundations of sovereignty, and hence sees the contemporary dilemma in some ways more clearly than those suffering intoxication by the New. 'Accident' would be an equally poor explanation for the fact that the most persistent and celebrated critic of devolved government in Britain over the last twenty years comes out of the same century. But I refer here to a living relic, not just an idea: Tam Dalyell MP (formerly 'Dalziel', pr. 'Diyell') of The Binns, in West Lothian. He dwells in the more amenable country north of George Lockhart's Carnwath, where his mansion has been turned into a temple of the sort of élite Britishness I was trying to describe above.[5] Since 1 May 1997 we have seen him remount on the umpteenth leg of his crusade to save the Union. Where his ancestor General (or 'Bloody') Tam used musket and sabre to underline the advantages of Britishness, today's Laird wields The West Lothian Question. He has laid about him with it for over twenty years now, smiting liberal smartasses and heeding no man lest the (nationalist) Devil steal his tongue. 'One day . . .' he recently told *Sunday Times* readers –

> . . . a government will come which will not tolerate a situation where my successor and the other West Lothian member, Robin Cook, will still be able to vote on housing, education and health in West Bromwich but not in West Lothian. A Prime Minister and a government which set such store by doing what is right in the long term cannot shrug off this problem by intoning: 'Sufficient unto the day is the evil thereof'. Just how will the White Paper address the problem of setting up a subordinate parliament in part – though only part – of a Kingdom which above all one wishes to keep united?

Did 'one' not know the context and the man, another 999 call might seem appropriate. This is at first glance the language of sandwich-board salvationism. *What* 'evil thereof', intoned upon which particular day of wrath? As for 'subordinate parliaments', is today's Europe not carpeted with them from the River Oder to the Atlantic? What Biblical doom can possibly be hastened by a few more in the British-Irish archipelago?

But of course what we have here is a familiar – a personal emissary of that darker sense in which he does indeed know what he is talking about. Being from the 17th century he bears Thomas Hobbes's Sovereignty in the DNA, and understands that 'subordinate' can so easily, indeed almost inevitably, come to mean 'insubordinate'. Beneath the studied phraseology of his West Lothian Question lies an invocation of terror and the Last Days.[6] There is in truth no way in which some sense of sovereignty regained can be prevented from informing any new Scottish parliament. It is not quite like most other present-day regions, *Länder* and autonomous entities. And hence, there is no way in which a counter-sense can be prevented from arising in the old British-English parliament. No way (consequently) of avoiding some kind of struggle over where the last word lies – on what, eventually, might be any number of subjects.

For the artificers and loyal servitors of Union, such a struggle must be prevented at all costs. The only sure way to do so was by abortion. Unfortunately, this particular abortion lobby has got used to phrasing its message in the deliberately quaint litany imposed by its author: the supposed absurdity, or impropriety, of future Scottish Deputies legislating on sewage, road-signs, toilet-paper, class-sizes and E coli outbreaks 'in West Bromwich but – once a Home Rule assembly is at work – *not in West Lothian*'. The vantage point of the tedious litany was invariably that of the rulers and legislators. *Their* sovereignty – in fact their entire lifestyle – would be intolerably impaired by such absurdities. Through the resultant fatal crack in power's façade, dark forces would then erupt. Ravening ethnicity on one hand, and upon the other the awesome prospect of English resentment: too many Scots at Westminster; too much being done for them, time they were taught a lesson. This bothered King James greatly too, gazing back as he did upon centuries of such lessons.

Such matters have of course been straightforwardly resolved by other regional or subordinate-national constitutions round the world. Viewed abstractly, since the British are not so different from the rest of the species, there should be nothing to prevent that here. Not, that is, *if* we had a new, general, written constitutional settlement to replace the 1688 version of Sovereignty. Surely a redrafted democratic Union could then build in some new 'quasi-federalism' – a confederal or other partnership scheme for the archipelago's *ethnies*?

I apologize for evoking this bedraggled old chimera once again. But it is Tam's real point, although one to which he has never wanted to draw too much direct attention. He has always used a heavy concentration on hypnotically engulfing detail to dispel the uneasy radicalism attaching to such notions. An obsessiveness over supposed illogicalities distracts argument from something more deeply uncomfortable. The truth being held at bay here is not simply that do we not have such a settlement. In itself that might just be a remediable accident. More importantly – and best not dwelt on for the sake of democratic sanity – is that in the Kingdom which 'one' (i.e. Tam, the Queen, Tony Blair and his party, etc.) wishes to keep united unto the world's ende, we almost certainly *never will*.

Farthermore, if we had it, it could not help being every bit as fatal to Tam, his class, Etonian Britishness, and all the paraphernalia of the previous Union-imperial state. An authentically *democratic* system would have equality as one of its pillars, equality for nationalities and minorities as well as for individuals. Thus what we now call 'Devolution' would still be part of it. It would still have to include England. But since the

English as a nation were quite content with the old arrangement, they would have to be persuaded – just as they have to
be now – of the need for such a 'costly, unwanted' (etc.) adjunct
to *their* idea of what democracy means.

Thus the West Lothian Question would merely reappear in
a different form. So would every other dilemma being posed at
the moment. Break-up is break-up, and for this particular historical inheritance, *easy* remedy is none.

Make Up or Break Up

At the end of his 1607 speech to the English Houses of
Parliament, James lapsed into an appeal to them all to trust his
own person:

> Studie therefore hereafter to make a good Conclusion. avoid
> all delays, cut off all vain questions, that your King may have
> his lawfull desire, and be not disgraced in his just endes.
> And for your securitie in such reasonable points of restric-
> tions, whereunto I am to agree, ye need never doubt of my
> inclination. For I will not say any thing which I will not
> promise, nor promise anything which I will not swear; What
> I swear I will signe, and what I signe, I shall with God's grace
> ever perform.

In the beginning lay the end. It is all too easy to translate the
above into a Blair speech, with appropriate spaces for the slight
but passionate fake-quiver which today's Sovereign has so perfectly mastered. His fustian resembles King James's so closely
because it articulates the same deeper problematic of
Sovereignty. There is actually only one cure available for West-
Lothianitis and the over-masticated quandaries of Devolution:

recognition of the sovereign character of the new (actually the restored) Scottish Parliament. If that is not recognized, it will end by imposing itself.

The 'New Britain' everyone has heard so much about for the last six months would require a new Treaty of Union. This has to be renegotiated. In 1998–9, it can no longer be imposed. But renegotiation is not consultation, the perennial placebo of those in power. It requires at least two parties, in order to guarantee consent, whole-hearted democratic agreement (and all the other Blairian watchwords). A substitute for equal partnership imposed by one side alone, via the ambiguities of devolution, can only end up as provisional, incessantly contested, and probably bad-tempered.

If there is anything in the longer-term perspective I have argued for here, then 'devolution' will be like the application of a plaster-cast to a leg broken but not reset. Thus far it remains founded (like Labour's previous 1978 Bills) upon solemn listings of discrete 'powers'. These may be either given to the new assembly, or (in the formula finally favoured by Blair and Donald Dewar) 'withheld' from it as the imperial responsibilities of Westminster. This choice certainly made a difference to legislative progress through the House of Commons but in no way affected the principle. In the light of sovereignty, both formulae are absurd. They disregard and offend the 'residual Scottish sovereignty' which Russell has rightly diagnosed in the post-1707 legacy.

The only way this can be avoided is by treating the resurrected assembly as a constituent or 'convention parliament', one of whose tasks – probably the most important – will be to strike a new deal with Westminster and replace the old Treaty, on behalf of the nation it represents. In 1689 convention parliaments redefined sovereignty after the Stuarts, and established the new system of representative, corporate Rights.

Farther ones are needed today to establish democracy, along the lines argued for by Charter 88 in England and the Constitutional Convention in Scotland.

A propos the latter (and in case people feel uneasy with the abstraction of 'the nation') let me remind them of recent concrete history. The Scottish Constitutional Convention was a broadly-based body which included the Labour Party, the trade unions, the churches, and representative of the most important institutions. Not without reason was it parodied as a constellation of the Scottish great-and-good, convened in definitely Godly style by a cleric of the Episcopalian Church, Kenyon Wright. This Convention met patiently for years in the 1980s and produced the over-modest home rule scheme on which the new legislation has been largely founded. But in 1988 – the 300th anniversary of William's accession – it also published a Scottish Claim of Right signed by most Labour and Liberal Democrat MPs, which attributed all sovereign rights in Scotland to the Scottish people, rather than to the Crown in Westminster.

Did they mean it? Well, presumably the signatories did mean it, at least while their pens were scratching the Declaration paper, and what they were defining was the principal task of the new Parliament for which they were agitating. These initiatives were all preambles to the framing of a new constitution for Scotland. A renewed Scottish written constitution will be needed to show just how those sovereign rights should be exercised, and the necessary condition of that is political independence. The refound political voice might decide to go on acquiescing in the multinational agreement. Were the advantages of the United Kingdom really what Unionists have been proclaiming for so long, how could they refuse? But they would certainly have to *decide* the matter democratically, in a way which was not possible in 1707.

Some of the signatories may now be telling themselves it is

irrelevant, or that it has been superseded by the newly Glorious & Bloodless Accession of 1997. What mattered under Sovereign Thatcher no longer counts under Sovereign Blair. But if so, they are mistaken. Blair is no Prince of Orange, and his ramshackle bundle of changes is no successor to the British Leviathan. I suspect such recusants often cannot help themselves. They have been struck down by the curse of the New.

I attempted to account for some aspects of this condition in Chapter One. Living inside a cadaver brings with it certain risks, including a belief in miracles. Since spontaneous regeneration is difficult (implying a revolution, a new constitution, and so on) the temptation is to hope that marvellous short-cuts, ingenious tricks and wheezes, might do instead. Thatcherism was a hothouse for this sort of thing, and a Left modelled by her influence has partly succumbed to it too. She did feel the need for change, and the hunger for it. But paradoxically, her government also rested upon an almost Tsarist-style resolve to maintain the old Union régime unchanged. Hence non-state or socio-economic transformations had to be feverishly stimulated or at least (where they turned out to be hard, or impossible) fantasized about: Crowned entrepreneurialism, America minus democracy and egalitarianism – everyone can recall only too well these and other halfwit formulae of the 'eighties.

An instant intelligentsia and formula-industry arose then to supply them. The authentic philosophy of the old Anglo-British domain had been empiricism, but in the 1980s this was abruptly (and maybe fatally) deposed. John Locke, Michael Oakeshott and nearly everyone in between were consigned to the bin. Where superior somnolence had reigned, artificers of the new mushroomed, and prophets power-breakfasted with Ministers – the process whose long-term culmination has amounted to the Musil-moment of British redemption.

I mention all this again not out of hostility to the post-modern, but to try and locate it better. It may not be so easy to distinguish death throes from the stirrings of the new. Any suggestion of this kind – that nation-states are the likely inheritors of the British Union – is bound to encounter the accusation of archaism. All today's think-tanks seem to have it in for nationalism and nation-states: outmoded, narrow, obstructive, reactionary, inward-looking and immune to alternative intellectual medicine. As a one-time addict of modernizing mania – not to speak of departure-lounge internationalism – I can't help sympathizing with much of this.

None the less, if the question of sovereignty is taken seriously, as it still must be in Britain, then the emphasis has to be put the other way. There may be a degree of anachronism inseparable from such solutions; but *that* may be because the context itself remains so deeply anachronistic, and cannot be wished away. There is no magic leap out of it. Democracy won a remarkable victory on 1 May, I agree; but so (unavoidably) did archaism. Even now, in 1999, it may not be quite clear which aspect will be the more important; but of course the argument I am advancing here really implies the second is likely to prevail. The evidence has been steadily accumulating in that direction.

Power may or may not corrupt 'absolutely'; it will as sure as British Fate tend in that direction. In such a backward-inclined framework, established solutions remain not only inevitable but *at least provisionally* desirable. If the President continues his successful appropriation of the former charisma of Royalty, and the framework gets even more old-fashioned beneath all the trappings of the New, then they will become that much more desirable. If a *de facto* English Parliament emerges to fulfil the West Lothian criteria, alongside the *de facto* sovereignty of the Parliament at Holyrood, then any more forward-looking formula will in any case have to be agreed between them – 'as between' two sovereign states. The 'as between' will lapse.[7] This is why the Convention and its Claim remain justified – and much more justified in principle than in the over-praised detail of the self-rule schemes which it and other bodies have so laboriously worked out.

Trapped in the Interim

The present British Sovereignty-system arose in the interim era between Absolutism and (with 1776 and 1789) the advent of democracy. Its terminal crisis is occurring in another interim: that between the national-identity states of 1789–1989 and the formation of a democratic European polity. I suggested earlier that historical and developmental location explains most of what matters about any particular variety of nationalism. The point can be put more crassly as well: things happen when they have to, and usually at the 'wrong time'. There is a deeply accidental side to progress, which has consistently mocked blueprint-makers from the Enlightenment onwards. On the other hand, the accidental is also 'essential', in the sense of inevitable. There was no way that anyone could conceivably have foreseen or planned the actual errancy of 'Progress'.

This has nothing to do with irrationalism or 'human nature' in the fatidic sense, though it certainly helps explain the formation of mythologies of that kind. The 'wrong time' which Ukanians of this moment happen to be in is the one between the endlessly-analysed 'decline of the nation-state' and a European successor still under construction, within which ethno-linguistic and political differentiation may assume renewed and stable – or at least longer-term – forms.

It would of course be awfully convenient if Scotland, Wales

and Peace-Agreement Ulster could somehow fast-forward into that regional/national condition of the future. It would be especially so for theorists, which may be why so many voices are clamouring for them to do so. Thus, it is suggested, they would avoid the perils of nation-statehood and atavism as well as the disenchantments of sovereignty in a globalized world. Abandoning old-style sovereignty can be awfully good for you. Best to disclaim it in advance, therefore – prove your innocence before anyone has a chance to accuse you of the crime. By renouncing Satan nationalism and all his mesmeric trappings, a calmer future will be guaranteed for all. Why, societies may actually gain in effective authority (as well as economically) through a pooling or merging of statehood – and this without sacrificing 'identity' in the psychic or communitarian sense.

Now all this may be absolutely splendid – *for those with sovereignty already*. They were (so to speak) the winners in the first round of nationalism. From London, Paris, New York, Ottawa, Brussels and other victorious summits, it is most enlightened to discuss the merits of dilution, cession, merging (and so on). For the first-round losers, however, those who came too late, failed or are still trying to put together a bid for recognition and modernity-status, the question appears differently. After all, they possess nothing resembling sovereign power to 'pool', 'merge' or gallantly sacrifice. They are simply being asked to forgo it. Metropolitans may enjoy such sovereignty snakes-and-ladders; their sovereignty-deprived satellites are bound to see the game in a different light. They wanted to get into the game. Now, relatively suddenly, they're told the game isn't worth the candle. Take the UK and French Leviathans of 2000, for example: not only did they at an earlier stage appropriate smaller-nation sovereignty wholesale – now they aspire to giving it away again, *still on our behalf*!

Scotland has plenty of its own fast-forwarders, some of them in the Scottish National Party (which has been brandishing 'Independence in Europe' for many years). As usual I suspect they actually mean something different by it, not necessarily appreciated from a distance. As a formulaic long-term solution the thought may appeal of being an autonomous Region, or Region-Nation inside European Union (whatever 'independence' turns out to mean there). In the shorter term, however, as a way of avoiding trouble, strife and secession, there is always another implication present, but possibly one less salient within the London/Home County conurbation. It is that *England* (or maybe even regions of England) must move at the same time towards some similar or equivalent status. Indeed – since that happens to be where Sovereignty is unjustly concentrated – it would plainly be both simpler and more appropriate for the Metropolis to (at least temporarily) lead the way forward in such noble sacrifice.

So on with the pooling and merging, Britons. *Until* this is achieved, however, and 'Sovereignty' decently buried, could we on the periphery please have some ordinary, boring, narrow, dangerous, egoistical, potentially atavistic (etc.) sovereignty? In an epoch of the provisional, the sole solution remains that actually attainable. Which means one that looks back as well as forward – sovereign statehood, that is, also known as 'independence', and prescribed by the general rules still prevalent in Europe, and in the world of the United Nations. Until 'the interim' becomes a good deal less interim – just to be going on with – a few more national states may be required.

The new Scottish parliament does have a sovereignty-ambit defined for it in advance by the history I have tried to overview here: from the 1689 Claim of Right down to the new 1988 one squeezed out under the pressures of Thatcherism. That is where it will really start from. In the new parliament there may also be plenty of 'good boys' (including I hope 50% women) who wish above all to conduct themselves with devolved propriety inside the pseudo-immemorial rules of Ukanian hegemony, antique and New. This has come to be known as 'making the parliament work'. I suspect they will be wasting their time. Seen in the sovereignty terms we have been looking at – the rise and fall of Britishism – ordinary nation-statehood and responsibility (also known as freedom) may turn out to be a lot less trouble.

Readers may have noted something odd about this manner of argument. It amounts to saying that a frankly sovereign parliament and its eventual accompaniment, a Scottish state, are both the most likely and the best solutions to the emerging dilemma, and yet employs no standard-issue nationalist rhetoric to do so. This is because in Scotland the case does not depend (and actually never has depended) upon such familiar motifs and incantations. It may also be why the latter sound a bit odd in the United Kingdom context, as if an important message was somehow getting mistranslated into the wrong tongue. The general (hence unavoidable) speech-mode of nationalism has never in fact accorded very well with the particular problematic of the England-Scotland relationship. It does fit Ireland, and half-fits Northern Ireland/Ulster. But that is because Irish 19th century and early 20th century development was so much closer to European and global norms: in those comparative terms, it was more 'modern' than main-island politics (not more backward, atavistic, etc.). The political die for that development was cast by the incorporation of the Irish Parliament in 1800 – across the threshold of nationality-politics, as it were, two and a half centuries after Welsh assimilation and one century after the Treaty of Union. The first national liberation movement of modern times was the American one of 1776. The second was the Irish Rebellion of 1798.

This can be put in another way, by asking what the Scottish electorate now votes for. In one sense, of course, it votes via the Westminster *table d'hôte* menu of different parties inherited from the long epoch of political incorporation. However it can also be seen as voting in a fairly unanimous (70%–80%) manner for a distinct yet ill-defined direction of affairs, described in innumerable surveys and polls as 'more say in our own affairs', 'home rule', and so on. With a degree of relief, some commentators regularly point out that only one part of this registers on the Thames-side Richter Scale as overt 'separatism' – the 20%–25% supporting the SNP. This is true, but the relief is misplaced. The point can be put more Irishly: in Scotland, Home Rule has been far too serious a matter to be distracted by Independence.

On the other hand, it now seems most likely to *mean* independence. What most voters may really have been supporting is (so to speak) the Sovereignty Party, a movement which has addressed itself to the people in many different party and non-party guises (including some open support from within the ranks of Scottish Conservatism). It could also be called the 'right-to-decide' party. The most important thing for the recalled parliament to decide (I need hardly point out) will not be raising or lowering income tax by a few percent. It will be whether to try and alter the conditions of its UK affiliation. Like many (possibly most) adherents of 'right-to-decide' I think that once it comes into existence only a Scottish parliament will have the right to decide such questions.[8]

Of course that body might meet only once, and decide to follow 1707 precedent, by requesting reincorporation at Westminster with a few modernizing touches. Curiously few seem to expect such a result. Personally, although disappointed by any such verdict, I would certainly accept it on democratic grounds. Democracy is what matters most here – that is, democracy not merely as head-counting but as the account-able majority of heads in their actual social configurations, including that of nationality.[9] But by the same norms, I assume opponents will accept any eventual verdict on disincorpora-tion, and on seeking 'independence in Europe'.

The right-to-decide party is about constitutional democracy, and forward-looking; it is not about ethno-cultural nationalism, and in that sense backward-looking. What it does look back to is the loss of 1707 – the surrender of a state, not the assimilation or defeat of a nation. At the same time, it recognizes that democracy retains its predominantly national configuration, something capable of transformation but not (or not yet) of supersession or transcendence. British Unionism was a short-lived pseudo-transcendence whose day is over. The 1997 election result opens the door to (at least) begin an escape from it. I hope we can get some way through that door before it closes again.

CHAPTER FOUR

Devolution or 'Virtual Liberation'?

Researchers in computer-imaging technology are developing systems by which users can experience a simulated three-dimensional reality. This simulated reality is known as virtual reality (VR). The term cyberspace has sometimes been used synonomously with VR but has by now gained its own meaning. Since the 1970s, technologists have learned how to produce animated computer images of objects that exhibit the colors, textures, and changing spatial orientations that their counterparts exhibit in the real world. The results can look as real as actual motion pictures. The further aim of technologists is to make it possible for persons to 'enter' and actually manipulate Virtual Reality.

The Grolier Interactive Encyclopedia (1997)

Virtual Politics in Ukania

Donald Dewar's Devolution project has added greatly to the momentum of change in Scotland. Since the referendum there has arisen the general sense of an incoming tide, carrying us forward into a new period of history. Like many others, I waited only too long for that tide to come, and still feel grateful for its very existence. No survivor from the days of interminable mud-flats and decaying seaweed will really feel otherwise, even if many of us feel obliged to huff and puff a bit, and complain about how much remains to be done.

The shift changed everything, for the victors as well as for the defeated. Indeed it did so more for the former than the latter. Those who have retreated muttering and groaning into assorted bunkers do in a sense perpetuate the older landscape. They want things to stand still – above all, they want *Britain* to remain intact. By kidding themselves it does so (like the Ulster Unionists) they at least retain a sense of where they are, and what they mean. Those who want out of Britain, on the other hand, are being compelled to acknowledge a new sort of *Angst*.

My view is that all too little has befallen UK Sovereignty since the advent of the Blair government. Much less has happened than first met the eye – and henceforth even less seems likely to happen. In a nutshell the argument is this: relatively big changes in central authority would be needed to make Scottish and Welsh devolution 'work', even in the modest sense of being less than an unceasing pain in the neck at Westminster. And yet, these now look like being more a matter of wilful rhetoric than of willing substance.

Causing national assemblies to exist is one thing – a fundamentally important step, and less irreversible than British Socialism has proved to be. But getting them to function as parts of a renewed British fabric of state will be quite another. It's for this reason I suspect that very soon 'Britain' may soon come to appear as reversible as its Socialism. And yet, there does not seem to be as yet any serious strategy for arresting this disintegrative trend. There is only the 'virtual strategy' of Blair's New Labourism. Of course there are some who believe Devolution to be itself such a strategy, but my argument here will be about the limitations of that. Part of this argument must be that probably no such real strategy is now possible in British terms alone – that is, without transferring the substance of the dispute into European terms, and putting Europe first. On its own, late-British political practice may simply lack the means to confront such problems.

It is not necessary to delve too deeply into the theology and lore of Sovereignty, and I raised some aspects of this in the preceding chapter. Let me just point out again that what matters is the contrast between 'government' and 'sovereignty' (with or without capital 'S'). I take that to mean the difference between the ordinary exercise and deployment of authority and the underlying assumptions of such deployment: the 'constitution' (with or without capital 'C'), the written and unwritten rules of the national game. These rules most often pass on unchanged from one government to the next. Power is a daily routine; while sovereignty is about who has the ultimate say, why they have it and (though not too often in the British context) how this should be altered.

Governments propose (one might also say) but it is the sovereign authority of the state which disposes. Disposes – often – not just with the sense of implementing government plans but pretty often with the sense of establishing what such policies 'really mean'. In 1997 the government proposed in the matter of Devolution to Scotland, Wales and London. It has since then done something analogous for Northern Ireland, but in close collaboration with others, especially the government of the Irish Republic. Are we now starting to perceive what these policies will mean? Yes, I think so; and yes, I think they are already showing signs of meaning something different from what was intended by the policy-process.

The Strange Deaths of British Local Government

In this context it may be salutary to recall something of the fairly recent past. We dwell in the afterglow of one extraordinary – and too rarely regarded – example of how British sovereign disposition may differ utterly from British policy-making. In that case the newly-minted policy did not just fail to be imposed, it was totally wrecked by the attempt to do so. The glistening blueprint, although think-tank nurtured and defended with vibrato in a thousand orations (now repressed from memory, if only to avoid death by shame) not only crashed, but brought down Mrs Thatcher with it. It finished off her whole phase of Tory-radical social engineering. In its dismal wake there came the Tory palace *coup d'état*, and then the seven-year régime of fag-ends and leftovers which endured right down to May 1997.

I am of course referring to the Poll Tax or Community Charge, of living if abjured memory. This is worth recalling, not for academic or historical reasons, and certainly not out of nostalgia. Not (either) to suggest that Devolution will be doomed to a similar débâcle. I am not suggesting for a moment that self-government in Scotland, Wales, Belfast or London will collapse in that kind of ignominy.

The point is much more modest. It may be that the attempt to implement Devolutionary policies by a central, sovereign and unitary power, itself essentially unreformed, will once more set up a partly unforeseen dynamic of change. And then, (though anything but 'disastrous' in their own right), these changes may come to resemble the Poll Tax in one important respect. They may be uncontrollably different from what the blueprint-forgers had in mind. It will then be said that the situation is 'unprecedented', and probably the sideeffect of malign peripheral tribalism. Alas, it is all too precedented, and has little to do with the periphery. A decade ago, it showed that the trouble was at the centre. If so, then the fish was already dead, in the famous metaphor, and was already rotting from the head downwards.

The Community Charge was not an isolated episode in either Tory or British political life. Its defeat and ludicrous side effects do not mean that it was actually a sideshow. Shame has done its work all too well, however, and today it does tend to be presented and dismissed in just that way. Toryism is seen as having 'gone too far' into a kind of lonely convulsion, a one-off epileptic fit from which they and everyone else mercifully recovered. The results were then safely shelved in the Westminster museum of State Folklore alongside the Gold Standard, the Eugenics Movements, Nationalization and the South Sea Bubble. Many people – not all of them hard-core Friedmanites or veterans of the Tory first hour – have conveniently forgotten that it was designed as the clinching financial armature of a much grander, and largely consensual, purpose. This was a broadly bipartisan aim of the post-1960s era. It was the idea of carrying out a general, reinvigorating reorganization of all the local government structures of the United Kingdom.

Far from being a one-off, that aim has been shared, supported, indulged in, and then repented of, by every successive British government for the last thirty years. It is worth pointing out too that Blair's 1997 government can be seen as busy extending the aim in new directions. After all, whatever other factors have come into play, the constitutional changes then in the air – Devolution, the new London Assembly and the more vaguely proposed English agencies and regions – may also be seen as farther examples of that same long-term trend. They are also extensions of 'local government reform', even if going beyond the original intention in various ways.

Widely differing formulae or recipes were of course employed over such a long period of time. Most will recall at least echoes of the bizarre and prolonged ideological clamour which invariably accompanied the process. It was launched by 1960s progressivism under the banner of making local authority 'bigger and more rational'. At that time much opinion still held to the old social-democratic nostrums – it continued to trust in élites, and believed some planning to be a good thing. So, Local Government was to be reforged, in order to foster a more modern and intelligible structure which could link locality and State together. It was also meant to make planning more effective and more cost-effective.

Some years passed. But bigness and rationality mysteriously failed to function, at least in Great Britain. Then from the late 1970s onwards planning began to wilt away in the heat of reborn market-mania and the idea of transnationalism, or globalizing neo-liberalism. While people were still wondering just what had hit them, another comet was seen in the east. It was travelling in the opposite direction. 'Make it *smaller* and closer to the voter', the sky-writing now announced. A segment of the Metropolitan clerisy was instantly converted. These neophytes set up preaching tanks to try and divine the comet's direction. The signposts now seemed to include old-fashioned community values, responsibility and the nuclear-family virtues. These bore an agreeable resemblance to what had once been put down as bad habits by visionaries of the sixties. The latter were always inveighing against 'anachronism', and the aldermanic or parish-pump mentality. But there it was: parochialism staged a triumphal comeback through the tradesman's entrance, re-robed in Tory slogans like 'Back to Basics' and the no-nonsense aboriginal morality of old Grantham.

The Reign of Ectoplasm

Not that these two avenues exhausted the illusionary potential of local-governance mania. It would be unjust to forget a curious variant which straddled both camps, and was for obscure ethno-geographic reasons visited upon the people of Scotland. Our proudly separate nature was in that part of the century acknowledged by a quite separate (or as people liked to say, 'distinctive') reorganization which tried, as it were, to make everything bigger and smaller *at the same time*. So the Scots ended up with Strathclyde Region on one side – half the size of Denmark – and microcosmic entities like Crail Community Council on the other.

I happened to be living in East Fife at that period, and recall quite vividly the inaugural meeting of the latter, one freezing night in the winter of 1981–2. It began with a prolonged discussion of the unexpected mission thus mysteriously signalled to Crail-dwellers. The still lamented (but at least partially understood) Royal and Ancient Burghs bequeathed from the time of the Scottish Kings had, it appeared, now been designated for rebirth. They were to become voluble hives of the truly and up-to-date local. Communities were to be made over into buzzing foci of popular initiative, enabled and spurred on by a broader range of interwoven support-structures reaching outwards and upwards through District and Region to the Scottish Office itself.

At that time the non-hereditary power structure of the local *habitus* was dominated by someone whom (to avoid embarrassment) I will call simply 'Mr East Fife'. Thus was he usually referred to by his electorate, hardly any of whom could recall life without him, and nearly all of whom (including myself) owed him some kind of favour. Over the next few years (until the final post-Thatcher reform-wave struck us all amidships) I recall with admiration this potentate's deft navigation of the reforming tides. When it came to keeping things unchanged, Count Lampedusa's *gattopardo* had absolutely nothing to teach Mr East Fife. He coordinated a seamless switch-over from draughts to chess, based upon calculations of just who was now responsible for what, how they could be got at, what the new tariff would be, and how in the end things would stay exactly and triumphantly the same. Beneath the water-displays of virtual reform, endemic clientelism quietly survived, and got the better of the systems which 'They' had dreamed up. Nor – as everyone now knows – was this really much different from what must have been going on at the same time in the new super-fiefdoms of Strathclyde and the industrial West.

Over the thirty-year period as a whole, one mission simply followed another, before vanishing forever from human ken. These were not effective or enduring reforms, reinvigorating Britannia's grass roots. They were unbelievably expensive tides of virtual reality, meant to reassure a distant ruling caste that all was being renewed under its vigorous and inspiring tutelage. Invariably designed to save Central Government cash, they invariably failed to do so, though it was regularly claimed they would in the 'long run'. This was a safe escape-clause, in practice, since in the long run some farther wave of reform was likely to have struck, depositing its own mound of debris and resentment.

'Roots' was the guiding horoscope of such missions. Rootlessness was their infallible consequence. Conceived under icons like 'participation', responsibility and integral health, British Local Government reform in fact put down few tubers and was most often vaguely resented by those who (in the 1990s) it became fashionable to call its 'clients'. Few of the latter ever half-understood what was going on, and even fewer cared – apart, naturally, from those local councillors and functionaries who found themselves repeatedly uprooted, promoted sideways, found surplus to requirements, chided, renamed, and then blamed for everything – both from Sovereign heights and from long-suffering below.

If there were so many ungrateful beneficiaries of these bracingly 'radical' upheavals, it may be because so much of them consisted merely in one aberrantly radical slogan succeeding another. 'We must make local government more *responsible*' gave way, as in the Red Queen's dream, to 'No no, *cap them* – spendthrift authorities deserve to have responsibility taken away' (or indeed abolished if the misbehaviour threatened to become chronic). Whole tiers of local government were created to deal once and for all with the extremely serious problems at the foot of the British rainbow. Then closer inspection of this site showed there to be far too many of the damned things, inflicting far too much bureaucracy upon a local citizenry chafing for freedom – know-it-alls, do-gooders, reckless spenders. 'Get rid of them!'

No doubt the abiding purposes of the United Kingdom are better served by drawing a veil over much of this story, and especially its cost factors. The veil certainly was drawn, and oblivion has taken over. More significant though, today no one seems much concerned with what it was all about. I admit to not really being up on contemporaneous developments in (e.g.) President Ceauşescu's Romania or the central African kingdom of the Emperor Bokassa. But somehow I doubt if, over the period in question, such astounding sub-state earth-tremors affected any comparable non-dictatorial state. Has any other country engendered a municipally-founded near-revolution – a fiscal egalitarianism so preposterous that masses actually erupted into the streets and invited imprisonment in order to denounce it? And yet, these were not accidents. The Community Charge was simply the most determined (and naturally the most 'radical') moment of this long-range strategy – a grand if unfortunately fluctuating vision, the impulse to endow Great Britain with an appropriately great lower-tier administration, once and for all.

Why? Well, the notion was always of Britain being thoroughly recast – pristinely renewed from its grass roots upwards. The dénouement of this vision in the Poll Tax disorders was in that sense the most elaborately prepared suicide note in modern political history. So there must have been, at least implicitly, some profounder purpose behind the process. That strategy was clearly continuous and repeated enough to be phrased in terms of the State, or even of 'sovereignty'. It was more than just successive governmental policies. Perhaps one could sum it up by saying that from the 1960s into the 1990s, as the United Kingdom state grew steadily more centralized in operation and unitary in practice, it sought with approximately equal constancy to counter-balance, conceal and legitimate this trend by the reconfiguration of local or 'regional' government.

Participation and Mutiny

Though done initially with an administrative rationale – efficiency, effective redistribution, cost-saving modernization etc. – as time passed and the world became steadily more democratic, the ideology accompanying the quest was retailored to fit altering conditions. When it started off, the United Nations Organization was peopled mainly by dictatorships. By the time of the post-Thatcher wave, democracies were in the majority, and the Cold War was ending. British low-political reform had therefore to acquire a stronger democratic camouflage – that of 'returning power to the people', whether as citizens or (Mrs Thatcher's preference) as entrepreneurs. Giving a say, a voice to the multitude, liberating them from bureaucracy and do-gooders – this became the ultimate motivation for the reform of local government. It started by imposing more effectual administration, and concluded by liberating folk from administration altogether, at least in the sense of officialdom and politicos.

The present Leader of Britain's Conservative and Unionist Party (and potentially of England's National Party to be) famously played his youthful part in these developments. No one old enough to have witnessed it will have forgotten the high point of the celebrated schoolboy oration in 1984, when the 17-year-old Hague concluded a Party Conference act by turning archly towards Thatcher and the assembled Cabinet dignitaries on the platform: 'Get off our backs!' the lad boomed (as nearly as a seventeen-year-old could). The importance of the motif was not displayed only in the delirious applause and benign smiles of the particular instant. The promising young fellow was acknowledging a deeper current, one whose longer-distance repercussions have undoubtedly helped put him where he is today.

Central Sovereignty rolled remorselessly forward, therefore, while claiming in ever more booming tones to roll backwards. But the real point of the latter was always the former. 'Power devolved is power retained' was how J. Enoch Powell phrased it in the 1970s (talking of Scotland and Wales) – except that 'retained' was never a strong enough term. Great-Sovereign States in retreat have to augment such power as is left to them, and not merely strive to retain it. 'Decentralization' is (or can seem to be) one way of accomplishing this, and the pattern has been followed in both France and Britain over the last generation.

In accordance with the differing character of sovereignty in the two countries, French reform was 'rational', uniform and consistent, while the British version (at least until Poll Tax dementia struck it down) was pragmatic, heterogeneous and revisable. But both were intended to reconcentrate authority and promote more effective *participation* (the same word applies for both tongues) within the regrettably shrunken command-structures of these ex-imperial states. Shrinkage does not lead automatically to fade-away. The contingent gets devolved, in order that the essential be re-empowered. In the terms used earlier, the state may shed certain levels or dimensions of governmental power, the better to keep up its sovereign authority and appearance: that is, its *standing* (another joint Anglo-French word) in the wider world.

In Britain that project reached its limit with the Community Charge débâcle. It then fell through the floor. But it did so in quite a useful way, which at least allows one to perceive the true parameters at work. This is important, because such parameters are still in place – and hence likely to affect the devolution story as well. The British Poll Tax was not defeated by sapient internal manoeuvres within the political élite or the parties (whatever gloss they subsequently put upon events). It was arrested by popular mutiny.

The French are supposed to be better at mutiny than the British, but the weird tale of local government casts a different light upon this and other truisms. The anti-Community Charge upheaval had a deadly effectiveness about it, and one thing this revealed was the true polarity of political life in the United Kingdom. On the one hand, a forever unchanging sovereign state (add capitals as required) which simply commands whatever grass-roots alterations appear required by the moment's captaincy. On the other hand, there is an opposing horizon of grass-root or below-decks revolt – the black hole of ultimate refusal. The 'Constitution' (here definitely requiring its capital letter) is the elaborate, but of course unscripted, pretence that in Great Britain there is really something in between the two.

'Mutiny' is a system-limit, a sufficiently massive decision that enough is enough. It was that limit which eventually (in that sense I mentioned before) defined the true meaning of the Community Charge legislation, and destroyed it at the same time. The entire political class then scuttled to obey, congratulating itself on its realism rather than apologizing for its own fickleness – behaving in fact rather as the British Royal Family did, after the scenes in London following Princess Diana's death in September 1997. Otherwise I suspect that most of us would still be grumblingly paying up. HM's bailiffs would still be selling off non-payers' furniture, and the first concern of Mr Blair's incumbent government of 1997 might then have been not Devolution but finding, at long last, some 'fairer replacement' for the 'appalling mediaeval tax'.

This brings me to the point: I suspect that Devolution too is likely to have its meaning defined for it by spreading mutiny – but (it should be added at once) by a mutiny of a very different sort. If forced to phrase it as a one-liner, I would say, this time it will be by an *equality-mutiny*.

Helpless Provincialdom

To recapitulate: since the 1960s a congenitally imperial state form has been struggling to adapt itself, not just to change but to accelerating rapids of transformation – above all since the end of the Cold War. And it has striven to do so without reforming its historical or constitutional mainframe. The nucleus has remained sacrosanct. Just as the Gaullist style-core of republican grandeur and *rayonnement* remained untouchable under Mitterand and Chirac, so the British equivalent persisted under Thatcher and Major. For Mrs Thatcher, especially, part of the explicit *raison d'être* of 'radical' upheaval was to preserve the core of British sovereignty as virginally intact as possible. It was because these upper layers of sovereignty were too holy to touch (at least until May 1997) that the standard route of political modernization has been denied.

The decline-dilemma meant that the underlying claim ('Best Constitution ever known', etc.) had to be made ever

more resoundingly, as one preposterous episode followed
another. Even the Poll Tax catastrophe did not change this.
One particular idea had proved itself bankrupt beyond belief,
yet the ideology it was designed to sustain continued to
unfold – and in a way, Devolution remains part of that unfolding. I suspect this is much more because of its links to the
ongoing dilemma of British sovereignty than due to the discrete and often diverse policies of one government or another.
The basic unity of the United Kingdom has to be conserved, so
that the traditional sovereign-power structure can go on punch-
ing above its weight in the international arena (immorally,
amorally or, as more recently, ultra-morally). '*Grandeur*' is
another common French-English term, and meaning. This is
usually put in terms of 'being stronger together' than as separate and possibly bickering parts. Truism is obliged to
underwrite untouchability.

But one of its implications is that everything else may be, in
a curious sense, over-reformed round about this untouchable
resolve. That is another sense of 'radicalism' in its late-British
formulation. Incapable of passing through the ordinary channels of constitutional, juridical and electoral reform, it is as if
the restless, increasingly resentful impatience inseparable
from both French and United Kingdom decline has to overflow in other directions. It happened in the economic field,
naturally, where central-planning mania was succeeded in both
countries by bouts of raging capitalist fever. Planning too has
been in a sense privatized. Think-tank blueprints were once
despised by British Establishment culture and identified with
smart-ass Parisian *idéologues*. Now they are taken for granted.
The boot-strap renovation of civil society on paper became a
respectable profession in London as well. The discrediting of
Socialism led to a supposed 'third way' of associational self-
help – new this, new that, New Everything, preferably

uncoupled from 'conventional politics'. I discussed this in Chapter One, above. Local government reinvention can be perceived as only one long-running symptom of this compensatory overflow. Unwillingness to overhaul the semi-divine apparatus of Sovereign Power ensured, and in a way still ensures, the diversion of such ideal energies on to the plane of the hapless British provinces.

This latter term is ancient yet appropriate. I use it here because the fact is these provinces combined two features crucial to the decline syndrome. They could be identified, in an imprecise yet rhetorically important fashion, with 'the people', or the 'grass roots', daily lives and so on – the latest climate or *sine qua non* of modernity. But they were, at the same time, almost entirely dependent upon central power and under our *ancien régime* possessed not the faintest mote, beam or echo of Sovereignty. Hence they were entirely unable to resist or protest effectively against being repeatedly reinvented. The older rural or patrician stratum associated with local and provincial power had declined or disappeared over the same period (nowhere more strikingly than in the ranks of Mrs Thatcher's party). Squires, lairds and tradition-minded notables had to give way to enablers, service-providers and managers.

But given the antipathy of British central power to formal, non-conventional reorganization, no statutory system had replaced the *ad hoc* old order. The abiding aim of UK stateliness is to avoid being 'pinned down' by that sort of thing. It continues to prefer the public-bar company of Edmund Burke to the saloon-bar rectitude of Tom Paine. Instead, the illusion was cultivated of a provincialdom reconstructable at will – of localities that could be remodelled, replaced, abolished or restored, with or without a semblance of 'consultation'. The grass roots would thereupon (in a revealing and endlessly reiterated phrase) 'settle down' once more, somehow magically transmuted by the sovereign recipe of the moment. These may be among the reasons why the death throes of the 1688 polity were first rehearsed at provincial or local administration level.[1]

The Nemesis of Britishness

Were I presenting the Devil's case (as Unionists are bound to see it) I think at this point the argument would get stronger and stronger. 'Don't think for a second the death throes are over . . .' I can hear Him whispering now, out there in the dark. The symptoms have merely moved away from that of the 'local' which prevailed from the 1960s down to the 1990s, and on to the far more perilous terrain of regional/national government. The system could re-establish its validity only by the massive electoral lurch of 1997, and this meant falling into the control of a party whose power-base had, in the intervening decades, grown over-dependent upon certain of these allegiances. The acquittal of such debts had now become indispensable to the consolidation – by 1997 one had already to say the 'restoration' – of central authority.

However, in spite of all the clamour for renewal and rejuvenation, there is likely to be far less ground for the negotiation of novelty into this system than appears at first sight. Is this not what the débâcle of local government reform suggests to us? A sovereignty built up over three centuries will go on tending, as it has been doing over the past generation, to consolidate or fall back upon its essence, even while it searches around frantically for new survival-formulae. The 1997 Labour government inherits easily the most dense, refractory and metropole-centred power-system in Europe. That historical unitarism was borne to a new level altogether by the reforming passion of Baroness Thatcher, who – as one commentator after another has noted – remains in important respects Tony Blair's heroine and model. He may want to move in different directions from her, but he also badly wants to do so *as she did*, in the sense of popularly and decisively (even ruthlessly).

Farthermore, he possesses something she did not: a new party. The new Premier's central authority rests upon the crucial vehicle of a modernized party where greater individual democracy has been counter-balanced by intensified core autocracy. I said something earlier about the implications of this – the 'new ruling class' in embryo inside Blairism.

To regain office, three successive modernizers (Kinnock, Smith and Blair himself) have been forced to transform Labourism along parameters which were (immediately) those of 'Thatcherism' but (more profoundly) could not help also being those of an ultra-centralist polity near the end of its tether. These leaders did succeed in the sense of turning Labour into a party of power rather than protest. But as we have seen, 'power' in the deeper, sovereign sense is not an abstraction. Once reconfigured in these British post-imperial circumstances, a party inevitably becomes the vehicle of actual or historical sovereignty. There may now be few left who wish Labour was still a party of moralizing and futile protest. But the risk of rendering it capable of wielding authority is that, in turn, an inescapable template of authority may come to wield it. Under such a sovereignty-order, governments and Prime Ministers think they exercise power. But *how do they know?* In any particular situation (and above all during crises or conflicts) it may be a pre-constituted sovereignty which is exerting itself through them.

Nor finally (Auld Nick concludes) ought we to forget how New Labour attained its power-objective: through the kind of absurd tip-over inherent in the ancient electoral system. By too great a victory, in other words, and one owing far more to the old mechanism of élite representation than to democracy. The electoral triumph of 1 May had a plebiscitary character which itself carried central authority on to a new plane of intensity. For the moment at least, we see a blatant presidentialism towering over a landscape almost void of opposition.

The Fakelore of Youth

As it towers, it talks (or occasionally blabbers) non-stop. The topic of such discourse is naturally radical change and (as with all its predecessors since the 1950s) the bestowal of undreamt-of power upon its subjects. But elementary caution and recollection should make one wary of this. Revolutions from above can happen; but feigned or non-revolutions from above have been more common. What these do is ostentatiously alter a few things, in order to preserve an essence, a creed, or a place in the sun. Admittedly, Blairism no longer officially fetishizes the State and Constitution. It has acquired superior public relations skills, as part of its modernization. However, it does not follow that the Labour Party will actually reform the very machinery on which its power has been founded. It is much more likely to reform some features of that government in order – like all its predecessors – to conserve or reinforce the essence of Britishness, and hence increase its chances of remaining in office, or of returning to office for an appropriately or Britishly long period of time – an 'era', as it were, rather than an electoral term or session.

I looked at this comparatively in Chapter One, suggesting that 'breakdown' may be the sole real alternative to honest (and not necessarily very popular) constitutional reform. The new Scottish and Welsh Parliaments may appear also as related to the same melancholy saga – that is, when set in its perspective of still accumulating, and still unreformed, central sovereignty.

The particular circumstances of the election of the Labour Government have made opinion focus largely upon power to the detriment of sovereignty. The personnel, rhetoric and the professed (or spin-doctored) intentions of those so over-dramatically returned to office have eclipsed consideration of structures. It was very noticeable how over the whole period 1997–99 most political commentary and debate has ended, seemingly inevitably, with speculation about the subjectivity of the rulers: what they (or increasingly what he) 'really means' or intends to do. If Tony Blair so much as winks at a journalist in the course of some perfectly anodyne remark about the constitution or the monarchy, it is sure to be read next day as a sure indicator of abiding radicalism (in *The Independent*) or impending sell-out (in the *Daily Telegraph*). But all this may mean is that the Anglo-British sovereignty-structure is reverting in its dotage to something like its origins – that is, to the purloined absolutism of William and Mary in 1688, at the moment when regal authority was so enduringly sanctioned (and reinstated) through forms of élite consent.

Blair and his government do their declaiming in the name of a new, reborn and once more youthful Britain. The United Kingdom is in glad-confident-morning mode once more – not for anything like the first time, as I noted in the Introduction and Chapter One. All that is implied here is the appropriate intensification of a rhetoric which has counter-weighted each phase of decline since Queen Elizabeth II was crowned back in 1953, as (literally) the symbol and radiant emblem of a rejuvenated land.

There is a successful chain of shops nowadays called Past Times, specializing in 'period' gifts to older members of the family and friends, Edwardian and Victorian nick-nacks, 1920s-style clocks and radios, and nostalgia books. But there is one volume still missing from its book section. Yet there could be money in it, once Blairism has subsided. It might be called *New Britains We Have Known*, and the cover-montage should be (e.g.) of a 1950s Mini, Harold Wilson in Gannex, Elizabeth and Philip, Carnaby Street, Diana's 1981 wedding-dress, with Peter Mandelson and William Hague squeezed into the bottom corner. As I noted earlier, the New Britain business has now been round quite long enough to deserve its own sepia-tone mementoes.

An associated Theme Park might transport visitors from Annigoni's famous 1953 portrait of the girl-queen in a Spring landscape, via the youngsters who 'never had it so good' in the later 1950s, into the White Heat of 1960s Technology, then on to the juvenile comet-like entrepreneurs of the deregulated market. Towards the exit a 'Get off our backs!' Pavilion could lead up into the Blair-Hague Gallery. An appropriate combination of conclusion and high point could be a simulacrum of the Greenwich Millenium tent, back in the Year 2000.[2]

The local-government and other fetishes of modern British politics have actually been ways of standing still, while appearing to be running extremely hard. Feigned social breathlessness has become the public relations of deepening catatonia. A government of actually youthful 'radicalism' would have binned the House of Lords in its first week. The virtual radicalism of Mr Blair and Lord Irvine, on the other hand, appears to be moving gracefully towards a removal of hereditary entitlements, quite possibly before the year 2002, while retaining some kind of 'balanced' appointee Lordship less likely to obstruct Britain's elective dictatorship. It is (so to speak) time that crude biology ceased interfering with the pure *Geist* of 1688, distilled to its final (though possibly terminal) perfection by New Labour.

Born-again Albion

Some years ago Christopher Hitchens published an article about Prague in the *New Statesman*, saying apologetically to the readers that though his ambition had always been to write something on Prague without once mentioning Kafka, here he was – failing again. In the same way, as someone who always wanted to write about Devolution and Scottish self-rule without mentioning Tam Dalyell's 'West Lothian Question', I must apologize in the same fashion. Yet again, the absurd yet fatal folklore obtrudes, the preposterous yet unavoidable non-question which, since it consists essentially in waving a scarecrow about, has never and will never receive an answer.

That scarecrow is 'England'. All defenders of 'Britain', a United Kingdom ruled to all eternity from The Binns (or places resembling it) always fall back upon England. That is, upon the supposed eventual resentment, discomfiture or intolerance of an English people provoked beyond endurance by Scottish or other interference, unfair representation or appropriation of resources – by wilfully ethnocentric egotism directed against the common interest. This common, negotiable interest can only be defined centrally, by the Union. The reason is that Great Britain is not a federation, a confederation, an asymmetrical quasi-federation, a crypto- or pseudo-confederation, or any kind of consociational hippogriff. It was built upon final rejection of such 'jests and chimeras', back in 1706–07.[3] It is a great unitary state, which happens also to be what an important recent book has called *A Union of Multiple Identities*.[4] In their comparative conclusion the editors underline how the UK's English-made unitarism has given such low priority to ethnicity and cultural assimilation, because –

In the United Kingdom . . . political discourse was broadly

built around the assumption that Parliament, not the people, was sovereign. As long as the inhabitants of the British Isles accepted the very English idea that change could occur legitimately only if sanctioned by the British Parliament, there was a limited need to foster unity by State-sponsored acculturation . . .

Hence 'political culture' was the crucially unifying element: Parliament and the parliamentary class or élite – a representative stratum itself rather than those it supposedly represented. 'Britain' was a multinational social class before it was a multinational state; and the latter remains in essence a manifestation of the former. Britishness was a stratum-phenomenon rather than a mass or popular one, but later on the élite-mass linkage was greatly fortified by an overseas command-structure in which mass participation was allowed, and indeed positively encouraged and channelled. Empire and successful warfare gave this class-forged link an iron durability.[5] At the same time, the monarchy was refashioned into an equivalent or simulacrum of nationalist symbolism. The chain was both gilded and strengthened by this transformation.

While in France revolutionary methods had compelled the construction of a socially sovereign identity through intensive or even terroristic acculturation, the 'very English idea' was able to acquire considerable institutional rigidity and some symbolic charisma without an English nation-building in that sense. 'There was a British *Sonderweg*', conclude the editors of *A Union of Multiple Identities*, most strikingly configured by 'the experience and management of empire', and it is this which gets celebrated through the endemic mythologies of 'flexibility', empiricism and English national indeterminacy. I spoke earlier about the Westminster state form being 'congenitally imperial', and this is actually the same thing. What counts as

'congenital' in this sense relies upon a range of societal equivalents for 'genes'. These are no longer reproduced by having
colonies, or oceans to command: they have to go on working
through the habits and instinctive assumptions of sovereignty.

But what the latter manifest has been a state-way rather than
a folk-way. Although powerful (in proportion to its success and
prestige) this diminishes and grows thinner with the passage of
time. The Anglo-British mode may have avoided the conflicts
and breakdowns of French popular sovereignty; but in the
longer run, it lacks its great resources as well. Just because
there has never been a British nation underpinning the state,
the latter's decay is likely to be terminal.

When the underpinnings of the British state-idea decay,
there is astonishingly little left. And anyone can see these have
now largely disappeared. The external command-structure, the
symbolism of regality, the old 'parliamentary class' and the rigid
prestige of the institution itself have either disappeared or
diminished. Their iron has turned to rust. The simulacrum
aspect of 'Britishness' as national identity inevitably stands
exposed. The post-1789 French nation always stayed much
stronger than its various Republican-state incarnations, however fragile the latter may occasionally have shown themselves.
In contrast, 'Britain' has been one continuous state-incarnation
of formidable *durée* and outreach, but – in the end – significantly less indwelling power and human resource.[6]

Over-identified with a single but extruded institutional form,
English nationality has consequently little political horizon
beyond that. When summoned to present its credentials at a
deeper level it has normally resorted to literature: English literature has often been made the vehicle of a national *Geist*.
The latter grew less accessible in the narrower terms of territory and institutions, after the overwhelming expansion of the
18th and 19th centuries. Such habituation to a wider – at one

time almost global – mode of political expression led to a compensatory internalization, a falling back on the spirit. The animating nation, when required, could now most easily be evoked via culture – by the English Word rather than the old English State.

We should not overlook the fact that the final act of invalidation did not take place until after Blair assumed office, with the return of Hong Kong. Nor that it was followed almost at once by the bewildering 'spiritual revolution' after Princess Diana's death, in the course of which, for the first time in history, a capital city was barricaded by poems and floral tributes rather than armed crowds and soldiers.

What Dalyell's West Lothian scarecrow relied on was this politically indeterminate or unfocused character of 'England'. It exploits it with the suggestion that restricting or provoking such a *Geist* can only generate resentful monsters. Thus the spirit which bestrode and (by its own accounts) civilized much of the world must on no account be encaged by mere nationality, or it will turn out to be the meanest and most resentful of enemies. Hence Blind-Brit preservationism is the one hope for the Scots and the Welsh – as, more obviously, for the Ulster Protestants. The periphery must cling forever to the cadaver of imperial Nurse, out of fear of something worse. Of course, there is also the secondary (yet quite vexing) possibility of an entire multinational, middle-management stratum of Parliamentarians, Lords and bureaucrats being not simply unemployed, but in a sense unemployable: how can they avoid being pensioned off, and condemned to a pitiable future of fête-opening, water boards and unpublishable memoirs?

I know West Lothianism is also conventionally 'answered' by a set of recommendations, utterly reasonable in themselves, about federalism, or the development of regional government in England. But the sheer reasonableness of all this has been just what's wrong with it. Things which happen everywhere else in Union Europe, and could (abstractly) quite well happen here, represent precisely the converse of the fated *Sonderweg* which seems to be still operative through Blairism – that is, the state-form attached to the 'very English idea', built up for so long around Parliament and Crown rather than citizenship. Concretely, they stand no chance because they presuppose a prior transformation of central power towards acceptance of the formal and statutory, and towards either cultural or legal homogeneity at the sovereignty-level. There is no blueprint-wand capable of switching from one mode to the other. That would need a central revolution.

But Blairism is far more like one more virtual horizon, prolonging the settled historic one of United Kingdom sovereignty. The fact that, like all its predecessors since Wilson, it gabbles unstoppably about galvanizing, modernizing and the virtues of youth is neither here nor there. As on all the previous instances of glad and confident morn, it is not simply a matter of the rhetoric outweighing actual reform – it is meant to *take the place of* effective reform. Virtual Liberation is intended to function as a surrogate of the actual kind – 'independence' and statehood. Delighting in Devolution, we subjects are also expected to confirm the State in its persisting self-estimation. Not only are we content, the Centre will be renewed by having executed the required and promised 'revolution from above'.

I realize such cynicism sounds suspicious too, since it's close to suggesting that nothing at all has changed – in which case the sense of liberation and possible renewal generated by 1 May 1997 must have been a delusion. No – things have changed all right. And we can be grateful both for the changes and for the régime which fostered them, whatever the accompanying absurdities and deceits. However, such shifts have not come

about because of Party Political Broadcasts and think-tanks.
They have shifted on a level far below that of Westminster and
the spin-doctorate – on that of sovereignty itself. That is, on the
plane referred to earlier, the structural underpinnings of the old
régime of 'multiple-identity' Britishness.

When the hollowness of earlier reform therapies – like local-
government resurrectionism – was exposed, there was still an
overarching traditional structure to fall back upon. A century
and a half of state-inculcated identity still counted for something. In the 1990s, by contrast, such reserves are low. The last
bout of shake-up – 'Thatcherism' – devoured them, at the
same time as it ate up the economic bounty from Britain's
North Sea petroleum. This is really why, after so many
rehearsals, the break-up of Britain is actually happening. In
1979 Dalyell's scaremongering could still hold it back; since
1997 it has merely served to escalate it. The springs of British
virtual reality are running out – by 1999, running out so fast that
it has become hard to keep track of them all.

Impossible Equality

One odd feature of Tam Dalyell's 'West Lothianitis' was an
unconscious yet quite obvious, even visceral, anti-
Englishness. Its depiction of the 'inevitable' English
response got away with something close to racism – all the
more daunting (and yet convincing) since it has been put
about by subjects so totally addicted to the ways of
Westminster. Unionists were thus permitted a virtual xenophobia for which any nationalist would have stood
condemned. Since 1 May 1997 and its impressive Labour-
Liberal majority in the South, no one will pay much attention
to that either. However, the true reason for apprehension

about resurgent English identity never depended on such equivocal fears. It is founded more simply, upon a recognition of certain *inequalities* inseparable from the demography and economics of the British Isles.

The British national minorities are too big to be simply ignored, yet far too small to count naturally as equals or partners. As we saw, they were subordinated through a system of informal hegemony, buttressed externally by empire. That multiple-identity order was *made* to cohere through close political union: 'Britain' was the label for the subsequent over-centralism of a ruling and administrative class, compensating for the persistence of national diversities. England's 'natural' dominance depended in turn on the absence of formal political voice among this system's components. The latter by its definition all became equivalently 'local', in the sense of sovereignty-less, and such a status was maintainable only under an 'unwritten' constitution. The rule of custom thus became, in effect if not in theory, the instinctive mode of English (or perhaps Anglo-British) nationalism.

It meant (for example) that one could do anything one liked with the 'local', while a subordinate legislature was a contradiction in terms – that is, within the *sui generis* terms of imperially-oriented nationality. The crazy vein of truth in West Lothianism is simply its prostrate acknowledgement of those terms: nothing will ever be allowable in between folkloric locality and Red-Queen Sovereignty – hence things had better stay the same. Federalism? Just a theory – possibly applicable where different instinctive modes prevail, but quite futile within the traditional reign of English-Britishness.

Were Charter 88 to succeed in its reforming campaign and install a modern written constitution, things would naturally become different again. However, the 'things' here happen to include England. Which means, they comprise the dominant national group configured by Sovereignty – unwrittenness, all the customs linked to not being vulgarly or narrowly English, the Monarchy and Shakespeare. Historical effect weighs more heavily than theoretical propriety. Instinctive modes of being can't be rewritten like blueprints. The constitutional question remains indissociable from the national question.

The Inevitability of Mutiny

And this is really why mutiny is unavoidable. The 'self' active in once harmless phrases like 'self-rule' has actually been mutated by the democratic revolution since the 1960s. Nowadays it harbours the yeast of equality. The resultant fermentation carries enzymes alien to the archaic body of Anglo-British sovereignty. I don't see anything too surprising about this – it would, surely, be far more surprising if the 1688 sovereignty-system were indeed gifted with the eternal life its worshippers used to take for granted.

The renewed Scottish parliament will (for example) naturally want to be taken seriously, in a sense which never figured in the local government saga. And 'seriously' can't help meaning something like 'equally', particularly in Scotland. This might be true anyway for the largest minority in the United Kingdom, even were that a 'region' without any previous state or a battling nationality past. But here of course it applies to a nation whose credentials are comparable to those of pre-Union England, and which throughout the multiple-identity era has clung stubbornly to notions of association or partnership – ideas of (in today's terms) 'virtual equality' in the absence of a separate political voice. I must say the belief that any devolutionary settlement will *not* involve a demand for and attempted resumption of equality in a stronger sense seems laughable.

However, this implies some kind of disavowal of the 1707 Treaty of Union – a qualification, if not an outright renunciation of it. Is this not why the draughtsmen of the Scottish Parliament Bill have been so careful to include it intact? Clause 1. – (1) reads: 'There shall be a Scottish Parliament'. But fifteen pages later, in Clause 35, 'Miscellaneous', we find it pointed out that: 'The Union with Scotland Act 1706 and the Union with England Act 1707 have effect subject to this Act.' Hence any new Scottish Parliament, capital letters notwithstanding, will not be *the* Scottish Parliament Mrs Ewing declared it to be, in the first words spoken within it after the first elections of May 1999. It is not permitted to be the sovereign body which dissolved itself two hundred and ninety years ago. The Union only persists 'subject to this Act': hence the Sovereign power behind the latter is unabated, and is merely being manifested in a new mode. Scottish political authority may look as if it should affect the 1706 and 1707 Acts – may indeed seem to imply revision or replacement of the Treaty – but in *Realpolitik* it does not (and in fact, judged in terms of the 'very English idea', it actually cannot).

Why not? As Clause 35 states, there were two Acts involved in the Union Treaty, one English and one Scottish. Now, however, the only one which counts is that of 1706, passed at Westminster. It may have required two State Acts to set up the resultant British polity; but only one of these has truly animated the successor State – it alone, therefore, now possesses the authority to repeal, modify or replace the Treaty of Union. And no damned local government will be allowed to assume that right, either. Since there is effectively no 'very Scottish idea' to contest the Bill's interpretation of the 1688–1706 moment – at least, not until the new Parliament gets into operation – it is the other idea which goes on determining its meaning.

For the moment, that is. Outside the universe of

Parliamentary draughtsmen, however, Scottish ideas do go on existing in Scottish minds. Before the new parliament even meets, about a quarter of the Scottish electorate seems already to support 'Independence in Europe', a slogan which took over from straightforward 'Independence' over a decade ago and explicitly asserts an alternative equal-rights formula. Nor is this only a matter of party banners or election rhetoric. Events since May (and even more so since 11 September) have illustrated how energetic the equality-enzyme is likely to be in the new situation. As a matter of fact every relevant event I can think of has underlined the same point.

Most people here will recall the incidents I mean. The dispute over future representation of the UK regions in Europe, for instance, and the possibility of Scotland's Parliament representing British interests in Brussels. Or the argument (at present unresolved) over the control of funds for attracting inward investment. Central control is meant to prevent supposedly 'unfair' competition among UK regions – the North-East of England is not supposed to undercut (say) Wales, in the way that Spain or the Republic of Ireland regularly do parts of Britain.[7] This is for fear of 'anarchy' (the sovereignty-enzyme) going to non-metropolitan heads. As part of its Ulster Peace Process, the government undertook a balancing-act of concessions to both sides, notably to imprisoned terrorists; and a Scottish prisoner, Jason Campbell, looked like benefiting from this by being transferred to jail in Northern Ireland.[8] The ensuing furore made it clear that *raison d'état* had either forgotten or ignored the fact that there was a separate legal system in Scotland, by which Campbell had been tried and convicted. It was a system not inclined to make the slightest concession to 'political prisoner' status.

A few weeks later, and the Scottish media were engulfed in

disputes over the general future of the Barnett Formula, the mechanism for allotting government expenditure to various parts of the UK in proportion to population and need. Since the Edinburgh parliament will raise only a small part of its income in direct taxation, it has to remain dependent on a grant from London, and hence upon the Formula. But will the latter be kept at prevailing levels once Scots are (non-fiscally speaking) 'running their own affairs'? First doubt was cast upon this; but then came a decisive stroke of pure virtual insanity. It was announced that the Formula is set to become as flexible as the Constitution: it might be reviewed *every year* in future. Until things settle down, presumably?

On all these issues (and too many others to list here without being tiresome) the reaction from Scottish broadsheet and serious media comment has been fairly uniform, and continuous. Eighteen months before the new assembly was even elected, public opinion was doing nothing but 'standing in' for it, or behaving as if it were actually in existence. And it was doing so on the basis of a single *Leitmotiv* – one constant complaint, voiced in different accents or with varying degrees of irritation but returning invariably to the same thing: 'Treat us as equals!' The psychology always incorporated (as Russell notes) into the Scottish understanding of Unionism has become virtually stand-alone in the new circumstances.

But when the parliament meets it will actually be standalone, and far better equipped than the media to voice resentment. Nor, judged by recent events and public arguments, will it have much trouble in finding subjects of complaint – every one of the arguments mentioned above was (or was perceived in Scotland as) the result of central arrogance, indifference, folly or worse. From the centre the perception was different, naturally: local prickliness and bias interfering with the broader perspective, parochialism best kept in its proper place, etc. These were obviously so many rehearsals for dramas to come.

The point here is not to adjudicate such rows, but to point out their structure. They derive from perceived inequities. Whether or not real socio-economic inequalities increase, there surely cannot be the slightest doubt that perception and resentment of them will. Democratic voices have been willed into existence, and must find something to say. Also, they are bound very quickly to say it on the plane of 'high politics' – not the prescribed one of 'low' or local-government and administrative affairs. This is because, however lowly the origin of any given argument, it is likely to connect with the terrain of rights and principles. It can hardly avoid touching on that non-equality between Sovereignty and locality which was the axis of the old state.

'Devolution' has attempted to project an authority-mode somewhere in between these two levels, but without a framework relating it to either. Such a 'framework' could of course only have consisted in a new, written constitutional instrument. This would at once distribute and codify 'sovereignty', limit central power and the Crown, and guarantee regional or dependent rights – the very things which 'multiple-identity' empiricism has striven to avoid since its bad time with them in the 18th century (notably in America). In its absence, a devolved authority can only oscillate between claiming sovereignty (like say Jersey or the Isle of Man) and sinking into locality (like old town and county councils, however the titles change). In Scotland, however, that choice is simply unreal from the outset: a long history, independent institutions, the Treaty of 1707, and the way in which the devolved status has been gained – all combine to make sovereign equality the only practical possibility.

This means that Devolution as a process or continuum is likely to be led, and in a sense conditioned, by a sovereignty-oriented movement of the largest UK national minority. Having been undertaken the wrong way round (from periphery to centre) it can hardly avoid being determined by the strongest tendency on that periphery. The Welsh parliament in turn will not want to be treated unequally, in spite of its more restricted range of powers. In England itself a mounting regionalism will then have to make the case – as representatives of the Campaign for a Northern Assembly are already doing – for not being regarded as inferior to 'what has been given' to the Scots and the Welsh. When Londoners vote for their new Mayor and Assembly, it will (as Lord Archer unfailingly reminds them) be bound to do so in terms of standing up for their own rights and status in this new context – and so on.

What will make this process into a rolling mutiny is not just parochialism (let alone insane nationalism) but the sovereignty-vacuum in which it seems condemned to unfold. In Great Britain as historically constituted, there is simply nothing to be equal to: the available, experienced modality of power is a Godly relic of the 17th century – by nature inimitable and over-arching. The Scottish Parliament can't (obviously) equal this poly-national statehood of Westminster. But it has no English-national equivalent to compare itself with either. The Welsh Parliament's wish to 'equal' Scotland would place it in the same insoluble dilemma of which the Scots are already complain-ing. As for Northumbrians and Londoners, given the absence of a national dimension to their autonomy, they will probably be forced to assert equality through an unlikely (and anyway aggravating) demotion of the 'privileges' accorded Edinburgh and Cardiff.

The sole other alternative would be the Cornish one – claim-ing or coining national credentials in order to underwrite equal status. This too is a stratagem likely to increase. One should not omit from the view those places mentioned earlier, Jersey,

Guernsey and Man – possessors of genuine sovereignty by a curious and special dispensation, and tolerated by the Britishness of past times because of their smallness and eccentricity. However, scale is not so significant these days, either in Britain or the world at large.[9] 'Being like' Singapore, Andorra, Liechtenstein or Curaçao stopped being an absurd aspiration decades ago; but international-relations 'Realists' and metropolitan Foreign Secretaries failed to notice this, and theory (regrettably) has gone on taking them too seriously.[10]

De Facto Sovereignty

As I pointed out before, it may be handy for theorists that there are abundant examples of vital regional and regional-national governments functioning elsewhere in Europe; but they are quite useless in Britannic practice. The latter remains ancestrally configured, and so far as incapable of domestic system-change as of any 'rash' dive into compromising European company. Unable to shut out the great social currents of post-Cold War modernity – equality, democracy, economic globalization and rediscovered nationality – it has sought to incorporate them 'empirically', according to the mainstream reflexes of its history and politics.

What the Devil's advocacy ends by suggesting is therefore simple: those who have lived too long by noble Empiricism are now dying by it. Philosophical empiricism and 'flexibility' were in truth complex ideal forgeries designed to garb and protect traditional English-British sovereignty. Yet that Sovereignty itself has been the opposite of empirical and flexible: as both Tam Dalyell and William Hague insist, it was (and remains) absolute, unqualifiable, and more divinely aloof than the most extreme of 'continental' doctrines. It has consistently deemed itself capable of impossible feats like the Poll Tax and Devolution. *Force majeure* has made Foreign Secretaries admit they no longer control the globe these days; in relation to matters still within its domain, however, the god like conviction persists – let it be so and, with a bit of consultation, things will magically settle down or 'work out' once again. 'Muddle through' was English nationalism's version of the world spirit, founded upon the supreme (if self-ascribed) reasonability of the class embodying it.

The contradiction of the 1999–2000 moment is that Blairism responds both to the urge for change and to that for replication. As with Thatcherism before it, the enactment of 'radical' policies appeared to require the assumption of the old and (supposedly) sovereign power-base – since the conviction and sway of absolute office will alone permit such drastic changes. Everything must be changed; but regrettably, it is always the genes of changelessness which have to be mobilized for this task.

I mentioned to begin with the general contrast between the levels of policy-making and sovereign execution. These are never equal. In the longer term (or when in confrontation with crisis and contradiction) the second has to prevail, and it is this thought which has informed my subsequent analysis of the prospects for devolved government. The Community Charge could for a time be confined to the timeless reservation of provinciality; but 'Devolution' is not, especially in Scotland. It cannot avoid reconfiguring (or at least trying to reconfigure) the *Geist* itself. In the longer run I suspect this will be just as true of Wales, Northern Ireland, Northumbria and Cornwall, as of Scotland. However, it is via the latter that the new syndrome is likely to be most clearly manifested.

One interesting note may be worth adding to the discussion of re-emergent Scottish sovereignty. The audience may have noted that almost nothing has been said in it either about

Scottish nationalism, or the familiar theme of the differences (real or imaginary) between Scottish and other British societies and cultures – for example, the frequently invoked 'corporate' character of Scots identity, Celticism, native egalitarianism, and so on. These tend to dominate the view from the South, and also from the angle of a certain kind of nationalism. But the odd fact is that they need scarcely be mentioned in the Sovereignty perspective I have concentrated on here – not because they are unimportant, but because the contradictions within United Kingdom Sovereignty itself are sufficient in themselves for an analysis of break-up.

The Scots themselves have generally argued things out within a spectrum of 'Home Rule' versus SNP-style Independence. I suspect the 'versus' aspect of the dispute is now fairly redundant. Within the crumbling clam-shell of British Sovereignty, everyone except Tam Dalyell and a few bitter-enders want 'serious' home rule; but such self-rule will find it hard to avoid *de facto* sovereignty. This category is for-mally unacknowledged by international relations ideology. But then, that ideology was evolved by and for *de jure* states, before the rise of European Union and the decline of Britain. Just how or under what conditions the *de facto* might in this case turn into the *de jure* would need another sort of discussion.

In conclusion: the reader may occasionally have felt as if some parts of the tale outlined above must have been lifted straight from Lewis Carroll or J.R.R. Tolkien. But in a way that is the point: Ukanian Sovereignty was indeed also such a story – a great public outwork of narrative collectively erected upon the foundations of English nationalism, in the course of the latter's subsequent adventures and travails in the wider world. But as the world has changed, that narrative has grown obsolescent. It has been retold too often, and instead of trying forever to upgrade it with ingenious twists and turns, a new start to sovereignty would be better: better for the periphery, but also (in the longer run) better for England itself. It is time the virtual became the real, within the new story of Europe.

CHAPTER FIVE

On Not Hating England

Who would have thought it, and not me, not me . . .
It was a long road back to this undeclared Republic.
I came by the by-ways, empty of milestones,
On the roads of old drovers, by disused workings.
. . . Allow me to pull up a brick, and to sit beside you
In this nocturne of modernity, to speak of the dead,
Of the creatures loping from their dens of extinction.

Douglas Dunn, 'An Address on the Destitution of Scotland',
St. Kilda's Parliament (1981).

At Dead of Night

Just over a year ago, on 11 September, a referendum voted
75% 'yes' for the Scottish Parliament to resume business (and
also to pay for it, by 65%). Knowing I would have to be up in
the middle of that night, I had gone to sleep not long after the
polls closed, and next morning wasn't awake enough to listen to
the car radio until around 5 am. And so the news reached me
while driving along the High Street of Forth, South
Lanarkshire (pop. 2523, alt. 286 mtrs).

A folk-tradition has grown up of recalling just where one
was and what one was doing at historic moments. It's important
to get the details right. On my way from Edinburgh to Ireland
I pulled up for a minute or so to listen to the news, near Forth
post office, between two dour-looking pubs, next to a family
butcher's over the road from the '1st For Convenience' shop.

Then I got out of the car and walked a short way along the road, uncertain why, just turning over the details in my mind. A lot of Bannatyne Street – the High Street – seemed to be up for sale, right down to the long southward bend with its splendid prospect across Clydesdale and the Lanark Hills. The sale signs made it feel as if the whole place was becoming disposable. Not that Forth had ever been there for the views. The council houses on this wind-torn shoulder of bogland had been built only to serve a coal mine, until burrowing gave way to late 20th century open-cast.

What did I feel? 'Tradition' usually implies some qualified reconstruction of the past, which I'm trying to resist. Actually it was rather formless and confused – but at the same time, uneasy – along the lines of: '*No more* damn-awful scenes like these, thank Christ'. Not one thing would ever be quite the same again, in Forth or any part of Scotland. The Proclaimers once had a hit single called 'Letter from America' which took off from the idea of 'Lochaber *no more . . .*' and then went into a litany of less familiar heritage-sites like Linwood, Renfrewshire and Methil, Fife. Just what was being thus wryly lamented, or exorcized? Old Jacobite Scotland, the rude shade of Scotch engineering, or both at once?

On the radio one could hear the excitement of hundreds of people in Edinburgh's new International Conference centre, where the final results had been counted and broadcast. And yet, I did not feel less in the middle of it that deserted morning, crossing Scotland's central morass in the hour before dawn. The road passed by so many fallen asteroids of the country's post-industrialism: Bell's Quarry, West Calder and Addiewell, then Breich, Wilsontown and Forth, places I know very few readers of these pages will have seen or heard of. I suspect they might be gratefully overlooked even by anti-guides to the solar system.

The cold, autumnal edge of the September wind was not

lying. In the dead of that night a landslip had begun that would carry most of our previous habitations away. In a time far shorter than that of Empire and the boiler-plate engineers, their legacy in turn would vanish, or become a heritage-site like today's New Lanark, or the old Pictish stones. It had been a long, quiet process, and ended in a completely peaceful revolution. Many hearts had been worn down or broken by it, but no one had died. Scotland had upheld its modern civic tradition, and in the end had also managed to emancipate itself from the limits of that tradition. Thus far, an equivalently civic and decent nationalism had prevailed.

This was a low-profile success, in a world preoccupied by the military high drama of Kosovo, East Timor, Palestine and the former Belgian Congo. But the fact was, not such a small one either. An old nation – one of the original 'nation-states' of the early-modern world – had embarked upon the process of regaining its independence. Although located on the outer fringe of geographical Europe, it would do so within two very significant polities: the one-time industrial giant and former Empire-owner, Great Britain, and the emerging European Union. Like Slovenia, the Ukraine and the post-Czechoslovak nations, it had been able to seek emancipation through political agreement and negotiation, not via warlike exclusion or the forcible assimilation of someone else. The 'destitution' (in Douglas Dunn's phrase) to be remedied was internal, institutional and cultural in nature rather than a by-product of colonization or oppression. It looked forward to liberal confederation of some sort, and not backwards into the maw of vengeance and blood-sacrifice.

While many felt such a process starting up in the Autumn of 1997, nobody could have imagined the astonishing speed of the collapse. Within *six months* the Scottish National Party was revealed by surveys as likely to dominate, and quite possibly to control, the first Edinburgh Parliament. By 10 March the Glasgow *Herald*'s System Three poll showed them overtaking Labour. 'Connery confident upward trend will continue' declared the front page ('speaking from his Los Angeles office:', etc.) Far from home rule 'killing nationalism stone dead' (as Minister George Robertson put it), the very prospect appeared to be lending it new momentum.

Mr Connery's confidence has since then continued to be justified, right up to September of the following year, when the most surprising evidence yet appeared. An Edinburgh *Scotsman* poll (4 September) added a religious affiliation question to the usual ones about voting intentions, and discovered that a majority of Scottish *Catholics* would now vote for independence: 58% as against only 51% of non-Catholics (mainly Presbyterians). To grasp how surprising this is, it must be remembered that the popular Catholic vote was the traditional bedrock of the British Labour Party in Glasgow and right across the central industrial belt.[1]

This was an electorate that had seemed doubly imbued with underdog mentality: proletarian by fate and still half-foreign (Irish) by descent, always suspicious of nationalists as both 'tartan Tories' *and* somewhat Protestant (or even Orange) in demeanour. Although accounting for only a minority of the Scottish electorate, probably around 16 to 17%, the Catholics occupied a peculiarly strategic position. Their much higher concentration in the old-industrial areas had made them crucial to Labourite hegemony there – that is, to the 'one-party state' set up in the 1930s, and which by 1997 had known a lifetime of unassailable (and unassailably corrupt) local power. It was this bastion which, in turn, had become so important to British Labour as a whole.[2]

If that has changed, then it is no longer an exaggeration to say that everything will. A 'molecular change' was under way, rather than a passing shift in voting patterns. The underground workings must in fact have been far more decayed than anyone could have known only the year before. 'Class' was being transmuted into 'Nation' before our eyes. It seems to follow that the overall dynamic of the Parliament will be quite different from what was projected by the 1997 White Paper and the legislation which followed.

These had proposed a self-governing region in (as it were) harmlessly National uniform. By the following year, eight months before the first elections, what seemed to be arriving was a Nation already bursting out of the regional and devolutionary constraints. Most observers agreed verbally that the referendum was launching 'a process' rather than a fixed set of arrangements – that Devolution would require (in what was then a customary phrase) 'fine tuning' and a good deal of mutual adaptation in order to work properly. Indeed nobody could seriously think otherwise, given that the new authorities in Scotland and Wales were promulgated without any new all-British constitution to contain and circumscribe them.

However, it is one thing to calmly hold a door open to 'possible developments'; quite another when the first entrant proves unexpected, disreputable, and thoroughly ungrateful for being allowed into what he thinks is in any case his own house. And when he is, in addition, the very lout which the Open Door strategy was intended to keep out for good, or even kill stone dead, things begin to feel distinctly out of control.

Beyond Cosmopolis

Back in the seventies – when the Proclaimers would still have been at school – I remember someone who used to invoke Forth in arguments. Whenever this character saw pointy-heids

like mine agitated by thoughts of rebirth he would lean stiffly
forward from his well-worn perch at the end of a journalistic bar
and object darkly: 'Aye . . . all very well that, but it's what the
man in Forth thinks that really counts!' The point was difficult
to deny: few could know where Forth was, let alone claim
acquaintance with its manful sagacity. But of course his point
was plain. Giddy dreamers should not delude themselves that
the stalwartly canny Forthite would ever heed such nonsense: a
Labour-voting Scot-Brit would he remain unto the end of time,
or even afterwards, as Caledonian delegate to Nirvana (a
spruced-up version of Glasgow Corporation). Man-of-Forth
stood for the unalterable cosmos of grittiness in which Scotland's
winning the World Cup (or even attaining the semi-final) would
always mean more than fairy-tales about independence.

Parochialism is not just a state of mind, but a social structure.
I had entertained theories like that before; but they became a
real feeling only at that moment, in a 5 am sensation of ground-
shift too full of puzzlement, and too big for gladness or
retrospective gloating. I don't know how many Forth electors
voted for the change, probably nearly all of them. Not a shred
of the old saloon-bar wisdom now remains. It is deader than the
West Lothian shale-bings and a lot less decorative. Never was
real defeat more utter, or reversal from a shaming like 1979
more complete.

Yet coming down from Forth to Lanark, then across the
Border and then the Irish Sea, it was the sense of uneasy puzzlement which weighed most. In longer retrospect, I think that
derived from something only half-formulated in my mind that
morning. Time alone could bring it out. It was the sense of
how, in fact, no side really wins or loses such big arguments – or
at least, not in any sense subjectively imagined beforehand.

For twenty-five years in Scotland Unionism and Nationalism
had contended amid notions of seeing the other side in flight,

or with luck dropping stone dead on the spot: justified triumph
with his foot upon the expiring, scaly monster. But history is
not a courtroom or a newspaper Opinion Page. Things happen,
and a die is cast – but always for partly accidental reasons, and
never in a way or at a time corresponding to previous forecasts.
Then the instant it occurs everything is too much altered, once
and for all. Most of the old software of both sides is outdated on
the spot. Although victorious, the dreamers then need upgrad-
ing almost as badly as would Scotland's nay-sayers and
'hairmless Harrys'.

Was this the cunning of history, in Hegel's sense, or just its
daftly accidental nature? Whichever: in those small hours a
country for too long too much outside itself would return into
itself. Its former parochialism rested on a temporary equilibrium between places like Forth – John Galt's Parish, Dr
Finlay's Tannochbrae/Auchtermuchty, Duncan McLean's
Blackden, Andrew O'Hagan's Saltcoats – and a spuriously cosmopolitical realm, long deemed the equally natural habitat of
Scottishness. On the one hand stood Blackden/Forth, 'the arse-
end of the giant' as McLean describes it; on the other, a
'universalism' which was really the British Empire imperson-
ating civilization itself.

During that age a genuine Scotsperson was a sort of human
shuttle, a back-and-forth composite of and between these
things. Our *Heimat* had been both together, a package deal. The
grimy, couthy old dump where nothing ever happened and no
one bore a name like Jelly Roll Morton – not just a place, but a
state of the soul. And then its busybody school-leavers, out
there in Hong Kong, Calgary or the Khyber Pass, explaining (or
vending) Testaments and guns to other aspiring natives. These
did not just gang thegither, they were an intimate condition of
one another. Jointly they framed the special and awful style of
parish-pumpery which was being condemned to oblivion last 11

September. James Buchan has called it the mental world of 'the Empire Scots', the imagined community of Scotland-at-large, a nation simultaneously far too wee and much too huge (or at least, over-extended) to require ordinary human statehood. It was the world of his grandfather John, and when that inheritance dies off (he concludes) '. . . with us will die a mental country that will astonish any future Scot who chances on this article' (Glasgow *Herald* E2 section, 7 February 1998).

Good riddance to it. Its cost was the blood of loss which I tried to evoke above (Chapter Two). It was that corrosive, underground stream which has seeped remorselessly down through the veins of one Scottish generation after another out of its source: 'the last day Scotland was Scotland'. The lands of George Lockhart of Carnwath were only a few miles southeast of Forth (in the area where Ian Hamilton Finlay's 'Little Sparta' temple and garden stand today). As we saw, those who accomplished the act could not have really known what they were doing either, in spite of the rhetorical warnings of Lockhart, Lord Belhaven, Andrew Fletcher and others in the last Parliament of 1706. Paid or not, for good and deplorable motives, they were opening a heart-wound that would run darkly underneath the whole span of the nationality-world lying ahead of them. However good it was to become British, this companion injury could only persist as well. As Lockhart felt, a nation could not cease being what it had become through such custom and the prolonged state-effort of centuries. It could only feign other and grander modes of existence, while simultaneously haunting all such departures with the question mark of its own origin.

Folklorists have thought of this souterrain nationality as the carrying stream. But this seems to me an over-romantic conception. Blessing and curse together, nationality is simply the fate of modernity. We know now how little genetics has to do with it, but the societal equivalent of DNA is another matter. There is a long-range transmission of community from one age into another, through a myriad of idioms and altering channels, which is too little understood. This can be seen as a cultural blood-stream too, sometimes blind or disguised in its impact, liable to assume unforeseeable shapes or even flow in reverse, and capable of rising to the surface when least expected.

I know that the literal blood of others counted too, alas, in the British-imperial existence which for so long ensued. Its charnel-house side probably had more impact on the Scots than anyone else.[3] But latterly more appears to have been pumped out of the national heart-stream itself. This has been symbolized through the belovèd, itching, scabrous wound of so much 20th century Scottish literature. The latter's prolonged sojourn in Hell stands at bottom for the same loss, become reasonless: a national abnegation no longer explicable or sustainable by participation in a meaningful mission. I suppose British Socialism was the missionary party's last throw. After such betrayal, remedy can be none. Well, none but (as Buchan ironically concludes) a common sort of Euro-prosperity via 'independence or provincial euro-autonomy' – that is, a normalization enviable by most populations on earth, yet somehow a bit ordinary to the Heaven-obsessed. To some of the latter, desertion by the imperium (God in disguise) leaves Scottish society beyond even the hope of redemption. It might as well blot itself out in drugs.

MacEverywhere, Farewell

In retrospect I can see that's what the prophecies of grittiness were (and still are) all about: explanations of how late it was, how late – vibrations from a parochial past rather than the

future of Holyrood. This accounts for their extraordinary viru-
lence, and their hatred of nationalism. They were extolling
Forth less for what it was than for what it meant: a Scotland
whose pawky misery was the reverse of Universality's coin, but
also betokened a Glory to come. In his novel *Lanark* Alasdair
Grey called Glasgow 'Unthank'. So, on the farther side of
Unthank stood a heavenly city, a miles-better Jerusalem to
which our nation should at all costs remain faithful. Nationalist
chatterers were wilful – hence hateable – despoilers of this
faith. They were a modern version of the Damned, protagonists
of 'the world'. Especially after North Sea petroleum appeared,
their selfish materialism enjoyed the kind of progress to be
expected of Satan's seed, culminating in the decade of
Thatcherite darkness.

To their credit, English observers never had much clue
about the underground topography. Had Captain Kirk and
Spock ever reached Scotland, their data-bank probes too might
have been baffled. The expectation would have been to find
nationalists frothing at the mouth and folk-dancing, pausing
only to flout sober cosmopolitical reason and measured
appraisals of the main chance. In this contraflow country it was
in fact often *anti*-nationalists who fiddled and ennobled folklore, with steam jetting from their ears. The Labour Party's
Norman and Janey Buchan presided over a prolonged anti-
Nationalist *ceilidh* in the 1970s and 80s, and the former even
composed and published a mock-epic poem about chauvinist
folly, *The Dunciad*.[4]

Mild, secular, and almost entirely philistine, the SNP-style
national credo exhibited by contrast a low-pressure if (in the
long run) incontrovertible rationality. At bottom the fulmina-
tions against its fairly reasonable self-interest (or its thoroughly
'*petit-bourgeois*' nature, as the Marxists said) were all because
this wasn't good enough for Scots. It was as if the latter had

been marked out for some special extra- or supra-national rôle: an elect folk haunted by a God-given universality, for whom political independence would be but a selfish distraction. Since their true *ethnos* was the cosmos, it would be folly to settle for less. There was of course a bizarre kind of super-nationalism cached away somewhere in such numinous notions, like an unconfessable Zionism of almost Serb intensity. But by that time it had (fortunately) nowhere to go, and could only be defended in mounting fury and frustration.

Such was the Grail-quest of which Her Majesty's Labour Party (West of Scotland Branch) had been made the custodians. The denominational input to this mindset was variable. I think the principal impetus must have come from the old Reformed majority itself, diverted in its thrust yet still inclined to moral absolutism. But there was a prominent Catholic presence as well, stemming from 19th century immigrants wary of Protestant hegemony. Until very recently (as I suggested before) they couldn't help feeling that secular British Socialism might be safer than a possibly Orange-tinged domestic corporatism.

It was this kind of deep-structure inversion which conditioned surface political events until the 1980s, and the lessons of Thatcherism. Until then the most extreme version of nationalism around in Scotland was always anti-nationalism. Most of its disciples were on the Left, and habitually danced in rhetorical circles around British Socialism, their ineffably commanding consciences, leaky council-house roofs, the supposedly 'broader' (internationalist) view, and so on. But these were fig leaves. Underneath there lurked that simpler propulsive intuition of the Scot as chosen, and indeed superhuman: a nationality predestined to superb exemption from the vulgar nationalist path. Its visible justification on earth was still the Socialist Phase of the Great-British imperium; and its most important duty was to prepare for that coming by keeping the ever-falling English in line, and up to the mark.

There could be no mere parishes for such a race. Since its parochiality *was* the universal, the gritty judgement of Forth was indeed guaranteed to floor romantic haverings. The *Sunday Post* too was divinely ordained, mocked only to be ultimately exalted, the bleeding stigma of a Christ-ridden *Volk*.[5] No doubt that was why the present writer once felt it appropriate to rid Scotland of both that newspaper and its last Minister together, in a single liberationary outrage. They did belong together, and resumed the aberrant parochialism of an age. Not that I had worked it out at the time, twenty-nine years before last year's referendum. In 1968 it was more of a querulous desperado's hunch, which today I would defend only in much more qualified and second-thought terms.

With rueful introspection, moreover, I see that I'm actually doing so because the General Election result of 1 May 1997 so unmistakably cancelled the last custodial duty of the Northern warders. Middle England no longer needs us. In fact it has grown distinctly resistant to sermons about moral backsliding and Socialism. In fact it probably never really needed them (or us) at all. So isn't it time we left them alone? Shortly after the election the entire imperium-pretence was formally wound up in Hong Kong. It is long past time for the wandering preacher to return from his moorland hilltop, find an ordinary job and (as James Buchan implies) give his vocal cords a rest.

Labourism has remained the midwife of the delivery which followed. But (as I will argue below) we must hope that by delivering self-government it will also go on to deliver itself. Its unco' guid and well-meaning managed to retard development for nearly twenty years, before reluctantly giving way and persuading themselves they had always desired the outcome.[6] They too now deserve a break. On that level it's time we drew a line and forgave one another, for new-political rather than old-theological reasons.

On Failing to Hate the English

What has been happening in Scotland? For the metropolitan media, the simplest available answer was that the Scots are now possessed by a demon. It is the fashion to call the latter 'ethnicity' these days. Two months after the referendum a nineteen-year-old lad called Mark Ayton was beaten up and kicked to death in the posh Edinburgh suburb of Balerno. At that time I lived fairly near there, and can recall reading all the details in the local paper.

I did so with special and personal interest because I happened to know a bit about the area. Years before, a former partner had come from Juniper Green, another suburb-village adjoining Balerno, and she often used to talk of life there. There had long been an abrupt social contrast between the working-class communities at Juniper Green and Currie, and the older and more select Balerno. Juniper Green and Currie had been paper-mill villages, dependent on the Water of Leith factories in a nearby river-valley. Balerno was a traditional Pentland Hills small town, located up-river well before it got industrial. In the 20th century it had become a typical executive and retiral outer settlement at just the right distance from Edinburgh – a semi-rural *banlieue* of stone-built houses and large villas, set well apart from the industrial wastelands of West Lothian.

One way of manifesting these contrasts was through traditional animosity between their respective schools, and tribal rules about who regularly drank in which pubs. Poor Ayton and his brother were caught up in a prolonged punch-up of that kind. Edinburgh as a whole remains, alas, chronically beset by such social chasms and resentments. Customary exclamations followed in the Edinburgh and local press about the surprizingly 'good background' of his assailants (i.e. upper-middle class, one of them actually *English*). They were given four years for 'culpable homicide', and Edinburgh's *Evening News* commented severely on the leniency of the sentences: 'Much was made of the accused men's claims that they didn't mean to kill Mark, and of their leafy, suburban background . . . The fact is that this incident and the ensuing court case would have been coloured considerably if it had taken place in Muirhouse or Pilton . . . , (2 June 1998 – Muirhouse and Pilton are parts of the city now linked in the public mind to *Trainspotting* and *Filth*). The *News* ended with a ringing condemnation of Appeal Judge Hardie as 'Lord Advocate for the Upper Classes'. Neither ethnicity nor race-hate were mentioned in the *News* account.

It was therefore a good deal more than surprising to read in May 1998 that there had been *a race riot* in Balerno. The *Spectator* brought out a story entitled 'A Very Scottish Death' by Katie Grant, in which she claimed that Mark Ayton died 'for being thought English', and that what the whole incident laid bare was 'a rising tide of anti-English sentiment'. Why the tide? Because 'behind the mask of Scottish middle-class respectability there lurks a racist monster'. It is now loitering with more open intent, since the referendum 'Yes' campaign had been 'fought by New Labour and the SNP on an anti-English ticket'. Although invisible to most referendum voters on 11 September, and undetected at the time even by London media correspondents, this had none the less 'given anti-English feeling a degree of respectability in middle-class leftish circles'. Oh yes, with hindsight 'it is easy to see how death walked down the road to meet Mark Ayton'.

Even without hindsight, it remains a bit puzzling to see how

the *Spectator* had given space to stuff like this, even when composed by Peregrine Worsthorne's niece. As Isabel Hilton
commented acidly in the *Guardian*, if she was right 'it is only a
matter of time before white-robed figures with burning torches
are hunting out English settlers from their beds and hanging
them from lamp-posts' ('The Ku Klux Klansmen', 10 June).
Nor was Katie Grant alone in her demonology. In fact she
seemed to have launched a mini-trend.

Monster-sightings were suddenly on the increase. The
Sunday Times of 28 June last, for instance, led with the headline
'Anti-English Feeling Grows in Scotland'. The pretext for their
front-page drama was another poll on the subject; but only a
resolute minority of readers is likely to have followed through
to the inside-page commentary on the findings. That was given
by Professor David McCrone of Edinburgh University, and
suggested that in fact anti-Englishness had 'grown' from the
trivial to the insignificant:

> The news for the pessimists is that there is not a lot of anti-
> Englishness about. Fully 83% said they feel no dislike of
> the English, and this is true for all ages, social classes, and
> among men and women. There simply is not the animosity
> around, with only 17% saying they disliked the English
> either a little or a lot . . .

But it takes more than this to divert a headline pessimist
with the ethnic bit between his or her jaws. Andrew Neil
returned to the assault in the *Spectator* the following month,
with a piece talking of 'a pervasive and growing anti-
Englishness . . . an outpouring of denigration and hatred'. He
felt that this sort of thing was stealing his own country from
him – the douce and decent British Scotland which he was
reared in, and wants to keep going. Such a verdict is clearly of

some importance, given that Neil is now Editor-in-Chief of Scotsman Publications (*The Scotsman*, plus what was then the country's only Sunday broadsheet, *Scotland on Sunday*). Not long before the incident Neil had also founded a 'Scottish Policy Unit' with money from his proprietors, the Barclay twins, in order to help stem the monstrous tide.[7]

At that time *The Scotsman*'s Westminster political correspondent was Iain Macwhirter, who was disturbed enough to reply to his own Editor-in-Chief with a testy 'Open Letter', in which he pointed out that there is so far no evidence whatever of increasing Anglophobia of the malignant or discriminatory kind which such tirades were signalling. Yet (he went on):

> *Spectator* columnists like yourself, Katie Grant and Bruce Anderson have been spreading fear and loathing in the Home Counties with tales of the tartan terror. You've become a kind of Scottish Tourist Board in reverse: 'Come to Scotland this Autumn, and be Beaten to Death for being English!' . . .

So (it seems right to ask) just what on earth *is* the panic about? Some people want there to be monsters. This must be because they explain, or seem to explain, something. The Scots appear to be going off the rails – that is, the rails of United Kingdom convention and expectation which all such critics (Scottish or English) took for granted, and to which they indeed owe their own formation and present status. A convenient way of accounting for the aberration is to imagine some kind of ethnic *Geist* or blood-instinct 'unleashed' by Labour foolishness. There may be little to support the idea in Scotland; but there is of course plenty elsewhere, not so much in the actual history of Eastern Europe as in mediocre journalistic musings upon its most violent incidents.

How inveterate such opinions are likely to be was shown
later on, when an article in *The Observer* repeated what was by
now the script, verbatim. Their reporter Dean Nelson wrote on
8 November 1998:

> There is a good deal of complacency in Scotland on
> racism . . . there was reluctance to believe that the killing of
> English youth Mark Ayton in a middle-class Edinburgh
> suburb this year was racially motivated. The police have
> kept an open mind on the issue, while lenient sentences
> given to his killers were greeted with outrage.

The last sentence is true (as I indicated). As for the rest, Mr
Nelson just hadn't done any homework, or read the cuttings.
He didn't need to. Like other recent 'revelations' of this kind,
his piece could hardly avoid ending somewhat differently – in
this case by again citing David McCrone's evidence, and con-
ceding that 'a sizeable number of English settlers in Scotland
have joined the Scottish National Party'.

But that was the small print at the end. The big print over
the top read: 'SOD OFF BACK TO ENGLAND: Scots no
longer ashamed to be anti-English'. The crucial part of the
message here is '*no longer*'. It means that things have changed
because of current events, and will therefore get worse. The
Union prevented (or at least restrained) such intolerance; hence
its loss entails a fall into ethnic hatred and discrimination.

Northern Nihilism

There is plainly a pathology here that calls for more searching
explanation. It seems to me there are two main causes for it,
one among the Scots themselves, the other located much

more profoundly, within the uncertainties of English identity.

It is remarkable in retrospect how much of the most strenu-ous opposition to devolution has been the work of Scots, and particularly of Scottish intellectuals. Ever since the late 1960s, when Winifred Ewing unexpectedly won a by-election in Hamilton and showed that nationalism might become a serious political force, an influential minority of educated Scots has vehemently agitated *against* the very prospect of political rebirth. On occasion it succeeded in sabotaging the process, most strikingly at the time of the 1979 home rule referendum. The passage of MP George Cunningham's '40% rule' at Westminster meant that the small majority won for devolution could then be disregarded by Mrs Thatcher's incoming gov-ernment. Although Scotland had become a left-wing country since the 1950s, and resisted the tide of right-wing populism that had overtaken England, it was helpless against British gov-ernment throughout the eighteen-year Conservative régime which followed.

In the end (we know now) this was to generate a stronger national reaction against Britain. But the point is, it was serious politics. This style of intellectual anti-nationalism had strong links with politicians, and it was noticeable in both dominant political parties. The question remains – what were such enduring and effective links founded upon?

One part of the answer lies, obviously, in the force of a fairly consistent 'rejectionism' in Scotland itself. The term 'national nihilism' may convey it best, by indicating what was being rejected. In occupied or colonized societies, intellectuals have most often been found on the side of the deprived population. There, nationalism has normally had the joint aim of political liberation and 'nation-building', a process requiring inclusion of whatever educated strata were available. The latter might be 'bought off' or distracted by the imperial power with honours

and trinkets, and seek to convince themselves (normally with
metropolitan assistance) that all this was in the true 'best interest' of their people. However, it is simply a matter of record
that such pretences were usually thin, and short-lived. They
rarely resisted post-1945 decolonization, and where they have
survived beyond independence (as in French West Africa) it
has been in a miserable *diminuendo* sustained at great expense
by the former colonial power.

By contrast, Scottish national nihilism was founded upon
being 'on the other side' in a far less usual sense. Although
apparently marked out (like Wales and Ireland) for conquest
and assimilation, the Scottish state sought to avoid that fate. It
did so first by its own national effort at the end of the 17th century, culminating in the abortive project of colonizing the
Panama Isthmus in 1698–9: the Darien Scheme. When that
was defeated, it agreed – albeit reluctantly – to a 'joint venture'
with the vastly more powerful English state in 1707. And it
was the success of this incorporating alliance which then provided a much stronger metropolitan platform for the
intelligentsia of the lesser country to occupy and (before long)
to exploit quite effectively.

This intelligentsia learned to reject its own country *in itself*,
as a land bearable only when 'merged' or extended by association with another – the England-Britain set up by the Treaty of
Union. From this mentality came the fervent Universalism I
mentioned above – that is, the identification of homeland and
cosmos which suppressed mere local statehood as an unworthy
side-issue. It then seemed to follow that the Scots could only
'be themselves' when thus broadened or leavened. Such postures have persisted strongly into our own time. Indeed there
could be no more striking testimony to the durability of the
pattern than the Blair government itself. Blair only became
Leader of his party through the death of his formidable Scottish

predecessor, John Smith, and in competition with the latter's equally impressive countryman Gordon Brown.[8] His subsequent government could not avoid remaining very Scottish, however. The Scots may have attached themselves to the Anglo-British state as supplicants in 1707. By 1997 they were surprisingly close to being its masters. This was testimony to decline, admittedly – but also (obviously) to the vigour of such a transplanted or reverse-colonizing élite.

Since the 1960s, however, taking 'the other side' in that sense has at least implied rejecting an alternative. Rejecting separatism just as a policy or strategy has never been enough. From the angle of the outward-bound élite, Nationalism was best presented as a vista of existential outrage. However quiet its language and aims, it was virtually a kind of damnation, propagated by fiends. Such has always been the sense (e.g.) of Labourite 'Nat-bashing', from William Ross down to the present régime's Helen Liddell. Whatever the pros and cons of a separate government it would inevitably threaten the life-support mechanisms of this quite substantial cultural and political stratum. It *is* a matter of life or death therefore – their own. Hence it is much more than a question of a few *vendus* or token metropolitan pets – the pretend-élites of most past nationalist dilemmas. A more extensive imbrication has taken place in this case, and one of its consequences has been this more visceral and impatient rejection, manifested in an emotive distrust or rage – itself so uncannily similar to nationalist passion.

Such anti-national 'nationalism' is certainly an unusual specimen in the ethnic gallery of modern times. But it may be more common than one would think. I think that varieties of its parodic humour are discernible in France and Italy, for example – other states of strictly forced centralism, where semi-alien élites have been co-opted into a majority hegemony. It was also found in the pre-1922 Irish-British rapport, much more strongly than is now easily recalled. But its most astonishing expression, surely, has been the UK one – above all on the British *Left*.

One should not forget that the Scottish branch of UK Labourism actually abandoned Home Rule *completely* in the early 1960s, in the period just before Scottish nationalism became politically important. Though a version of national autonomy had traditionally figured in Scottish-Labour mani-festos from the 1890s onwards, it was formally renounced just as British decline grew unmistakable, and (simultaneously) campaigns of born-again *redressement* and greatness-support became more important in London. Scottish Labour's initial contribution to these was a renunciation of what it then dis-missed as 'the Home Rule Shibboleth'. Thus it led the way to becoming more demonstratively British, as the trumpets of imperial distress sounded more loudly. Surviving elements of this same stratum are still pursuing the same campaign, under Blair. The 'shibboleth' has become reality (and they now claim to have always desired it); but it can still be prevented from 'going further' (and leaving England quite deprived of Northern moral guidance). Not long after the original save-Britain campaign got going, London was compelled to remonstrate gently but firmly over such excess of zeal – by pointing out how Britain's interests might be best served by *some* measure of local differentiation.

Southern Opportunism

Monster-viewing excursions are unlikely to tail off during the early years of the new Scottish Parliament. So it may be worth stocking up with some obvious facts. First of all, the Scots are *thinking about* England more, for obvious reasons. The subject occurs to them now, in a way which it previously did not, or not so often. How could this fail to be true? It is natural to wonder – not necessarily with antagonism – how Edinburgh-London relations will develop under the new circumstances. Problems *are* likely in what was, until 1997, an unnaturally changeless and stultified rapport. The Scots enjoy arguing, and ever since the referendum the Edinburgh and Glasgow media have indeed resounded with such speculative disputes. Some have interpreted this benevolently, as a sign of returning political life and intelligence. But with adequate ill-will it is also possible to see in such animation nothing but 'looking for trouble', or even looking for a fight of some – any – kind.

Secondly, there is *of course* antagonism towards 'England' among Scots (though far less towards English individuals). It has been there since long before the Union, after which it set-tled down into a sort of steady-state grumbling and narkiness, a 'chip on the shoulder' due to the structural inequality which opposes 80+% of 'Great Britain' to (now) less than 10%. As I pointed out before, Conrad Russell has shown how the Scots have largely supported the Union, more consciously and delib-erately than the English – but have also read its meaning differently. What they wanted most was the one thing it could never supply – *collective* recognition and equality. They needed some kind of federalism, but found they had signed up to an intensifying unitarism – to an historical over-centralism, in fact, which would attain its unsurpassable climax only in the Thatcher years. Again, how could some ill-feeling fail to arise from that? But the 'England' being blamed here is in fact the British state, and the individuals who get its rough edge are *almost invariably* those easily identifiable with the ruling *moeurs* – i.e. the 'upper class', 'snooty', those automatically knowing best, and so on.

Undeniably, all this has fostered a rankling and cantankerous streak in modern Scottish identity. It is most liable to surface against what I suppose should really be called Home-County Englishness. But in my experience this is rarely understood by the English (of any class or region) who encounter it, and is then all too often aggravated by being ascribed to 'unreason-ableness', or some kind of recalcitrant ethnicity. There are also liberal techniques of over-compensation – striving to avoid the slightest suggestion of superiority. However well-meant, these can of course be in turn profoundly exasperating. Having little overtly English identity to call on, and unwilling to strike British attitudes, southern commentators of that kind some-times resort to a facsimile of pure reasonableness – regrettably, the most superior of all postures. Thus instead of two ordinary national identities or points of view confronting one another, the result can sometimes be non-dialogue on an almost astral plane.

These are ugly dilemmas, and truly a part of 'the Destitution of Scotland' in Douglas Dunn's meaning. To my shame I can recall many incidents at University, or before that in school playgrounds, where such resentment would come helplessly to the surface and at least suggest the kind of violence which Iain Macwhirter's 'anti-Tourist Board' is now scrounging around for with bell, book and candle. Yet the main point about all this is as blatant as its historical diagnosis: the incidents I can remember occurred (alas) thirty or even fifty years back. *They were part of 'the Union'.*

Far from being novel, or in any way linked to post-referendum consciousness, they were side effects of Britishness, and completely incurable within the latter's anti-quated terms. By contrast, the current vogue of monster-hunting *is* linked to the notion of change: these intrepid scouts feel that the wish for 'devolution' or, still worse, independence *must* have provoked such reflexes – if indeed the whole business wasn't caused by them in the first place. Hence the Union must have been better because it restrained such barbarity. The uncomfortable truth is that the Union *caused* the 'barbarity' – that is, a petulant sense of frustration and incessant put-down which, under the old conditions, had no political mode of expression and sometimes assumed such irrational and personal forms.

Now, all these may indeed have been pretty small beer, compared to the kind of oppression suffered by most colonized countries; yet they were pretty disagreeable, and our own. Far from being a manifestation of 'nationalism' in the new, post-1960s sense, they provide a very powerful incentive to making nationalism more political – in order to at last escape from, or at least redefine such noxious dilemmas more tolerably. Scotland badly needs a cure for 'anti-Englishness'. But she can only find it civilly, by her own efforts. Here, what the ethnic-scare scenario does is to confuse cure and cause. All efforts to achieve equality imply heightened consciousness of inequities and prejudice; but such awareness (including a greater awareness of things English) is then ascribed exclusively to prejudice itself – an unreasonable will to be different, as it were (or even better).

I have mentioned some of the motives for the prominent Scottish collaboration in this new brand of witch-hunting – the fear of death, or at least of demotion and uncomfortable redefinition, among an émigré élite. However, the underlying sting in the process comes from a conjunction between such fears and the *emerging question of Englishness* itself. After all, a far deeper uncertainty attaches to post-British England than to any dilemmas currently experienced in Scotland, Wales or Ireland.

But one way of manifesting such anxiety is simply by displacing it, and projecting it upon others. The 'explanation' of troubling incidents and attacks then lies not in failures of state, or in the political system sustained by the UK majority, but in the ill-will or backwardness of minorities. The peripheral tribes are bringing trouble upon themselves, through unreasonable hatred of *us*; the childish dreads and charms of ethnicity lie within their nature, but never in *ours*. Such a form of self-exorcism requires the evidence of 'incidents' – or even their invention and (as in this case) heedless reinvention. The aim is reassurance: that is, peaceful certitude that the country of Stephen Lawrence and of so much malign Euro-scepticism is *not* succumbing to its own brutish prejudice or post-imperial exclusiveness. What Southern-liberal opportunism demands is above all to see ethnic cleansers tooling up for business . . . somewhere else.

The Lawrence case is especially relevant here. Alongside all the hand-wringing of summer 1998 in Scotland, the same readers and viewers were simultaneously being shown in dreadful detail just what 'racism' meant in practice, in a London suburb. Does anyone really think that people were less moved or enraged in Balerno or in Aberdeen, because Mr and Mrs Lawrence are *English*? On the contrary, I would like to think most of them knew the best of England when they saw it.[9] The English (like the Scots) have to get rid of their own venomous dregs – largely the deposit of a joint British imperialism which has been formally wound up yet still festers in the unconscious of both countries. However, the exposure and anger of the Lawrence affair have also been a way of combating that legacy. Would it not be *absurd* to see only ethnic monsters looming through it? Had Scottish pundits used such a diagnosis glibly to predict an advancing Bosnia in the streets of London and Birmingham, they would have been properly ridiculed. But that's the point: somewhat different standards were supposed to apply to 'ethnic threats' materializing in streets elsewhere – in non-heartland areas, even improbable sites like Balerno, where ethnicity is supposed to have a naturally higher profile.

A plausible overall depiction of what lies at the back of the different standards was given by columnist Magnus Linklater in *Scotland on Sunday* last November. Linklater is an informed witness of such matters. He lived in London for many years, where he edited English papers before returning to Edinburgh as Editor of *The Scotsman* in the 1980s. Looking back over this 'concerted and damaging campaign, conducted mainly by expatriate Scots' to convey the impression of a Scotland increasingly 'infected by anti-English racism', he pointed out that in the background had lain always 'the general idea of the Scots as a fairly mutinous lot – and growing more so'. Hence the profound constitutional argument being fought out around the Scottish Parliament, crucial to the future for England as well, gets by and large dismissed as peripheral bickering. Ethnic ill-will has become the standard way of accounting for it: 'they must hate us', rather than loving us for all we have given them:

> The prevailing English attitude remains, in short, a colonial one. It is condescending, biased and largely ignorant. Above all, it serves to fuel national prejudices north as well as south of the Border. It seems clear that much work will have to be done if Blair's vision of an inclusive Britain is to catch on. And at least as much of that will be needed in England as in Scotland.[10]

Region into Nation

It is now clearer in retrospect that the referendum vote of 1997 was for a direction of affairs, rather than for any precise model

of devolved government. The double 'Yes' was broad assent to
a movement, and not (or not necessarily) to the delimited goals
of the government's White Paper. And the movement in question was not that of a party, or even a coalition of parties. It
included all the parties except the Conservatives, and reached
far into the institutions of Scottish civil society. The latter have
been the main support of national identity since 1707, so it is
not excessive to claim that most of 'the nation' was involved.
The Claim of Right (1988) and the Constitutional Convention
were the obvious vehicles of that involvement – it was they
who did most of the work on the self-rule scheme which finally
turned into the Scotland Bill. But although the SNP had stood
apart from that process, it was clearly that party whose influence (or 'threat', as both Labour and the Tories saw it) held
such movements so firmly on course.

How conscious the electorate was of this became plain
during the referendum campaign. A key episode of the latter
was the agreement between Scottish Labour and the
Nationalists on obtaining a 'Yes' vote, and the deep reverbera-
tions which that generated. I was not the only observer to be
struck by the feeling – sometimes almost the fervour – shown
on the matter. It was like a kind of deep relief. A profound
paralysis was being undone. After decades of snarling strife
and denigration both movements had compromised on a platform enabling everything to move forward. But 'everything'
meant the country, or the nation. It did not mean (or only
mean) the autonomous region or the devolved local government foreseen by Westminster's final blueprint. Anyone who
doubts the difference between region and nationality should
study this alteration more carefully – and the history which has
followed.

There was nothing dishonourable or wrong about Blair's plan
(most of which had been thought up by Scots anyway). The

only thing 'wrong' was that it had finally been conceded to a people which, in the course of the prolonged struggle to obtain it, had recovered an identity and confidence going beyond what the plan finally allowed for. The final, vital touch was given to that confidence by the referendum campaign. It was as if a kind of subterranean fusion occurred, around a new-found sense of unity and legitimate common purpose. Once *that* had happened, however, farther progression was automatic – and passed, inevitably, a lot farther than what had previously been thought possible. All commentators have been struck, and rightly puzzled, by how rapid and near-unanimous this development has been. After all this was the nation which, in 1979, had suffered cold feet over dustmen's strikes and the antics of Alex Douglas-Home (he preached a 'No' vote at the last minute of the referendum that year). Yet only a few months after the 1997 vote, the route to independence was being taken almost for granted.

A lot happened in between to contribute to the eventual big shift. Before the 1997 election (for example) the Conservatives tried to make a mega-production out of taxation fears. They towed huge posters around showing Britain being torn into two parts by the imposition of a 'Tartan Tax': North Britons would lose their Union as well as their hard-earned cash, etc. When it came to the referendum, nearly two-thirds of them voted to pay the tax and were relatively unconcerned about the Union. What the Tories had suppressed from recollection was an earlier imposition which North Britain had mutinied against in significant numbers: Mrs Thatcher's Poll Tax.

I discussed this episode in the previous chapter. The mutiny in England then became even bigger, and was responsible for its defeat (and Thatcher's fall from power). But the point is that both the way it was done and the resultant revolt had had a differential impact on Scotland. We see now that this impact must have sunk in, and left a living trace. There had also been a national element in the aversion to Thatcherism, strongly revivified by the anti-Tory campaigns of the 1980s, and still being borne forward in 1997.

When after the referendum vote Tony Blair came up to Edinburgh to thank the people for supporting him, he was still thinking in terms of gratitude. How could it fail to mean what he (and the Scots in his cabinet) wanted – reinforcement of Labour's ruling power in Scotland, and hence some strengthening of the UK? But on this point he was already being carried away by his own public relations and self-image. Many of those he glad-handed up and down Edinburgh High Street then turned to the SNP. But such 'ingratitude' arose from a different dynamic, quite unforeseen by his lawyers and constitutional experts. It derived from an abruptly repoliticized national identity – and not from 'democratic deficit' and regional economic needs alone. No one had known quite when or how this would take place in Scotland. But now it had, and irreversibly. The land of supposed 'ninety-minute patriots' had carried the game outside the stadium, ignored the final whistle, and intended playing on to a real conclusion.[11]

New Labour has also been consistently deluded on this score by mistaken analogies with national and regional movements elsewhere in Europe. What all such comparisons ignore is the crucial historical differences between Britain and most other states within today's European Union.[12] With the exception of Sweden and Ireland, these are post-war régimes founded on elaborate written constitutions making provisions for devolved government.

On one hand the acceleration of a rediscovered national identity; and on the other an essentially unreformed framework making no real provision for containing or adjudicating clashes with the new centre of power – these are the divergent parameters at work. One need only set such internal and external conditions together to see how things are likely to go. But it is surely these structural factors which are also being registered by the electoral slide against Labour in Scotland, at least to some extent. An electorate long inured to British attitudes and political customs is perfectly capable of sensing its unease and decline over such a crucial issue.

And at the same time, one disintegration is also being spurred on by another – the local decline-and-fall which it was for so long intimately associated with. This is the fall of the old and corrupt 'one-party state' in Labour's Western-Scottish fiefdom. Scotland's first electoral campaign in 1999 has been preceded by the open rebellion of its most important city boss. Patrick Lally, Glasgow's Labour Lord Provost (Mayor), sued his own party for illegitimate removal from office, as part of the clean-up campaign. Spin-doctoring stands helpless before that scale of damage.

Scotland does have a great deal to be ashamed of. Douglas Dunn writes in 'The Apple Tree' of how 'Men' (including a lot of Scots) '. . . moaned of Scotland that its barren air and soil couldn't so much as ripen an apple':

> I can hear their croaked whispers reproach the stern and
> wild of Alba,
> Naming our Kirk, our character, our coarse consent
> To drunken decency and sober violence,
> Our paradox of ways . . .

But it's not so bad, he concludes. Apples could ripen there like anywhere else – if only it would regenerate itself, and do more to unravel such paradoxes by its own efforts. The trouble is that 'Devolution' has only limited value for this. It isn't up to deep-identity concerns like 'codes of courtesy' and ways of describing love, or constructing a better-natured land. For that (as argued below) it's independence or nothing.

In another poem, 'The Dark Crossroads' (*Northlight*, 1988), Dunn describes being cornered in an awful English pub by a gang of suede-shoed gin-swillers, delighted at finding an uppity Jock on their turf. He curls up in the corner, trying to ignore the jibes with 'dreams of the moss-trooper, the righteous horseman', and feeling a bit ashamed of himself for it. 'Unwanted thoughts, but unaccountable', he concludes, a dark parting of the ways which nobody would ever want to cross again. 'Unwanted' is right, but they were never unaccountable. However, they will be brought to proper and civil account only via independence. The alternative can now only be the rediscovery of a re-dimensioned civic nationalism *on both sides of the Border*. It can't remain the hopeless preservation of a Union which, in spite of the Blair rhetoric, is rapidly losing all purpose and direction.

CHAPTER SIX

The Unmaking of Scotland

For our nature must change, said Hugh to himself. That was his great feeling. He had grasped the politics, grasped the materials, but only now, with his advocacy of the high flats, did he come to grasp the central thing.

'We must make ourselves all over again.'

Rub out the past.

'And what are we here for if not for progress? If not for change!'

Join the air. High over Glasgow we can look down on who we were before. Who our people were. And by climbing high we escape our troubles. We leave the past and its rubble below . . . Closer to heaven, closer to God and his big, blue hand. Tower blocks: nearer the saints who know our failings . . .

Andrew O'Hagan, *Our Fathers* (1999), p. 119

The Latent State

To make a new Scotland, the old one must be unmade. Perhaps the same might have been said of any other decolonized, liberated or newly emancipated society. However, the Scottish example of national liberation does have one important peculiarity not replicated anywhere else. This is something easily overlooked or taken for granted. Yet it should always be kept in mind, since it conditions everything else. For the Scots, the 'old' society – the one needing renewal or replacement – *was largely their own work.*

Andrew O'Hagan's novel is amongst other things a record of the last mighty effort of unmaking and reconstruction in Scotland, that associated with the Labour Party. It began during World War I, gathered momentum in the inter-war Glasgow of John Wheatley and Tom Johnston, and attained its culmination with the high-flat mania of his central character, the visionary architect Hugh Bawn. The tower blocks and New Towns of post-World War II Scotland are its legacy today. *Our Fathers* encompasses that nobility as well as its ultimate degradation and final lingering collapse into the fitful half-reforms of New Labour. If anyone needs reminding, this book recalls the visionary sources of the Labour Party's modern hegemony, how what now seems stultifying dependency and sleaze was itself once a great effort at unmaking and renewal. Hugh Bawn ends his existence on the eighteenth floor of a crumbling tower block, complete with leaks, graffiti, dead lifts, drug-pushers and Councillors on the take.

Scotland was not really nearer the saints, the past had reasserted itself. The narrator is led to look ironically back over his family tree: 'Each was a good liar. Each could inspire love, and yet feel unloved. Each was a problem for all of us . . .' A 'native duplicity' seemed inescapable, death for a country these ancestors had not understood, interspersed with plunges into drunken oblivion. Like the Labour Party itself, Hugh Bawn was 'a truth-maker who turned his back on the truth; a high-minded pioneer who degraded his vision for the sake of expedience (and) died without too much honour on his side'.

It is salutary for anyone hoping for new starts to remember that history. It serves to explain the persistence of Labourism across the divide of Thatcherism, but also to underline the folly of undertaking to 'rub out the past' once more in an analogous fashion – that is, without revolutionizing 'Home' itself. Scottish Labourism and the town-planning tradition of Patrick

Geddes sought redemption in terms of civil society and moral will alone – not through a recapture of the state, and the constitutional reframing of their nation. They still belonged to the Enlightenment, and believed that the United Kingdom was quite close to the saints – close enough, at any rate, to tolerate being subverted by a saintly will-power equipped with the right ideas.

Our Fathers were mistaken in that view. My own father held to it as strongly as 'Hugh Bawn', although he didn't swear as loudly or (being a schoolmaster) have much cash to stuff in the back pockets of builders. But like Bawn, he recognized that the Scottish society of the long period between 1707 and 1997 was not imposed on us, or imported *en bloc* from a distant or alien metropolis. Development was not forced upon Scots by foreign plantation or factory-owners, they were not blown into submission by artillery or compelled to acquire an unfamiliar tongue, nor were their traditional leaders imprisoned, deported or 'civilized' against their will. They were neither colonized nor put down in less crass ways – on the contrary, for much of the time in question many of them were intensively occupied in colonizing and subordinating others, beyond the British archipelago.

It may also be true, and important, that a deeper kind of subjection and imposition remained inherent in this old situation. I have referred to it often enough in other parts of this book, and *Our Fathers* is like a fever-chart of its later stages. That was certainly 'national' in the sense of affecting everybody in Scotland, in ways that simply never applied to provinces or regions of England. Unionists have always made much of obvious resemblances between Lowland Scotland and parts of Northern England: high urbanization, industrial and proletarian traditions, Labourite fidelity, and so on. But such comparisons ignore or discount a wider framework of

institutional dissimilarity, which has given a different meaning
to both social policy and political mobilization in the two areas.
These distinctions have in the end asserted themselves as
more significant, producing both Devolution and a different
reaction to New Labour in Scotland.

But whatever these deeper differences are, it must be conceded that they have been accepted (or at the very least, put up
with) to an historically unusual extent. In spite of the amount
written about it in the past, this is something which remains
insufficiently understood. I remarked earlier that the short-cut
pseudo-explanation of 'ethnicity', though popular in England,
in fact explains nothing. It merely re-states the issue, or com-
pounds it with the suggestion of some mysteriously inherited
(and therefore sinister) native psyche instinctively resentful of
English (or perhaps any outside) dominance or influence. Such
diagnoses belong to the realm of superstition or astrology,
although the very fact that they can be so easily made may justify some exasperation with the attitudes underlying them. It is
rarely thought (for example) that there might be any corresponding English inheritance of exclusionary self-love,
alien-hatred or superiorism, which might have fostered the supposed resentments of the periphery. The English majority
ethnie is often judged exempt from an ethnocentricity otherwise
deemed universal.

But actually 'nature' in this inscrutable sense has nothing to
do with it. We are talking second nature here. What surely *does*
have everything to do with the problem is this 'second nature'
of institutions. The term is usually applied to everyday or
lower-level social bodies: a club, an association, a school, a
church – or, with a touch of metaphor, to 'the institution of
marriage', the institutions 'of state' or 'of civil society'. In a
more fundamental sense, however, higher-level bodies or entities like states, faiths, nations or the internet can also quite

comprehensibly be entitled 'institutions' – i.e. complex and interrelated organizations involving a lot of individuals, and requiring adherence to common rules or customs, either codified (written down) or informal (understood in practice or through imitation and observance).

The most important of such grander institutions in modern times has been the state, and it is the fate of that institutional level which has been crucial for the Scots. What the 1707 Treaty produced was a state 'merger'— in today's business terminology it was also a 'takeover' – whose effect was very unusual, if not unique. I have argued throughout the book that it led to a suppressed state, rather than to the more normal consequence of an assimilated, subjected (and then renascent) nationality. Institutional distinction and bifurcation was the key to the success of the Treaty arrangement. Such permanent distinction had to be soldered together by a homogeneity of stratum: the 'class' of the former imperialist hegemony. That implied acceptance of the new arrangements by most of the minority country's institutional cadres (as well as by its aristocracy), and would include those set up long after the Treaty was concluded. The nature of such acceptance was vital to the style of 'dependent development' which finally imposed itself.

'Self-colonization'

Sometimes people have spoken of 'self-colonization' to account for the Scottish phenomenon. The term is paradoxical, yet in this context unavoidable. After all, it is possible – and indeed very common – for subjection, marginalization and inferiorization to be self-imposed. That is, 'chosen' as a fate – maybe not ideal, yet preferable to others on offer. We all appreciate such possibilities as individuals. A lot of psychiatry deals with them, as do everyday ironies, mother-in-law stories, and Jewish-style family jokes.

However, equivalent dilemmas, pseudo-solutions and apparently impossible knots can also exist on the scale of larger groups, and even of nationalities. In the latter case (as many aspects of Scottish tradition demonstrate) 'fate' may then be bolstered or excused by ideology. Indeed with some help from religion and a compliant school and university system, as well as from imperialism itself, a form of servitude could even be converted into a kind of superiority. It was (or could appear) better to be a small, if inadequately acknowledged, part of a conquering dragon than to be one of its victims, or else a side-lined and marginal country. Regrettably, the imperialism of the Lieutenant could be worse than that of the General.

Today, naturally, no one would maintain that democratic Scotland really 'chose' that previous state of affairs. By modern political standards, it arose from the decision of an averagely disgraceful pre-democratic élite. As far as one can tell, the Union with England was probably opposed by most of the non-élite in 1707. Yet not too much should be made of this, once it is recognized how the Union did come in a sense to be posthumously 'chosen'. Of course such retrospective choice remains as odd as 'self-colonization'; yet both were equally real in their effects.

In Liberalism and the Limits of Justice Michael Sandel suggests a 'constitutive conception' of community as part of the explanation:

> On this strong view, to say that the members of a society are bound by a sense of community is not simply to say that a great many of them profess communitarian sentiments . . . but rather that they conceive their identity as defined to some extent by the community of which they are a part . . . '[1]

People 'chose' the way they did because their powers of choice were increasingly, and often unconsciously, configured by the institutions in which they (often 'proudly') dwelt. The indus-trialized, urban Scotland of the 19th century ended by colluding very actively with a destiny which, at the time, seemed to be at once manifest, immutable, and in harmony with the sub-state institutions of Scottishness.

Memory and retrospect were amended accordingly, along the lines imparted by the schoolroom history of the times. Unity with our (pre-destined) neighbours then appeared nat-ural; a stand-alone Scotland was made to look like nobody-country, a peripheral dead end which, without Union, might have been cut off from the great adventures of modern times. It may be true that 'England' has never ceased to arouse a sort of inner resistance, occasionally suspicious and resentful. But Britain could in contrast be adulated with a compensatory and justifying love. This was never mere sup-pression or oblivion. As now seems more obvious in retrospect, the shame of loss remained part of it, but was con-verted into a sincere (if occasionally wry) avowal that 'it was all for the better'.

The resultant alloy showed it had great strength. Yet it never acquired the 'natural' force which an unqualified British nation-alism would have demanded. There was always something stilted, over-rigid and self-conscious about Scottish Unionism. This has remained the case right down to its last gasp – for example in the strident 1998–9 columns written by Andrew Neil, Editor-in-Chief of Scotsman Newspapers. These hector-ing mixtures of Britannic nostalgia, economic platitude and ill-concealed resentment at defeat were uttered as the new Parliament was preparing to meet. Even as the coffin of dependency slid into the grave, its occupant was urged to brace himself for a glorious reprise of Thatcherism. But the funeral crowds had already melted away, now far more concerned with their own English future. The rulers of England had in any case never taken the Scotch rhetoric seriously. To their inner ear it never rang true.

Walter Scott was the most influential literary representative of the old posture. Like many other voices of the long facing-both-ways era, he learned to set off ineffectual (hence emotionally exaggerated) regret against a 'level-headed' (and all too effective) acceptance. Boring-bastard heroes were required for that job, and he was notoriously good at inventing them. More alarmingly, such traits soon came to be incorporated into Scottish 'national character' and were eventually awarded ethnic status. One such character would attain global fame by ending up in charge of Gene Rodenberry's Star Trek engine-room. Both here and in Wales and Ireland, it was voices like that which extolled, vindicated and apologized for the British state, often a good deal more eloquently than the English majority did.

The Dead Monkey Society

And it was one such who decisively saved the Westminster State in 1979. I mentioned him previously – Labour MP George Cunningham, the librarian who thought of the 40% rule in that year's referendum as the device most likely to prevent devolution. What that relied upon was a range of impulses in the Scottish electorate Cunningham knew could still be counted upon only twenty years ago: unwilling recognition of Labour failure, mounting apathy and – above all – a clinging to the known devil of routine provincialdom. He counted on them being still like the dead monkeys of Henry David Thoreau's metaphor:

The way in which men cling to old institutions after the life
has departed out of them, and out of themselves, reminds
me of those monkeys which cling by their tails – aye, whose
tails contract about the limbs, even the dead limbs, of the
forest, and they hang suspended beyond the hunter's reach
long after they are dead . . .

'Self-colonization' is like 'self-censorship': a chosen and pre-
emptive suppression, undertaken to avoid something worse.
When institutionalized into a sufficiently general habit it of
course becomes 'instinctive' and can appear as nature – in this
case, the canny, circumspect (etc.) people that Scots are known
to be (when not being uncouth, England-hating savages, etc.).
I know the issue has been raised already above; but it may be
worth re-emphasizing some of the causes, if only to get a sense
of the scale of this particular phenomenon.

The co-option from above engineered by the 1707 Treaty
made Scotland into a satellite of one of the metropole-states,
rather than an oppressed nationality which (eventually) might
be forced to fight back. Like the Croats within the later Austro-
Hungarian Empire, the Scots partly adopted a stance of
'servitor imperialism' rather than of national liberation, thereby
inflicting a guilty conscience upon subsequent generations of
the intelligentsia. Hamish Henderson's great left-wing hymn of
national emancipation (post-World War II), the 'Freedom
Come-all-ye', refers with appropriate shame to 'the lands we
harried' for United Kingdom imperialism, and to the amends
for this which are still due.

Self-subordination has always played some part in colonization proper: there are striking accounts of it in (for example)
Frantz Fanon's classic *Les damnées de la terre* (1965). But where
it *predominated*, as in Scotland and Wales, later circumstances
were bound to be equivalently distinct. 'Ethnic nationalism'

was the normal longer-term, deeper reaction to enforced submission – 'damnation' in Fanon's sense. It sought to both
emphasize and romantically distort native cultural and customary traits, in order to foster a popular basis for political
resistance and revolt. Indeed this is where 'ethnicity' originally
came from, to be generalized as a norm of late 20th century
existence. As its precondition, the justification of difference
has required a long and differentiated struggle, on the whole
more successful than not, and conducted on a world scale.

Self-colonization, by contrast, had the opposite purpose of
limiting such traits and mobilization. It was a kind of opt-out, in
conditions necessarily rare (and hence difficult to generalize
about). Its aim was that of acknowledging ethnicity-traits but
simultaneously confining them to a 'reservation' separate from
political affairs – and so preserving or reinforcing the overarching status quo. This is why even today any Scottish landlord or
Tory (or Labour) Minister may so easily proclaim himself an
irreproachable Patriot . . . *and* an unflinching upholder of the
Union. The normal accompaniment of such marginalization
was in fact (as already noted) some style of adulation of the
status quo's civilizational merits and achievements. The virtues
of the imperium were customarily hymned and exaggerated in
Austria-Hungary, Tsarist Russia, Great Britain and France in
order to justify continued subordination. This grew more
important in the more and more insubordinate wider world of
the 19th century. National liberation was becoming the norm,
and one way of countering this was with a fulsome (and still
popular) mythology of 'dual identity'.

In one sense dual or multiple identity is merely a standard
human condition, more significant in modern or industrialized
societies than previously. There is nothing at all amazing about
(say) being a Serb, a 'Yugoslav', a Communist, a football fan, an
Orthodox Christian and an ardent philatelist all 'at the same

time'. Modern social conditions favour the multiplication of such 'allegiances', which exist on quite different levels and usually contradict one another only marginally. Few individuals turn out to be so dumb that (in Lyndon Johnson's supposed jibe at President Gerald Ford) they 'can't walk and chew gum at the same time'. But the ideological or heavy-duty sense of 'duality' was quite different: this decreed that two or more key (national) allegiances were compatible, and that it was preferable to be thus enriched.

This may be true; but it is an abstract kind of truth, which has had limited relevance in modern history. Historically, such combinations have in practice been rare cultural balancing-acts, mainly designed for the sustenance of inequality and empire. In the longer run, they were also mostly acts that failed. 'Dual identity' has depended in truth upon a simultaneous denial or curtailment of democracy, either directly (as under Tsardom or the Austro-Hungarian empire), indirectly (as under Great Britain's class-based parliamentarism), or constitutionally (as in the USSR and Yugoslavia). Nor is the reason for this obscure. What suited the intellectuals and political élites did not work for 'the masses' – the peoples being transformed by industrialization and urbanization, and seeking a democratic voice. The latter had to be 'national' – and hence, to give priority to one tongue, 'allegiance', 'imagined community' or another.

Such 'priority' has not necessarily entailed exclusionary politics, discrimination, ethnic homogeneity, and other sins, though these have been common. Differentiation does not have to be damnation of others, although it does involve being prepared to damn *some* others (the dominant power or nationality) for some time, or to some extent. Just when and how this happens depends on particular circumstances – we have now seen it assume vastly differing forms over more

than two hundred years. Those accompanying the decline of
the United Kingdom are just late entrants to the race.

Within the group of (claimed or supposed) multi-allegiance
polities, there was only one dependency where the societal
basis of the dual-identity claim was not only solidly established,
but completely institutionally configured, and guaranteed by
treaty. It was guaranteed, in fact, by what was originally international law, although this became effectively 'internalized'
within the legal system of the post-1707 United Kingdom. Nor
is there any doubt where the principal *locus* or *habitus* of the
resultant social order lay, and still lies: in the institutions of
Scottish 'civil society'. It was the allegiance of these dead monkeys which kept the terminal stage of the British Empire going.
It took a Mrs Thatcher to pry loose their clinging paws and
tails, and thus undo the old 'secret' of the Unwritten British
Constitution. At the end, it was a blind counter-revolution
which undid the latter's laws, rather than any of the old scenarios – so often evoked and elaborated in past times – of
proletarian and/or national liberation.

Its civil-society institutions have indeed always been the
principal boast of modern Scotland. They loom somewhat over-
large in all accounts of the country, and of Scotland's place in
the United Kingdom and the Empire. Twentieth century protagonists and opponents of independence have emphasized
their significance equally – the first as evidence of continuing
nationhood, the second as proof that nationhood can perfectly
well be continued without separate statehood (but with
enrichment of 'dual identity', etc.). The Church of Scotland,
the Edinburgh-based system of Scots Law, and a distinctive
school and university hierarchy were the original trio of institutional life, all consecrated by the 1707 Treaty as
unassimilable features of the Scottish nation. What was guaranteed by this at the time was of course the native social

authority of the aristocracy. But it meant that later the same 'self-managing' authority would be preserved and developed in other native hands – 'for all time coming' (as the Treaty put it).

As time actually came, and Scotland was urbanized over the following two centuries, the core bodies have been joined by a vast number of analogous or ancillary bodies, councils, boards, associations, clubs, societies, committees, churches and unions – all 'Scottish', frequently self-consciously or assertively so, and commonly irradiated with a sense of 'our own', as if some fragment of the nationality-*Geist* had been interfused with committee minutes, charitable works, sporting activities or stamp collections. Outsiders are often astonished by the interminable lists they find under 'Scottish' in the Glasgow and Edinburgh phone directories.

In the present century, probably most would agree that the main addition to this beflagged corpus has been modern local government – a veritable fourth limb worthy of (and larger than) the primordial three, now employing thousands of people within an utterly Caledonian labyrinth stretching from the Scottish Office administration on Leith's Victoria Quay to the dark glass cube of COSLA (the Confederation of Scottish Local Authorities) at the Edinburgh Haymarket. In its day (c. 1965–95) the Strathclyde Regional Council used to be proclaimed 'the biggest local government area in Europe' and once housed an equivalently huge western functionary-imperium in Glasgow.

Another key modern addition to Scotland's institutional armoury came with the Labour Party. Scots had played a disproportionate rôle in forming the United Kingdom Labour Party from the outset, and this disproportion has continued right down to the present. Indeed it is present in Tony Blair's 1997 government as never before. Without it, the devolution measures of 1997 would be incomprehensible, as would some

internal problems of the Blairite régime. Inside Scotland, however, the Party has of course also figured as a new-native
institution. Like the others it has combined tutelage of indigenous matters with the service of the multinational State. But as
a political organization not engaging with a distinct national
body, it has inevitably concentrated on local government.
There it obtained a degree of dominance rarely seen in contemporary societies. It easily controlled Strathclyde and later
Edinburgh and Lothian. After the local government reforms of
the nineties it won an even more striking victory in Glasgow,
still Scotland's largest conurbation. Up until 1999 (when new
elections were held alongside those for the new Parliament), in
a city of extensive conservative suburbs and a sedate middle
class, there was the astonishing result of sixty-three Labour
Councillors against only seven from all other parties.

Kirk, Law and education were thus the templates of what
grew into a much broader institutionalized sub-state. The original models were established by Union in a sense not too
remote from the 20th century idea of 'Establishment' – that is,
as a self-perpetuating and to some extent self-serving control
unit. But while England's social establishment was built for
imperial governance and against the lower classes, the Scottish
one had a third purpose. It was also designed for immunity
against the 'foreign', above all in the sense of English personnel and influence. Takeover by a Southern form of
Protestantism was actually prohibited by the Treaty conditions,
and the abolition of Scots Law by an alien system was also
impossible. That would have required an assimilationist will
which was simply not there, on either side of the Border. The
emergent imperial state relied on class, not remixed or (in the
kitchen food-processor sense) 'blended' nationality.

The same would never quite be true of other institutions,
admittedly. There would be English teachers and Professors (a

lot of them, in the 20th century), as well as civil servants and
public sector managers, alongside non-Scottish businessmen
and other professionals. But in spite of 'Englishing' (as it has
come to be called over the last decade) nativism has none the
less easily predominated in institutional existence. It was part
of the Union deal, and in the main has been consistently identified as a national right by the majority opinion of Scots.

But we have seen there was a constant, if often invisible,
precondition for such native institutionalism. It had to be *self-
alienating* as well as self-preserving. While the Scottish *chasse
gardée* had to be conserved, both as corporate privilege and a
redoubt of nationhood, the conservation went hand in hand
with a constant (but less noticed) self-limiting or non-political
observance. It entailed above all a refusal of leadership, or any
deviance liable to disrupt orderly working. This never meant
complete inertia and conformity (though admittedly, the legal
profession may often have approached this ideal). The Church
of Scotland, for instance, remained in the Union period constantly prone to dispute and schism. This ended with the
founding of a rival, non-established body in the 'Disruption' of
1843: the Free Church. It took over half a century to recompose
their institutional quarrel. However, what mattered most during
the theological war was that the 'freedom' inspiring it should
stay non-political – i.e., religious or social, resolvable in terms
which refused political translation. The disruption was of the
spirit and morality, and not of the United Kingdom's empire.

'Canniness' is one popular rendition of this attitude. It can
also be seen as a kind of collective and consistently sustained
immunization against charisma – that is, individual, disruptive
or 'unsanctioned' inspiration. 'Absence of leadership' is the
thing probably most repeatedly noticed, and complained of, in
the Scottish politics – including nationalist politics – of the past
thirty years. An individual or inspirational headship of affairs

came to be automatically identified with trouble-making, with being 'big-headed' and running needless risks. Sometimes this attitude has been ascribed exclusively to the influence of Presbyterianism, historically the majority Scottish faith. The latter has certainly always combined a strong egalitarianism with a committee-mentality, and distrust for 'being out of line'.

Yet it seems doubtful whether such a prevalent *mentalité* can be explained on that basis alone. After all, there have continued to be commanding reasons for it in all fields of national activity. 'Keeping one's head down', corporate 'consensus' and a some-what stifling version of 'moderation' were in effect a national survival-strategy. In Scotland we find them simply carried for-ward into the age of big private and public-service corporations. That is, into the arena where, as J.K. Galbraith puts it: 'In any great organization it is far, far safer to be wrong with the major-ity than to be right alone'. By guaranteeing the continuity and respectability of Scottishness without 'trouble' (i.e. without a politics of Scottishness), they have both reflected and endorsed the underpinning circumstances of self-subordination. The compensations for abstention had been great, indeed much greater than imagined in 1707. And even when they dwindled, the tails could react (now 'instinctively') by clamping more firmly around the dying boughs.

No doubt such an attitude is to be quite widely found among cadres and functionaries everywhere – it was notorious in Communist countries, for example, and indeed in all bureau-cratic systems. A century ago Max Weber identified it as a general symptom of statified modernity, and warned against its insidious diffusion. However, I doubt if it has been 'nation-alized' anywhere else quite as much as among the Scots – that is, nationalized and institutionalized in accordance with such long-sustained parameters of participation. In Scotland it has been legitimated and instilled for so long that it became (as suggested earlier) virtually 'national character'. In that sense, it became something like the *ethnos* of modern Scotland (or at least a substantial part of it).

Sometimes this Caledonian institutionalism has been carelessly identified with 'socialism', and sometimes with an imagined native (or even clannic) propensity towards the collective. These supposed traits are then depicted as the cause of a supposed anti-individualism in Scottish society – distrust of success and personal wealth, and unwillingness to take initiative. During the period of Thatcherism this kind of critique naturally gained in popularity. As one government after another tried to make capitalism more popular, and to instil an entrepreneurial outlook, it became tempting to ascribe their failure to some sort of inherited recalcitrance or incapacity. In reality, what such change was running up against was also the old half-life of Union Scotland: that is, a sub-state corporatism now irrevocably over-identified with the preservation of nationality and difference. Simultaneously, 'difference' was of course growing in appeal. But 'nationalist' outlook and culture in that sense could only take the existing channels, at least initially. The cramps and impediments to free-range enterprise were also 'community', familial 'customs in common', caring for the less privileged – and so on.

There was probably never the slightest chance of Westminster government altering such attitudes directly, either by rhetoric or by enticement. The possibility of such 'revolution from above' had perished alongside Empire, Monarchy and the old style of Welfare State. The Scots had now to either get rid of or develop such inherited complexes by and for themselves – that is, via their own government and example. But in their case (which is not necessarily that of Catalonia, the German *Länder*, Flanders, or Ulster) this is most likely to require the resumption of statehood.

Pickle-jar Parochialism

We can see that such resumed statehood will have to confront a very special kind of indurate parochialism. As an adjective, 'indurate' means that which is made hardened or callous, but also stubborn and resistant – which seems not a bad rendering of the downside to Scotland's 'civil society'. Civism has been inordinately lauded in Scotland, as a route preferable to ethnicism, romantic mythology, idealized ruralism and violence.

But without decrying this – or for a moment suggesting the other way is preferable – its downside also deserves to be more openly recognized. Low-political persistence and self-replication were not just a triumph of quiet survival. They also acquired aspects of a constricting fate, of a dire mediocrity tolerated for far too long and too grimly. As the outer circumstances of such toleration have disappeared, those features appear more evidently intolerable. The deterioration of Britishness has been accompanied by the rise of participative democracy on the home ground itself. The cost of pickle-jar statehood was always a kind of stagnation: one generation after another has felt oppressed by this, and sought to escape from it. It was like a fixed cost of that style of dependency. But since 1979 the costs have been unfixed, for which one should be grateful. On the other hand, as soon as they were questioned, these preconditions very quickly came to feel insupportable.

On the world's developmental scene 'nation-building' may have counted both failures and successes; but it has normally been a galvanizing and exhilarating process, at least to begin with – a society taking its place in the world, establishing its credentials, and doing its best to make a self-conscious rupture with past cultures of subordination and shame. It is best frankly conceded that nation or state-*conserving* has had few of these redeeming aspects.

What Walter Scott originally called Scotland's 'quiet way' had an utterly different existential basis. It was forced to emphasize continuity, native observance, precedent, protocol and repetition. New nationalism is by instinct anti-authority, resentful and in quest of new air to breathe. But conserving or reservation-nationalism always had a radically different temper: authoritarian, circumspect, distrustful of anything but its own air, odour and tradition. Its profound function was always compromise and survival: to concert an inherited national identity with wider-world presence and aspirations. But this had to be done in a unique *habitus* where passage to the universal was controlled by someone else, upon a high-political plateau where nativism had no official place whatever, save as ornament or nostalgia. Union was an arrangement most useful for the English majority, and above all for its governing caste, which most (nearly all) of the time could simply forget about such curious underpinnings.

For the minority, in contrast, Union was a permanent dilemma, which even in times of success they could never forget about for an instant. They had to quite consciously and continuously adapt themselves to it over about nine generations (by the traditional calculation). During this long time neither horn of the dilemma could ever be escaped. That is part of what 'structural' means here. It is also why one of its end products might be labelled 'pickle-jar nationalism' – an identity-structure within which certain inherited elements have matured too much and for far too long in their own company.

Thus Scottish virtues – in a sense the 'old country' herself – were still being advanced, made to count and noticed in the world. The old pickle-jar could seem justified after all. From a background often described as 'humble' – a milieu of positively Jurassic backwardness – Sir/Professor/General Secretary/Minister Alex MacChancer has emerged to bedazzle

the metropolitan and imperial élites. His gruff principles seem
to lay down the law.

'Self-colonization' contains the possibility of a limited
'reverse colonization' of élites. Thus the periphery comes to
contribute more than just manpower and mass emigration, and
the point of view of its successful minority is correspondingly
influential. The latter perceive as exemplary their own trajectory from unbearable narrowness and kailyard prejudice to
exalted status. In roseate retroview all robust inherited virtues
appear justified. Such a system obviously merits preservation.
However deplorable, the old reservation is both seed-bed and
launching-pad for future MacChancers. 'Unionism' for this sub-
class is less a political principle than a rooted life-chance
conviction.

Just as self-colonization differed from occupation, suppression and assimilation, so its end, self-liberation, is bound to
differ from the attainment of the standard forms of self-
government and independence. This has always been
confusing for stereotypes, and may well become more so.
There is no escape from identity-stereotypes in modern conditions. On the other hand, they rarely mean what they seem to,
and least of all what they consider themselves to mean.

'Display Identity'

Seen from outside, there is bound to remain something puzzling
about this argument. For it is also true that the identity of
Scotland has been regularly displayed to the rest of humankind
in a drastically different way. In that other perspective, it is not
castrate civility which predominates but a highly-coloured image
of defiant ethnic wrath. In the immediate past Mel Gibson's
Braveheart may have been mainly responsible for diffusing

this idea, but there is a long and relevant history preceding it.

The history in question here is of course that of a national 'identity'. This exasperating successor to 'nature' and 'national character' is today often awarded a wilful or even an aesthetic dimension, as if identities were primarily what individuals (or societies) chose or wish to be. It may be true – I certainly hope it is – that in post-Cold War conditions there is more space for such choices. It ought to become easier to 'decide to be' what-ever-it-is, or 'to become' a so-and-so. However, this real possibility remains quite distinct from the metaphysics of 'identity politics'. For the latter, the assumption is that identity itself is (and hence always has been) constituted by such deci-sions. Because collective (like individual) self-imagery has always possessed an imagined or even a fantasized aspect, the assumption then comes to be that the imagination was of their essence. 'Identities' were then viewed as cultural artefacts, more or less in the modern sense of self-conscious or adopted 'culture'. Hence they may appear suspiciously simple to re-fabricate in the present, for use in the future.

This is bound to have some appeal in a country where (as observed above) so much of society has remained 'our own work' rather than being imposed, and so much of the collective mental furniture is civic-institutional. Institutions are by definition non-natural, more 'built up' than unwittingly grown. The temptation to adopt an uncritical version of identity-politics is likely to be quite strong. Civism and identitarianism gang thegither, as it were, somewhat to the confusion of eth-nicity.

Another support for this style of ultra-civism is provided by the notable crudity and low status of *ethnos* itself in Scotland. No one would have said this quite so lightly sixty or seventy years ago, when ideas about the 'Scottish race' (Protestant, Teutonic, energetic and masterful) were prevalent enough to inspire crusades to expel degenerate Irish immigrants (Catholics, Celts, slavish, lazy and unmodernizable). During the entire period when imperialism has dwindled and political nationalism has grown, however (the 1960s to the 1990s), such ideas have become vestigial. As I pointed out earlier, far from ethnic infatuation having informed the rise of Scottish political nationalism since the 1960s, the contrary is closer to the truth. Ethno-cultural or blood-descent nationalism is today the preserve of cranks and ideological gangsters in Scotland. The conjunction of this with international alarm over recent conflicts in Eastern Europe, Central Africa and elsewhere, has made it easy to counterpose the virtues of civil-institutionalism against the real and supposed vices of ethnicity, or even of 'nationalism' *tout court*.

But I suspect there is also an element of *trompe l'oeil* in this counterposition. It is brought to the surface, oddly, by the imminence of self-rule. As I pointed out earlier, 'ethnicity' is a range of ideas relating to origin and pre-existent nature, and deriving from the past two centuries. More specifically, that derivation emerged from consciousness of the impact of modernity on agrarian and tribal culture, whether as 'Enlightenment', industrialization or political and military empire. Although contemporary usage may have stretched the ideas to include urban living, it was originally peasants and 'natives' who represented the ethnic: those who preceded the great change, human nature as yet supposedly 'untouched'. Modernity's alteration has been perceived alternately as 'progress' and 'degeneration' (or sometimes as both) but always with reference to such anterior conditions – the time before, by comparison 'changeless', authentic and given.

Since origins grew much more significant in the post-1789 world of nascent nationalism, they were naturally cast in the same mould. Crushed, threatened and reawakening identities instinctively awarded themselves an 'immemorial' source, the justification for new struggles and demands. Since the old faiths and dynasties claimed eternity, so would they. Ethnic nationalism was founded upon that kind of historical (or pseudo-historical) retrospect. That is, it was founded upon something itself quite novel, and quite distinct from what folk-mythologies and creation legends had previously been 'in themselves'. The 'folkish' was made out of how folk appeared after Enlightenment – when the peasantry had begun to quit the countryside, and the enormous convulsion of societal mod-ernization had been launched. Long before the appearance of heritage sites, 'inheritance' was itself a kind of icon.

It should also be recalled at this point that for the greater part of its hold over the modern imagination, all too little was understood of actual inheritance and its rules – either natural or social. In fact, from the 1750s right down to the 1950s, very little was known which affected these prevalent attitudes. Genesis in the sense of genetics was a mystery, into which any sort of story could be projected – from 'In the Beginning was the Word' down to crazy 20th century tales of Aryan suprema-cism. Given the limits of scientific investigation over most of that time, the foundations of human culture might indeed have been 'in the blood'. In which case some part of all 'identities' could indeed have proved immutable, or at least gene-dependent and hence capable only of very slow change. Only recently has it been finally understood that this is not so.

But with this emancipation come new problems. In response to liberation from 'nature', identity politics has tended to exag-gerate farther all the conscious or deliberate factors of identity. They have fallen over in the other direction, towards assuming that 'social' implies 'invented', even in distant historical retro-spect. All ethno-cultural boundaries can then be made to appear chosen, functional or 'negotiable'. But what this overlooks in turn is simply the depth, persistence, and largely non-conscious character of social inheritance itself. The mysteries of DNA and genetic patterning may be yielding at last to scientific investigation in the present. Unfortunately those of their social equivalents remain more mysterious up to the present.

And yet, few things are more evident from everyday life and politics. Few individuals spend much of their time consciously worrying over their own or their community's 'identity', while many spend none whatever. Social (including national) collective consciousness is none the less constantly transmitted onwards. In fact it may be powerfully transmitted, over surprising periods of time, and against great apparent odds – for centuries, rather than just generations. 'National identity' has in this sense to be described as a non-genetic but long-range socio-cultural inheritance, capable of persisting even although its salience and manifestations vary greatly from one time or situation to another. While of course it must pass through consciousness, its residence within any social fabric is largely 'unconscious' in the familiar sense of being 'taken for granted', as feeling, presupposition, reflex or fall-back mechanism. Were this not true, perfectly ordinary incidents like realizing (with dismay or gratification) 'how Dutch one is', 'what it means to be American', 'suddenly feeling like a foreigner', or 'being proud to be English' would be incomprehensible. So would most Jewish jokes.

The stereotype-rules of the nation-state world require individuals to be 'proud', or at least reasonably pleased, about being a so-and-so; but since very few pass much of their time in a trance of subjective gratitude, this 'being' must be a steady-state attitude which 'comes to consciousness' as and when needed. Were that not so, it would before long interfere with anyone's sanity. Steady-state means effectively 'unconscious' –

by analogy with computer language, it means registered on the hard disk rather than being forever present in the random access memory, on screen (even though the permanent or hard-disk memory ultimately exists to serve the latter).

Like individuals, nations are not, or are not only, 'what they think they are'. What they *are* (using the same computer analogy) is more like a package or bundle of long-range, resident programs transmitted and maintained in a great number of ways. These range from family and kinship to higher education and statehood, and surface intermittently in individual and shared consciousness, in an equally various (and not necessarily acknowledged) number of ways. Among the latter, self-consciousness is a rather infrequent display-mode – as in saluting the flag, swearing allegiance to a constitution, or being moved at *la ligne bleue des Vosges* or the white cliffs of Dover. National character ('identity') is all these levels together, with the background inevitably most important, most of the time: the structure or 'depths', as is sometimes said. But such depths are necessary, and they are only 'mysterious' in the sense that we know far too little about how they are accumulated and transmitted.

The display-mode was obviously a peculiar problem for a national society like Scotland's – that is, a country which had shed the usual display-mechanisms linked to modern state-hood, warfare and international 'representation'. These are normally provided by 'high-political' identification, as well as by 'official' art, architecture and centrally-organized commem-orations or rituals. With no political centre to oblige, and no ethnic movement to recover such a centre, 19th century Scots found themselves to be a potentially display-less nation.

Their civil-society institutions provided in themselves no substitute. It was simply not feasible to manifest 'Scottishness' by a proud unfolding of the Scottish primary-school system, or by disquisitions upon the Court of Session or the glories of Presbyterian pulpit and Assembly. Actually people did constantly attempt these things; but they now obviously fell below the mark required by 'identity' in the post-French-Revolutionary sense. The latter demanded much more visible, cultural and high-political insignia – phenomena capable of registering somewhere on the modern political equivalent of the Richter Scale.

It was, unfortunately, no use dismissing such representations as 'mere display', unimportant to sensible people concerned with more material matters (though this has been constantly attempted too). The truth is that in modern times 'sensible people' are also concerned with identity. Social anthropologists have shown how significant the display of identity was in earlier, smaller societies. It may be that in feudal or early-modern times 'identity' counted for less – I gladly leave historians to adjudicate about this. What seems to be beyond dispute, however, is that literacy, industrialization and urbanization have fostered the conditions of revitalized communal aspiration. The 'modern' is in that sense partly an augmented sense of 'meaning', which populations live by, and indeed may become obsessed by. 'Meaning' belongs alongside democracy and individual rights, and seems to be a precondition of them.

After all, it is the combined threat and promise of 'identity' which has itself given rise to the philistine's universe – that is, to the narrow, pseudo-rational world where material 'good sense' supposedly renders people indifferent to the glamour of faith, nation and causes. This is itself just another imputed 'identity'. The endorsement of such 'common sense' tends to be made principally by those in charge at any particular moment. Philistinism is itself a cause, in other words – usually the constricting and damping-down cause of keeping things the way they are, or even the way they were. Were that theoretical construction as true as its invariably complacent protagonists claim then (for example) no population would ever have gone mad about sport: there would be no such thing as 'football patriotism', or in certain cases football chauvinism.

But obviously they do, and there is. People live by and for 'identity' as well as for job-security, non-leaking roofs, making ends meet and being able to pay for their funerals. Damned awkward, of course, above all from the point of view of blueprint-forgers – but probably just as well. It is worth recalling that most science-fictional dystopias depict an intolerable future for humanity from which it is that side which has been somehow excised. In the long epoch of ascending nationalism, new standards of identification were created, and themselves became in turn inescapable facets of collective and individual existence – the sustaining obverse of democracy's coin.

Inescapable, that is, *for most people*. There may have been individuals, or even small populations in frontier zones or extremely remote locations, who could resist or sidestep the new modes of identification. But for everyone else it was a necessity. It was 'functional' for modernity, although in a much wider sense than is sometimes recognized. Industrialization, literacy and town-life demanded nation-states (as Ernest Gellner argued in his *Nations and Nationalism*). However, such societies had to constitute communities, and community in turn affirmed its own necessities. And one of these lay in being and appearing distinct, in a universe of similar (and frequently competing) entities, where minuscule élites were ceasing to retain their exclusive command over 'matters of state'. Nationalism never consisted only in a nationality asserting its own place and rights; it was also a way – and for long the sole way – in which the larger world was 'brought home' to less determinate and pre-political societies. It was that two-way process which generated 'identity' – the law of modern societal breathing, as it were, and the true invention (or 'imagination') of community.

A great deal of this process could not be escaped, even by a society locked into the Scottish reservation-dilemma described previously. Identification with Britishness took up some of it, naturally, most obviously during the high moments of overseas empire. But Britishness itself was a deliberately composite identity-mode, which (as I argued before) sought to subsume rather than to assimilate. It relegated rather than exalted 'ethnicity'. Placing class above nationality entailed the creation of 'reservations', of which Scotland was the most important, and the best endowed with institutional traditions and culture. One purpose of the Scottish and Welsh reservations was to keep nationality alive; preferably without politics. In the altered conditions of the 19th and early 20th century, this demanded an equivalently 'autonomous' strategy of identification – it was no longer enough just to manage surviving institutional modes and a backyard culture.

It was these changes which added another decisive twist to the 'self-colonization' dilemma: that of *appearing like* a nationality (and preferably an 'ethnic' – easily identifiable – one). Since actually becoming one was self-prohibited, it was all the more necessary to look like one. The answer to this dilemma is something which has become famous, and helps explain the disconcerting contrast of appearance with reality in contemporary Scotland. It was the phenomenon of Gaelicism, (or perhaps 'Highlandism'), a style of collective representation deliberately evolved into a mass identity from (approximately) the time of the Napoleonic Wars onwards. Another shorthand for the same thing has been 'tartanry' – the assimilation of all things Scottish to a clannic (hence plaid-clad) origin, and linked by association of ideas to Northern scenery, Celtic speech and artefacts, the Battle of Culloden (when clannic society was defeated alongside the Stuart dynasty in 1746), and a twilit Ossianic past. Not possessing a sufficiently distinct majority tongue, the Scots invented a 'language' of assertive display in other modes and forms.

Most Scots had no actual connection with earlier clannic or Gaelic society, and hence no 'folk' or other recollection or tradition upon which Highlandism could easily be grafted. On the contrary, Gaelic culture had often been despised by Lowlanders, and perceived as a badge of backwardness. None the less, the required recollection and 'traditions' were soon synthesized. This was possible because, with all its absurdities and unrealities, the process rested upon something real.

All intelligent visitors to Scotland have been conscious of the contradiction: a 'phoney' identity-claim to which perfectly un-phoney people cling, and with genuine passion. The contradiction has always been obvious, but its persistence manifests a fundamental wish: the will to continue 'being something', and hence to go on presenting a new image both to the outside world and to oneself. Historically, this societal instinct simply took up the material available – the real, if often tenuous, inheritance of tribal social formations and the population movements from Highlands to Lowlands (above all Glasgow) which occurred throughout the 19th century. Thus, the national society which had generated the staid, pure reason of 'civil society' also ended by creating a fantasy *alter ego* for itself – a simulacrum of ethnicity, as it were, intended to fulfil at least part of the socio-political rôle which, elsewhere, was being assumed by national revolution or liberation, armed struggle, chauvinism and racist delusions.

The real purpose here was always the preservation of

nationality – something which, by implication, civic institutionalism by itself would never have sufficiently achieved. However admirable, distinctive and successful, Scottish 'civil society' could not hope to be enough for mass identity purposes. But 'mass' in this context also means (at least potentially) 'democratic'. Approaching the return of a Scottish Parliament, it is important to keep that in mind too. A modern nation has first and foremost to be a 'community of citizens', in Dominique Schnapper's deliberately contradictory phrase. Democratic citizenship must be its principal armature: but it has to be a community too – social survival and reproduction, from which there is no escape, demands it be simultaneously a 'felt' association resting upon deeper and longer-range motifs linked to culture, emotion and transmissible 'instincts'.

Scotland returns to statehood in a world altered in all these irreversible ways. It does so weighed down by the detritus of its inbred institutionalism, and also by a partly aberrant identity code of fake Celticism. These are like the Siamese twins of an abnegated polity. A new parliamentary process will have the task of disentangling them from one another, and transcending both of them. It faces the problem, I will argue, of 'reconstituting' a nation rather than that of straightforwardly building one in the historically more familiar sense. Neither nation nor state have ever disappeared or been suppressed in Scotland. On the other hand, both have collapsed into a miserable and parlous condition, through dependency, mediocrity, routine and habitual pretence. The new instrument of self-government confronts tasks of 'identity' and unmaking, simultaneously with those of settling its new relationship to London and to Europe. This is why (as I will go on to argue) the returned *de facto* state vitally needs another instrument to support it through such turbulent waters: a separate, written constitution of its own.

Blaming the Other

Not having been subjugated or assimilated in standard fashion, Scotland was never likely to liberate itself in familiar ways either. Although it remains surprisingly hard to see just what these differences will be, there is one overriding reason for trying to do so. If we don't, then, in the context of clashes with the British government, it will obviously be too easy to pretend that *all* Holyrood's problems derive from Westminster. The formerly extolled could then become the presently and incessantly reviled. This could be all the worse since, naturally, *some* problems are bound to derive from that source. The 'chip on the shoulder' has been around for centuries: it was an integral aspect of the 1707 Treaty world. Now, however, resentment at inequality has an instrument of effective complaint and redress. Particularly at the beginning, the Auld Enemy's remaining hold over Scotland's political liberty could easily be exaggerated into the root of every evil.

No one should doubt that a new retrospect on Scotland's history and institutions will arise. In that sense at least the existence of the new Parliament is certain to 'change everything' (and is already doing so). Yet many in Scotland are curiously reluctant to admit the shift – a farther symptom, I would suggest, of the very malaise which self-rule must aim to put right. In the year before the event there remained a sense of over-continuity about too many current attitudes, deadening rather than reassuring. Not having been disturbed by war and revolt, it is as if society had somehow not, or not yet, disturbed itself enough.

Yet it has to: this seems to me a penalty of Scotland's curious past condition. For when things do alter, the new retrospect will make it seem that the former quiescence was intolerable – indeed almost inexplicable. On 12 May 1999, Winifred Ewing declared from the forum that the Scottish parliament, adjourned on 24 March 1707, '*is hereby reconvened*'. That was the quietly accepted sense of the event among Scots – not that a new regional assembly had been set up to attend to some specific, local tasks. For a country, her words changed the firmament, and Ian Bell of *The Scotsman* put it better than most:

> History is memory. This moment was memory reclaimed, a right restated, a truth reaffirmed. The nation of Scotland, with all its thrawn suspicions, numberless confusions, apathy, clumsy rivalries and disparate hopes, had remembered. (Thursday 13 May 1999)

Once such business is resumed, it is the three-century interregnum that will appear strange. Not being simply a new devolved administration, the Scottish Parliament did not seek to avoid the label which fitted – that of an ancient form of state.

In the longer run this may actually strengthen a settled relationship to Europe and England. But in the short run it could also strengthen the temptation to suppress the recollection of servitude, by a kind of exorcism. And the simplest way of promoting that is bound to be by exaggeration of the opposite – that is, by present-day non-acceptance, by irascible touchiness, or pre-emptive aggression. A certain vein of Scottish nationalism has always leaned in that direction anyway – the 'fundamentalism' caused by prolonged frustration and marginalization. The presumption of such wrath is likely to be that Scotland is already (inwardly) liberated and truly herself – and hence only (and unfairly) constrained by the remaining external shackles, and by interference from England.

Yet we know right now that this is not the case. The moment to anticipate the situation and its arguments is in the present.

The Parliament's business cannot consist only of continuing to 'run things' with a few minor changes, in the sense prescribed both by the Scotland Bill and the present British government's game-plan. It will not be – and must not be – a version of the 'local government' mentioned previously. Modern British government as a whole has suffered from over-continuity, traditionalism and complacency. These traits may have been denounced often enough in the Blair régime's initial rhetoric, but they have not been slow to reassert themselves. Before the new assemblies actually meet in Edinburgh, Cardiff and Belfast it seems likely they will once more predominate in London. As we have seen, a new central constitution for the United Kingdom is even now being farther sidelined – or at least, left to 'emerge' in the fullness of time, which (after the passage of enough actual time) could be another code-word for 'never'.

From a Scottish angle, the worst feature of this prospect is that it may yet furnish ideal and prolonged conditions for 'blaming-the-other'. Proponents of limited and well-behaved devolution have been disconcertingly slow to appreciate this fact. They are over-accustomed to the proverbial stability of the broader framework – to a United Kingdom itself 'well-behaved', and almost changeless in outlook. Even today they find it extraordinarily difficult to believe we are no longer in the smooth mill-pond of imperial times.

During that truly *longue durée* external havoc had been coupled to domestic constancy and state-level equilibrium. These were destabilized in the 1960s and '70s, before being shattered in the 1980s, through Thatcher's upheaval. In the same decade, what had really been the sustaining external supports of Cold War immobilism vanished as well. After Thatcher's deposition the mill-pond turned into the mill-race. Yet such was the decrepitude of the old order that it took a proverbial seven years of decline to react – the span of John Major's régime of funereal complacency and intensifying corruption.

In truth, what Scotland's Parliament returns into is a good deal worse than a faltering multinational state. It is a United Kingdom in which both socio-economic and constitutional renovation have been loudly spoken of, but then half-abandoned in disarray, leaving all the most crucial modernization-problems in limbo. No formula for 'stability' is visible here (other than robotic conformity to the will-power of Blair's 'project'). In fact it looks more like a motor of cumulative instability.

Yet, as if paralysed by nostalgic retrospect, the partisans of dependency appear perfectly unable to think beyond the passing moment of 'Blairism'. Just as observers sometimes found it hard to think that 'Thatcherism' would not last forever, today they believe that Blair's conjuncture of pretence and compromise – or something like it – must go on supporting any foreseeable British future. They fail to appreciate that the government in charge of such essential indecisiveness is merely one which has let one particular delusion get the better of it. Because constitutional change is not a popular enough issue in England, New Labour felt it simply could not be put and kept at the centre of affairs. As mentioned repeatedly above, they still believe it can be postponed, compromised away, or in the end used merely as a bargaining chip in the Labour Party's uneasy partnership with the Liberal Democrats.

Thus for heartland folk, reform of the state is a postponable, secondary matter – a way of remaining in office, and propping up what is really a surrogate British Establishment. It has not yet occurred to New Labour that this could become an inescapable way of tumbling from office, once the glamour departs from Blairism and 'Middle England' despairs of him in turn. In the first chapter of this book, I was arguing that nothing else is likely to ensue. Beyond Blair's parody of Britain a renovated England is certain. No one ought to fear that; *in itself*. But of course the condition of 'in itself' is not so easily attained. The ruins of Britishness are another matter altogether: here is an inheritance which, it seems to me, one may reasonably fear. During the week the first Scottish Parliament was elected, part of it exploded as nail-bombs around the centre of London – fearful reproaches against invaders, aliens, 'degenerates' and all who have injured or betrayed a certain idea of Anglo-British nationhood.

Ancestral Dreads

The fears associated with resurgent nationalism are usually seen as 'ethnic' – springing from popular resentments, detestation of 'the Other', instinctive preferences and folk-memories (real or simulated). Kinship, faith, tongue and popular culture are deemed responsible for the shift, and become the prime objects of dread and censure. Yet extraordinarily little of this appears to figure in the Scottish scenario. As we saw, there have been repeated attempts to 'lay bare' such horrid truths, or (frankly) to invent them for the edification of an audience which, after the events of 1989–99, thinks it knows what to expect. When invention fails, the critics then sometimes say: 'Just wait!' – time will tell, surely, once English heartland opinion gathers its resources and (following the prescriptions of West Lothian's soothsayer) focuses its resentment upon peripheral unreason and pretence.

I have already indicated the falsity of this perspective, which applies standard formulae to what was always an anomalous history and prospect. However, that history does have its own dreads, which will have to find their separate and peculiar answers. As for the repercussions of Scottish self-government on

England, these may well be far greater than even the most dole-ful West-Lothianers have imagined – but I suspect they will occur on the plane of the state, the constitution, and Europe, much more than on that of spontaneous popular resentment or culture-clash. That is, they are likely to occur in the area where British government has historically been at its weakest, and least concerned: constitutional politics. Nemesis looks most probable upon this terrain which it has for so long neglected – neglected and then, when forced at last into action, treated with a traditional inconsequence and 'absent-mindedness'.

Devolution has been a range of minimalist responses to sup-posedly discrete, 'peculiar' questions. But it was also a way of doing next to nothing, about the one question which mattered absolutely, that of reforming the British Constitution. And yet the plural challenges of the periphery lead inexorably back to this centre, and to the ever more belated dilemma of changing things there. A decade ago bold federal blueprints were pro-jected by Charter 88 and the other protagonists of constitutionalism, as Anthony Barnett reminded us in his *This Time*. Now – with Scottish, Welsh and Northern Irish govern-ments coming into operation – we find the London political machine distractedly wondering what on earth to 'do about England', or about the English regions. Will a Mayor for the Londoners be enough? Or might it merely make things worse? What style of non-elected 'Lordship' will provoke least cyni-cism and international ridicule? Queen Elizabeth II remains untouchable; but will the populations of a decentralized Kingdom really want to put up with her son?

In Scotland, the old pickle-jar mentality would have 'loyally' put up with anything. But that's the point. The ancestral dread afflicting the Scotland of a returned Parliament has nothing to do with genes, Celticism, new song-lines of the blood, or a suppressed thirst for ethnic vengeance. It has everything to do with fear of farther confinement in the Unionist pickle-jar, and determination that 'things should be different' – freer, more directly open to the world, more egalitarian, more participative and (in a sense impossible under dependency) more self-respecting. 'Democratic' is the usual term employed here, but it has a specific and very strong charge in this context.

Escaping From the Reservation

I pointed out earlier how Scottish 'reservation identity' was linked to the special stasis of 1707's institutional provisions – the closed circles of provincial self-management and establishment, a self-reproducing sub-state locked somewhere in between the (problematic) nation and the (unproblematic but remote) State of Westminster. One feature of this autonomous 'quiet way' was its incredible smallness. During the recent electoral campaign for the first Scottish Parliamentary session, a number of more cutting analyses focused on the clique-like aspect of the Scottish power élite, invariably with the implication that this Parliament had to do something about it. Scotland's power-brokers, explained Ian Bell in *The Scotsman* (1 March) were like a test-tube exemplification of 'democratic deficit':

> Change is upon us now . . . with a chance, finally, to let in a little light and a little air. Success and enterprise are not the issues or the argument. The Establishment constituency is too narrow, the connections too intimate, the lack of incentive for radicalism too small. This could only have come about in a small country without self-government and with a tradition of castes, private dealings and personal understandings . . .

Between fifty and one hundred individuals 'run' a country of over five million, Bell explains, at a tangent to the half-democracy of Westminster and local-authority representation. These individuals mostly know one another, often closely, and encounter one another almost daily on innumerable committees, boards and councils, as well as privately. Their combination of wealth, know-how, connections and national status renders them invulnerable, and also bolsters what Bell rightly calls 'the myth of the Scottish consensus'.

This consensus has too often been exclusively identified with approvable norms of community and cooperation, or even an indigenous socialism counterposed to English indifference or individualism. But as Bell points out, it can also be seen as pathological constriction, and a thinly-veiled authoritarianism. Over the last century, this country's *ancien régime* featured a Secretary of State whose real duty was to breathe down everyone's neck every day of the week, including Sundays. In the 1980s and early '90s, thanks to hyperactive Tories like Malcolm Rifkind and Michael Forsyth, the blighters never left the population alone. Their instructions, imprecations and dazzling (if transitory) notions occupied every front page and invaded every living-room with the evening TV news. Inaugurations, blessings, walkabouts, momentous conferences, visits to school and fish-farm and the reception of Royal or foreign personages produced a daily pantomine bizarrely like life in pre-1989 Eastern Europe.

I recall thinking often at that time, with a degree of bitterness, that nobody down in England had the faintest idea of what this pastiche-Gulag was like. Only some immigrants there knew anything about 'being ruled' in that sense: the impotent eternity of it, the crazed fantasies of escape, or the fulminating internecine conflicts fostered by impracticable formulae of redemption – policies forever 'out of the question' (since no political means existed for trying them out).

Such was 'stability': the celestial peace of the British Union, bestowing responsible administration by the extremely few, and co-opted by a Father-figure invested from the British Heaven. He could be of 'Left' or 'Right' indifferently (and the régime never managed to invest a female). Whatever banner the Satrap bore from the distant sun, there were phalanxes of moderate businesfolk and charisma-free trade-unionists, professors, landlords and clerics who dwelt or slumbered in his Committees before bearing his message loyally outwards to lieutenants, secretaries, non-investigative journalists, taxmen, foremen, policemen and barmen – all capable of imposing it with the minimum of protest, or indeed damned nonsense of any kind whatever. Such was the Land of Mountain and Flood, during that long exile from herself now at last ended. It was (in Bell's words) 'the small-country syndrome . . . the village network of power' marked from one end to the other 'with the hieratic devices of status and influence – the knighthood, the chairmanship, the honorary degree, the Cabinet seat, the charity board, the bank balance – as surely as any tribe'.

But one can't simply let a little 'light and air' into such a tribe. The Scottish Establishment did not suffer from 'democratic deficit'. Its essence was the *stifling* of democracy, in the joint names of nation and class (and often accompanied by odious protestations of a supposedly native equality, or even meritocracy). Adding some electoral legitimacy to this concoction would make it even more intolerable – the East-European syndrome again, which eventually allowed power-élites there to remain in office by manipulating an untried party system.

The ancestral dread which counts in Scotland has therefore nothing to do with woad, memories of distant battles, and instincts of native communalism. It has a lot to do with perfectly realistic apprehension of resurgent half-life, re-engineered mediocrity and sanctified marginalization. No one really thinks the shade of William Wallace will reappear at Holyrood. A lot of people do think, with appropriate despondency, that Councillor McDinge, Provost McBaffie, and Mrs McGrunge will not only be in there but could soon swamp the place. Such authentic representatives of the modern Scots 'ethnicity' are known to be tenacious of life, good at simulation, and never short of an offended principle. Scottish Old Labour had been their own. New Labour has been but a mid-morning snack to many of them – something to set them up for the permanent high tea they could perceive advancing with a Parliament 'of our own'.

In the early phases of the first Scottish election campaign (the second and third weeks of April 1999) it suddenly looked as if tea was as good as on the table, with the possibility of an outright Labour Party majority. Fortunately this induced a certain shock, even among the most blinkered of Unionists. There followed a reflux of sobered-up opinion which ended by at least confining Labour to largest-party status. Hairmless Harry was (as it were) held up on probation at the lunch trough – cause for apprehension, certainly, but not yet outright despair.

Here above all, Scotland has to be unmade by an eruption of democracy. In a wholly unusual twist to the story of national liberation, national 'deconstruction' should take over from 'nation-building'. The first elected government since 1707 (and of course, the first democratically-elected government ever) is confronted by the need to undo much of the existing nation, as a prelude to constructing something better, more European and contemporary.

But existing élite structures will not simply give up and retire, as happened to post-colonial countries. There is no alien governing stratum which can be dismissed or 'go home', or into comfortable exile. On the contrary, we know that stratum all too well: a parcel of rogues, yet undeniably our own – and something of them is inside all of us. Their customs and reflexes are almost wholly native, 'proud' and tradition-steeped. They cannot help representing a form of long-term adaptation to external hegemony, and now equally – through reflexes long since 'national' – they cannot help carrying on the act. They will carry on adapting, in order to avoid being replaced, and going under. What they really mean by 'new' is that the old half-life should continue, energized by a little more of Ian Bell's 'light and air'. In their reading of it, 'making a success' out of Devolution means avoiding the extinction of themselves by climatic – which in this case really means 'constitutional' – change.

More precisely, it means constitutional change with the aim of installing democracy in Scotland. This was not achieved by the Devolution legislation alone, nor by the initial plans for running the Holyrood Parliament, let alone by the first Scottish general election on 6 May 1999. In fact it was not attempted by any or all of these moves. The essential aim of all these was the perpetuation of the United Kingdom, and the reinforcement of its artificially renewed governing stratum – 'Blairism'. This is not (of course) to claim that all those involved in the change (nationalists, liberals, conservatives, non-partisans and cultural militants, as well as the Party faithful) consciously sought that end. They wanted it for all sorts of reasons, and with every imaginable qualification. However, the institutional sense of the shift is another matter. As Mary Douglas points out in *How Institutions Think* (1987), institutions are like languages: to some extent they determine the meaning of what individuals do, think and decide, and it isn't so easy to switch to a new one.

Individuals in crises do not make life and death decisions on their own. Who shall be saved and who shall die is settled by

institutions. Putting it even more strongly, individual ratio-
cination cannot solve such problems. An answer is seen to be
the right one if it sustains the institutional thinking that is
already in the minds of individuals as they try to decide . . .

Nor are shallow graves much good for them. Institutions and
their dead monkeys are (as can be seen in the first weeks of the
new Edinburgh Parliament) perfectly capable of rapid resurrection and new life beyond what should have been their tomb.

I referred earlier to Jean-François Revel's acrid critique of
Mitterand's rule in the Fifth French Republic. His concluding
damnation is worth quoting here too. He points out that however gifted, politically astute, courageous and visionary a
modern leader may be, in the end it is the structure that matters most:

> The sixth condition of statesmanship is not a personal asset,
> but something which constrains his own will, a salutary and
> external obstacle imposed upon him. He must acknowledge
> that his own wishes are in certain matters a poor guide, and
> must make way to a more fundamental law, that of heeding
> whatever criticisms, objections and contradictions are prop-
> erly raised against his actions on constitutional grounds.
> Without that, in a few years even the greatest political genius
> will flounder into blind arrogance and uncontrollable sleaze.
> There is a precise name for this sixth condition: democracy.[2]

Reconstituting a Country

Constituting democracy in Scotland is not a question of law and
principle alone. It is also one of popular identity and culture,
and that implies going beyond the old division between 'low'

(local) and 'high' (state-identity) politics. Which in turn brings the need for 'constitutional grounds' in Revel's sense. It may be that things hung together differently in the setting up of regional-national governments elsewhere in Europe – like post-war Germany and Italy, or post-Franco Spain. I have argued the case below, in the written evidence of the *Appendix* (p. 294). But in this case they hang together in a way which seems to make the case for a proper Scottish constitution irresistible.

Since it began functioning in May, every session of the new Scottish Parliament has resounded with pleas from every party in it to be 'different'. Nor is there any doubt about what it has to differ from. The unvarying object of censure and reproach is the other Parliament which created it in the first place: Westminster, the adversarial law-court on the Thames, with its almost geological coagulation of imperial self-importance, dismal flummery, schoolboy abuse, cadaverous party-spirit and antique servility. Everyone in Edinburgh – Labour and Liberal as well as Nationalists – wants the new body to be 'modern' in this sense. Its members are constantly exhorted to behave like citizen-representatives seeking agreements on a common good, not tools of the exalted Sovereignty momentarily bestowed upon a Leader, his Cabinet and his 'back-bench' Army.

Though often phrased in moral and personal terms, this attitude is plainly not just an advocacy of polite conduct. Implicitly it rebukes and rejects the unwritten Constitution which created it. That is, the Constitution which (beyond the literal terms of the 1707 Treaty of Union) the Scots once agreed to submit to. Having no alternative or new Constitution of their own (at least in a formal sense) the new Scottish representatives are however unable to counterpose their will to Westminster in this structural way. If they are compelled to emphasize modernity of spirit and deportment, an ethical will to be and appear different, contemporary and European, this is because a more serious

mode of expression is still lacking. Yet it must be found, for the
Scottish parliament to assume full existence.

In the broader public and journalistic debate also, the same
attitude often takes the form of a sometimes inordinate emphasis upon culture: the vital spirit of novelty and innovation, as
distinct from mere politics and law. Without dismissing this
stress upon subjectivity (which has obvious value in its own
right) its limitations need to be observed. No doubt the
Parliament of a restored state could have asserted up-to-date
practices very effectively and without much conflict – in a
wider framework itself being reformed along parallel lines.
That would (for example) have been the natural condition for
a United Kingdom federalism, or even confederalism, of the
kind so long urged by Liberal Democrats.

But of course, it is exactly what is *not* happening in the
United Kingdom. Instead, the real context of Devolution was
initially peripheral radicalization in consort with a half-hearted
central reform-process. Now the latter has defaulted back
towards outright conservatism. It is this perfectly objective contradiction which now underlies the rhetoric of the new
Parliamentarians in Edinburgh, Cardiff and (possibly) Belfast.

In theory, the dilemma could certainly be resolved by
renewed central advances. *If* the Blairite hegemony was (for
example) to be followed by a coalition where Liberal Democratic
ideas were more prominent, or even in command. *If* electoral and
constitutional reform was given new priority, and all the archipelago nations were urged actively to follow the Republic of
Ireland's lead, by moving jointly and finally into European
Union. *If* this were to be so, then of course apostles of the New
would be back on approximately common ground. 'Britain'
might be on the way to actually meaning something new, in a
sense far more interesting than the public relations 'branding'
exercise of 1997–98. The trouble is, none of these 'Ifs' currently

apply. And there is a decreasing likelihood of their ever doing so.

If on the other hand – as I have argued from many different angles previously – this common cause is in unavoidable disintegration, then the terms have to be changed. If the terrain is shrinking and increasingly treacherous, a new one will have to be found. In Scotland this can only take the form of a written constitution: the statute of a Scotland returned, and compelled almost from its first breath to found a legitimate basis for its existence. Legitimacy is no longer bestowed by an increasingly *de facto* Kingdom, or by the pre-democratic Treaty furtively resurrected within the *Scotland Act* (1998). As the subjective spirit of the new parliament acknowledges in its own way, these are offences against both democratic sensibility and the prevailing temper of a European polity in formation.

The spirit of the latter was very well expressed by Vaclav Havel in a recent declaration: 'Union Must Turn to the Written Word'. He points out that the construction of Europe began during the Cold War, but now proceeds in an utterly different environment. It started life as an economic recovery project, overshadowed by NATO and the threat of annihilation. It has ended as a project of democratic confederation where equally different priorities should apply. Openness is crucial to this:

> Openness needs to be enshrined in a way that mobilises public allegiance, otherwise the Union will be perceived as merely a complicated administrative enterprise, a task which only a special caste of Euro-specialists understands . . . So if the Union wants to get closer to citizens it must write the Union's principal law. A comprehensible constitution with a cogent preamble describing the EU's purpose and core ideas, and which defines its basic institutions, their areas of competence and mutual relations, is essential to stimulating broad public support.

He goes on to propose (in effect) a school-level cult of
European constitutionalism, and a revised two-chamber parliamentary structure along broadly American lines. But the detail
of this counts for less than the spirit behind it, which is here
clearly that of an aspiring candidate-nation:

> New candidates, of course, must meet common standards. If
> they comply, however, nothing must postpone accession . . .
> I am convinced that what I have recommended here opens
> more space for executing the will of individual nations and
> an enhanced assertion of their identity.[3]

These views seem to me to express almost exactly the spirit
in which any 'new candidate' country should approach the
framing of a constitution in today's Europe. Under Blair, Great
Britain seems to want into Europe rather than completely out
of it (if not too inconvenient, disadvantageous to the Pound
Sterling, etc.). But this wish remains simultaneously preserva-
tive, rather than innovatory. 'Europe' is simply one choice
amongst others for the already existing Anglo-British identity to
continue. It is emphatically not what Havel envisages for the
Czech Republic – an *enhancement* of will, real freedom and the
manifestation of identity.

But the reconstitution of a Scottish state-nation demands
just this enhancement – even more forcefully than the Czechs
are likely to. It signifies all that he refers to, *plus* a guarantee of
escape from the overweening former influence of England.
The meaning of 'escape' should not be misinterpreted: in
effect, it denotes not flight, resentment or hatred but *equality*.
The entire saga of the late Union and its recent unfolding
shows how difficult it was to attain the latter (some would
argue, impossible). On the other hand, in a wider European-
Union framework, and alongside a spectrum of comparable

polities, it would surely be *comparatively* easy to reach. The broader circumstances of a continental confederative structure might favour what the native ethnic imbalance of the archipelago has made so persistently difficult.

Building on Tradition

So, the first reason for determined constitutionalism in Scotland is Europe. The second is simply that a powerful *tradition* of constitutional claim and definition already exists there. It has been 'civic' demands and action which have brought about the return of the Scottish Parliament – not ethnic assertiveness associated with violence, exclusion or discrimination. But 'civic' here really means 'constitutional'. What has always been at stake is a protest for democracy, understood as a democratic and juridical *system* corresponding to the institutions and culture of a distinct society.

It is often said or believed (particularly in London) that Blair's party and government 'gave' Scotland its Parliament. But everyone who lived through the actual process of 1988–98 knows this to be a travesty. One need only look through some of the documents mentioned earlier in this book to understand why. By and large, the Scots have given themselves back the power to rule themselves – even although, after 1 May 1997, the prolonged campaign for a Scottish Parliament was indeed enabled by a fortunate capsizing of British central authority.

The *conclusion* of what is already a tradition, however – supported in the later 1980s and the '90s by most political parties, and indeed by most organized civil opinion in Scotland – can only be a new national constitution. The framing of such an instrument will be inevitable anyway, in the longer run. It is important to keep in mind here that a constitution is not just a set of principles, or a document. The argument is that Scotland has already half-joined the ranks of 'constitutional countries' in which such statutes of self-rule are accorded a special veneration and centrality: France, the United States, the German Federal Republic, Australia, Switzerland (and others). In such nations, the constitution is not a remote, dry-as-dust set of regulations, but a part – and often a crucial part – of popular identity. Civic nationalism has been the nerve of Scotland's political revival; and that style of affirmation is its only logical conclusion.

At this point, it must be said, genuine innovation contrasts with the phoney Great-British revivalism practised by Blair. The latter has ended by colluding with the relative constitutional backwardness and isolationism of 'Middle England' – an option fortunately no longer available in Scotland, Wales or Ireland. Worse, it has fallen into this trap just as English identity shows signs of wakening up, and demanding some kind of new life. The year before the reconvening of the Scottish Parliament saw the publication of no less than four significant contributions to a rapidly broadening argument about England's own future: Jeremy Paxman's *The English*, Simon Heffer's *Nor Shall My Sword: the Reinvention of England*, Kevin Davey's *English Imaginaries* and (on a deeper historical level) Adrian Hastings's *The Construction of Nationhood: Ethnicity, Religion and Nationalism* (mainly devoted to English problems).

Were such changes of attitude confined to the ideological and journalistic plane the change would still be striking. But of course they are not. Over the same short period William Hague has been scrambling to reinvent English Conservatism as a viable party, and even New Labour has had to respond to a climatic shift much greater than the one foreseen in Jack Straw's timid regionalist proposals, *Alternatives for England* (1997). By January 1999 we find Blair announcing a revived 'Committee on the Regions' for English MPs. Actually 'reanimated' would be more accurate: a genetic ancestor of the Committee did meet in 1978, only to be totally forgotten in the intervening years. But never mind: everything in England must have a precedent, and it was immediately and loudly declared that the Government 'had no intention of allowing the committee to become an English Parliament' (Margaret Beckett, as reported in *The Scotsman*, 15 January).

Thus formally debarred from all slippery slopes, the Committee of Regions – which should eventually include most members of the House of Commons – came blinking into the light just six weeks after publication of the Scottish Affairs Select Committee *Report*. This had attacked the Government for being hopelessly piecemeal about reforming the Constitution, and underlined how little provision it was making for English interests. Mrs Beckett put her project before the plaintively-titled 'Modernization Committee' of the Commons . . . which *may well meet* (I quote the same newspaper coverage) 'before the summer'. Who but an idiot would conclude that this Committee was *not* a prelude to some kind of 'English Parliament', and certain to accelerate its growth-rate as (in the same summer) the new Parliaments on the periphery come into being, begin to assert their identities, to argue with London and New Labour, and to set up for business in Europe?

All slopes are now slippery, in fact. The Constitution of old England-Britain once stood like a mighty dam, preserving its subjects from such a fate; nowadays, leaking on all sides, it merely guides them to the appropriate slope or exit. Blairism has reformed just enough to destabilize everything, and to make a reconsolidation of the once-sacred earth of British Sovereignty impossible. As if panicked by this real-ization, his government has then begun to run round in circles groaning that enough is enough, and that well must now be left alone: that which is not broken (e.g., dear old first-past-the-post) need no more be officiously fixed. The trouble is that *everything is now broken* – at least in the sense of being questioned, uncertain, a bit ridiculous, lacking in conviction, up for grabs, floundering, demoralized and worried about the future.

In other words, the mystique has drained out of all Ukanian 'tradition' as it previously did from the Monarchy. But in Scotland there is a new tradition – the one forged by the thirty years of Home Rule and nationalist agitation and organization which have produced the recall of the Scottish Parliament. Because Great Britain has decided against giving itself a new written constitution, it would be absurd for the Scots to do so. They are already more than half way there. The nucleus of a new constitutional order was set up with the 1988 *Claim of Right*, and the subsequent Scottish Constitutional Convention. A comprehensive overview of the development of constitutional thinking in Scotland is given in Lindsay Paterson's *A Diverse Assembly: the Debate on a Scottish Parliament* (1998), notably its concluding section, 'Towards the Parliament, 1992–1997'. The earlier high-point was probably Bernard Crick and David Millar's *To Make the Parliament of Scotland a Model for Democracy* (1995), but the debate was also to conclude on a similar level, in the remarkable document that appeared after Paterson's anthology was published: *Shaping Scotland's Parliament* (December 1998). This was the 'Report of the Consultative Steering Group on the Scottish Parliament' – often referred to, inaccurately yet much more truly, as the 'Constitutional steering group'.

It is this 'tradition of the new' which made self-government possible, and which (logically) ought to continue guiding the strategic development of Scottish parliamentarism. But it will also be required simply in order to obtain the sort of stability any new democratic system needs. Part of the work of the Scottish Parliament will have to be 'constitutive' in this sense. A constitutive assembly is one which decides upon its own constitution, principles and modes of operation. Inevitably, much of what is attempted will be making up for the deficiencies of United Kingdom centralism. The newly written will have to supplement the anciently unwritten – conventional, ritual-blessed, 'changeless' and utterly shifty.

Until (naturally) the forthcoming Parliament of England comes to itself, and decides to be born (after all the Blairite confusion). Then suddenly an *English* tradition of the new will be required. It will be the only way of sorting out the 'anarchy' created by irresponsible minority demands. At that point it will be indispensable to redefine Britain – more or less what ought to have been tackled at the outset, pre-Devolution. But at that time the ruling class (both ancient and pot-noodle) had still been unable to shake off the delusions of Sovereignty and having the Finest Constitution in the World. After the Devolutionary deluge it will all look different.

Disputes and Constitutions

After Europe and an already functioning 'tradition of the new', the Scots have a third reason for Scottish constitutionalism. This was mentioned earlier too. It lies in the likelihood (really the certainty) of incessant conflicts of interest between Holyrood and Westminster. That is indeed the question which has won most attention in the pre-Parliament period. It has been the thing which worried the settling-down and no-rocking-of-the-boat faction most, for obvious reasons. Without a new United Kingdom blueprint, including some judicial machinery for regulating disputes, how could the two Parliaments resolve differences of policy?

The British Constitution was supposed to accomplish this by sapient deployment of common sense and reasonableness. Her Majesty's Constitution: the trouble with this dashing fellow is that, although quite impressive in emergencies or crises (when action is called for without too much reflection) he has become difficult to pin down in all other directions. In fact since Blair arrived he never seems to stay in the same place for more than a second. The friend to whom this book is dedicated recently suggested founding a new Society, the 'SDPUCBC' or Society for the Detection and Prevention of Unadvertised Changes to the British Constitution. These have grown so numerous, and are now so feebly signalled, that actually nobody knows where they are. The subject-body might for example (he has pointed out) just switch on the News at Nine or Eleven some evening, and discover that an English Parliament had rematerialized (formally or informally) earlier the same day. One can be pretty sure that on the same occasion it will be declared (but more or less *en passant*) that the British Constitution, Monarchy, Lords (or neo-Lords) are all to continue as before.

The Constitution which North Britain has been ordained to live with by the *Scotland Act* contains references to a defiantly obscure body known as 'The Judicial Committee of the Privy Council'. This is the entity designated to consider and regulate differences of opinion between the Scottish and British Parliaments. To describe it as 'little-known' would be a huge understatement. On first discovery, some commentators surmised it to be a Tudor body; but in fact it turns out to be *echt* first-generation Norman, and hard at it since the Conquest. We owe this knowledge to an intrepid journalist from the *Financial Times*, Nicholas Timmins, who in April 1999 set out in a fit of exasperation to track the thing down.

He eventually found what he calls 'one of the capital's best-kept secrets' behind a door near the Horse Guards end of Downing Street, in 'a 30-foot tall oak-panelled room with gold-leaf centre rose' in Gothic Revivalist style. There, judges 'unwigged and in lounge suits, write precise fountain-pen notes on the submission of bewigged Barristers', and eventually deliver verdicts on a mind-numbing range of subjects: appeals against the death penalty in Trinidad, for example, land disputes in the Turks and Caicos Islands, insurance claims from Pitcairn or Dunedin, and protests from doctors struck off the General Medical Council. This Committee was once 'the final court of appeal for one quarter of the globe'. Today the only general heading its cases could possibly be ranged under is 'relics of empire'.

There are 109 people on it, including nine from Scotland and *fourteen* from New Zealand. This is because the New Zealand government and others have opted to retain it as an ultimate court of appeal. No doubt similar expeditions to New Zealand and the Turks and Caicos Islands would be needed to determine why. However, we do know that the Scottish Parliament has not so opted. But it is to have it none the less. Timmins reports SNP Leader Alex Salmond as saying that no Scottish Executive would stand for this as a substitute for a constitutional tribunal, and that 'We will simply have to find a better mechanism'.

But whether or not Mr Salmond has understood the implication, the only 'mechanism' capable of undertaking such tasks is (of course) a constitution. 'We' (the Scottish Parliament) cannot create such a mechanism on behalf of Westminster. All it will be able to do is suggest one better than what has been offered by the Finest Constitution in the World, and hope that eventually the House of Commons will agree. In other words, hope for a sort of negotiation – as between two Parliaments equal in status – which is inevitable anyway. But if that is the case, then the Treaty of Union stands very effectively undone. Would it not be simpler to recognize the fact, rather than clinging on to it as the Devolution legislation has done? This is one of the more important dead monkeys still hanging around. Perhaps prising it loose might encourage many others.

Constitutions and Independence

The argument implies that the newly created Parliament of Scotland is (in spite of Government assurances) incomplete – and not just in the trite sense of having many things to do. It is essentially or structurally incomplete. In the normal processes of setting up a regional or sub-state government a *constitution* is the foundation. The written central statutes of post-Independence India, Canada, the *Bundesrepublik* or post-Franco Spain provided an armature for such governments to work with and by. Their own sub-constitutions were written into the action from the outset. They may of course have been defective, and no human guarantee will ever fix polities into eternal life. But at least they were all launched from an intelligible blueprint, which any literate citizen in them could consult in his or her public library.

In the UK there are plenty of public libraries, but nothing of this kind to consult in them. Since there is no 'written constitution' there is no reliable 'Constitution for Dummies' either. The study of British Constitutionalism demands the acquisition of what one has to call a 'lore', and access to several imposing shelf-loads of related astrological material. Some of it was composed by lunatics. But since they were lawyers nobody paid much attention to this. Elite informality is tolerant of eccentricity, preferring it to vulgar divulgation and plain speaking. Once things get written down, any self-taught pundit or rabble-rouser can have his say. Emphatically, Devolution was *not* conceived in order to encourage these street-corner cranks. Its aim was like that of local government reform: rejuvenation through good sense and reasonableness, and the more effective dissemination of centrally-cooked wisdom.

'Settling down' is the disablement of democracy. The enablement of a national democracy, on the other hand, requires a constitution. It needs a distinct statute related to history and national identity, and (nowadays) it needs to be approved by the citizen body. In fact people become 'citizens' via such approval. Reconvening a parliament was one thing, but there was no constitution to re-enact along with it: that has to be created. The circumstances of constant disagreement and variance are likely to provoke moves in this direction anyway. Would it not be preferable to address the question directly, as a key part of the Scottish Parliament's new business?

Naturally, it will immediately be said that those supporting the constitutional process are nationalists (overt or closet). 'Wrecking' or withdrawing from the British Constitution, challenging its omnicompetence and Sovereignty, would surely lead to independence pure and simple? Those who want to make informal Devolution work, in the Conservative and Labour Parties, and those who want to formalize dependence in some kind of federal or confederal formula (the Liberal Democrats) are certain to view such constitutionalism as either unnecessary or precipitate. At the moment they all believe in time – time for settling-down, or time for Great Britain to take farther the grander process of constitutional reform, and enter a European Union in which all sorts of non-sovereign governments seem to flourish.

'Separatism under another name'? But the time is now long past when the United Kingdom state stood for a self-explanatory power and glory. The British Constitution has deteriorated into a shifting pattern of stratagems and *ad hoc* arrangements, where it is becoming harder and harder to find fixed points of reference. All that was fixed has already melted into air – or is on the way to doing so: Monarchy, Lords, the venerable pattern of the House of Commons, trust in the Law and the Pound Sterling, *The Times*, and the regulatory ethos of a rooted class. One of the strange by-products of the Belfast Agreement was the idea of a *Doppelgänger* for the whole archipelago, to be named 'The British-Irish Council' (in honour of the two accredited states it contains) or else 'The Council of the Isles' (in recognition of broader aims and greater future diversity).

Thus Lord Dacre's pessimistic forecast of nearly twenty years ago – cited at the beginning of this book – has now itself been left far behind. 'The people of these islands have seldom been united, politically or culturally', he noted, and from 1922 onwards 'the process has been reversed'. Slowly, in fits and starts, with long periods of apparent consolidation (or even reversal), the multinational unitarism of the former Kingdom has foundered – to the point where a single Leader and his cohort-Party strain to keep most of it in one piece. European Union on one side and a spectral Islands Council on the other are bidding for different parts of what was once its indivisible burden and identity.

Epilogue:
The Last Day

The Little White Rose

The rose of all the world is not for me.
I want for my part
Only the little white rose of Scotland
That smells sharp and sweet – and breaks the heart.

Hugh MacDiarmid, *Stony Limits and Other Poems* (1934)

On the last day it rained. I wakened at 5 am, with the Lothian sky drumming windlessly down upon our roof in Livingston. In a midwinter gloom, the lawn was a chain of huge puddles. The birds that usually wake people up on May mornings were inaudible, sheltering in the evergreens or under the garden furniture.

'My God, and this is the day they're voting', groaned M., pulling the quilt back over her head. 'Trust this country . . . !' (she comes from a different one).

'Well, maybe it'll clear up later', I replied helplessly; 'It cannae go on like that all day.' Foreboding has been the everyday horizon for too long among the Scots, never more so than when cheerily contradicted. Yet if you just say nothing, that too feels like giving in. Somehow you always felt you just couldn't win. Not on your own, anyway.

Downstairs making coffee, I could hear that the front guttering had once more given way under the strain. There was the familiar sound of a Highland torrent sluicing down the doorstep. As I was wrestling with the toaster the phone rang, far too early.

'Jean's very poorly' said her relative from Fife, '. . . gone down a lot. I just thought you ought to know.' I thanked her, already inwardly rescrambling my plans for the day. The tone was unmistakable. On this day, the first in history that the people of Scotland were to vote for their own Parliament, Miss Jean Robertson of St Monans was dying about forty miles away, in a hospital at St Andrews. We had been to see her a week before. She was then ailing noticeably, but still in command of hospital staff and visitors alike, and talking loudly of her plans for going home. Now there would be one more chance to see her, and I had to go on my own.

On the ridge road above Ecclesmachan there is normally a commanding vista over the Forth, from The Binns right down to the bridges at Queensferry. But on that day the [West Lothian] view was non-existent. Round the sharp bends over the Union Canal, the recently-installed traffic lights winked feebly through a tenebrous mirk, and beyond them the rush-hour traffic towards Silicon Glen revved impatiently, tailing helplessly back towards Newton and Edinburgh. I stopped in Newton Main Street and dodged across to the shop for the newspapers.

Just after the village there is another famous bridge view-point, which is also a quiet place to scan headlines and editorials. On 6 May these were largely historic-day material. Britain's Balkan war was for once off the front pages. The tabloids hyperventilated for Labour ('A Double Dewar's!', etc.) with *The Herald* moving in the other direction. It was giving readers a last dose of the grand impartiality between Labour and Nationalism which had recently overtaken it.

But a weird spasm had overcome *The Scotsman*. Its personality had long been split in two, between the granitic Unionism
of its proprietors and Editor-in-Chief, and the nationalism of so
many contributors and columnists. Unable to recommend that
readers vote both ways at once, the agèd *torchon de cul* had
opted for principled retreat to the womb. It reproduced its
founding editorial pronouncement *of 1816*, the year after
Waterloo. This turned out to be terribly and self-consciously
British, and all for the safely New. Hence Britishness – and
possibly the whole of history – is culminating in Blair. Now was
the day and hour, and the drumroll of antique Whiggery was
meant to arrest separatist misconduct among Edinburghese
voters.

Feeling helpless again, I looked up into the mist. It would
not have been too surprising to see James Hogg's Reverend
Wringhim writhing about out there, and groaning of the day's
awful portents. In fact justified sinners of a sort had been at
work since the previous week, when we took the same route to
St Andrews. Two bays along now stood a burned-out Escort
XR3 on its hubs, surrounded by broken glass and beer-cans.
The bridges remained invisible, with the rain hitting harder
than ever.

Over the bridge into Fife the fog thinned slightly, and traffic
speeded up on to the new dual carriageway to Kirkcaldy. But at
Markinch it closed in again like a wall. In the villages of the
Howe I crawled past two little schools turned into polling sta-
tions, with the regulation poster display (one per party) and
policeman in attendance. There were few voters about. It made
me think of twelve years previously, when I had broken election law by pinning up 'Vote for a Tory-Free Scotland!' posters
on the corner opposite Jean Robertson's house. 'Eh son, the
bobby was right on yer heels . . . He had them doon again as

soon as ye were back in the hoose,' she told me with some pleasure. 'Ye'll never change things that way, son!' (she and her sister called most people either 'son' or 'ma lass').

It was about eleven when I got into St Andrews from the Old Course side. 'She's sometimes conscious,' the Ward Sister warned me, '. . . but don't expect too much.' It was a shock: the silver-white rose had been stripped bare in one week, tumour and kidney-failure leaving only a shred. Nobody else was there, for which I felt grateful. I leaned down close to the parchment face, the eyes flickered open and she moaned faintly. I remembered smooth-pink cheeks and brightly mocking grey eyes. You can never say what you mean at such times, or be sure it's heard; yet nothing matters more.

Jean had indeed served the Lord in one of His most formidable metaphysical statements, the Auld Kirk of St Monans. Both its brooding spirit and its rising damp had benefited greatly from her decades of bring-&-buy sales. When I moved to the village she knew very quickly that I was disaffected from the faith, as from other ancestral causes like the Scottish Conservative & Unionist Party. There was no escape from her kind irony on such matters. More important by an unmeasurable distance was the great, repressed sweetness of her nature. The rauch tongue hid, yet also nourished, an underlying warmth and expansiveness. This music of the soul was linked to imperious impatience. Jean wanted things done each day, and usually got her way: it was like having a small, bullying angel on one's side.

But on my side she remained over years of setback and failure, and in the end of shipwreck. In those days St Monans was still 'Holy City', famed for its proliferation of sects. The Open Brethren bellowed tunelessly next door to her, and the Closed Brethren (who feared all music) held their blunt conversations with God at the other end of our street. I once observed to her how odd it was that the same meek flocks invariably voted in a very different sort of fundamentalist as their Provost: an anarchic Nationalist who boasted of breaking every rule going, and getting away with it. Jean disapproved of him terribly. 'That rogue's back again!' she would say, 'Thae folk dinnae ken *whit* they want!' There was no way of knowing whether she secretly voted for him too. He too has now died; but only after being re-elected for a last time, on this same day.

Were they awake at prayer and dreaming at the polling station? Or was it the other way round? I leaned still closer to her and tried to talk about the days of light she had helped us to know, just by being there. There were others who had loved her, unable to be there or say anything. I felt them beside us too. Something rises out of the deepest well of the past at such times. It feels like an impossibly astringent cry of gratitude, for which at last platitudes just have to stand in. Jean's family had come from Glasgow a generation previously, and taken over the general shop near the school. They were 'the Dearies' to the whole village: they used this term for all their customers, and everyone ended up owing them something. However, the joint burden of care for ageing parents and an all-hours shop also prevented Jean and her sister Margaret from marrying. Many had tried to pick the white rose (or so it was said) but the only one she fancied had been carried off by the war. Instead the girls came to form a close sisterly bond. As well as being like catalysts of the local community, they for long sought to steer it along the holy ways of Margaret Thatcher, and away from the Provost's influence. The former's fall in 1990 was a terminal shock; I never heard them say much about John Major or the Party afterwards.

Jean had lapsed into deep sleep again. The Sister explained the coma would soon become terminal; they had given up fighting it. From the hospital window there seemed to be white rents in the clouds to the east, with seagulls wheeling in and out of the haar. Around midday I left her with a sense of fatality, to take the slow coastal road back round Fife towards the bridges.

> You will go into the heaven
> Of unforgotten things . . .
> *Hello, my love. See?*
> *This thorn has cut my lips.*

Past Kilrenny, I turned almost without thinking leftwards down what we used to call 'the windmill road' towards Cellardyke, as if clinging instinctively to the edge of the sea. The long, narrow main street of Cellardyke has houses practically on the stony beach, and it was in one of them that we lived briefly in 1940. My father had been promoted to a job in West Fife but the house there was not ready for occupation, so we had to rent another temporarily. It belonged to Provost Carstairs, who also owned the smelly little oilskin factory up on Cellardyke braes. Coming abreast of the house, I pulled up for a moment. With an inexplicable shock of memory, it came back: right there in the street-side kitchen of this brown-harled house with three steps in front, we all sat around the walnut-panelled radio-set and listened to Winston Churchill. Fifty-nine years ago. The house had gas-mantle lighting, with the warm yellow glare my mother always preferred to electricity. I thought the place was heaven, it had a backyard with a gate straight out on to the beach. At night the North Sea roared one to sleep.

In those days the wireless was life itself, everyone listened to the news over and over again for fear of missing something, and never forgot the Prime Minister. He said: 'Our British life and the long continuity of our institutions and our empire' were at stake in the battle now upon us; if it all lasted for a thousand years, men would still be saying '*This* was their finest hour'. One lifetime later something of that hour remains, he was not wrong; but almost everything else has gone. As I realized when I looked up the speech later in the library, everything except the 'union of common citizenship with France' (which he had extolled at the same time). For both Scots and English this still remains some years off, but it will happen. At the time and for long afterwards it was regarded as the great man's identity-whimsy, an impulsive aberration to be overlooked.

Of course, what I could actually recall were very small things: the look of the radio, the warm smell of gas, my mother's tears at abandoning the seacoast for somewhere far inland – and above all, the excitement of being so close to a favourite fishing pool among the rocks. The long continuity of our institutions meant extremely little then. And yet, this does not imply it was all really 'over our heads'; on the contrary, I see now *that* was how it got into our blood, without missing a single beat over the generation which ensued. The minnows which any individual can recall are like pilot fish, beneath them swim far greater ones, at different and unsounded depths. Often these are sustaining and deadly together; and difficult to get rid of.

In his 'First Elegy' Hamish Henderson writes nobly of the German dead after a battle in Cirenaica. What had really mattered to them too was not race, Leader and realm indivisible but –

The lost world in the memory of letters,
an evening at the pictures in the friendly dark,
two knowing conspirators smiling and whispering secrets . . .
someone whose photo was in their wallets.

But such great humanity can be mistaken too: for the gods

and heroes were not really absent from that friendly dark, or
from the smell of gas and oilskins in Cellardyke. No, it was the
companionship of little things which helped bear those intan-
gible shades forward, and transmute them into identity. Thanks
to such banal alchemy, in time 'the vague imperial heritage'
would seem as precious as the sea's roar or the recollection of a
smile. 'No such thing as society'? I suppose the phrase's
wretchedness came home so sharply then because I had just
seen 'death making his incision', into more than an individual
soul.

Farther along, the narrow streets broaden out into the har-
bour front of Anstruther, which I remembered as a primeval,
ever-shifting landscape of herring-boxes piled up to twenty or
thirty feet high. We played war games among them, covered
with fish-scales and salt, making fortresses, machine-gun
redoubts and hidden caves, constantly chased off by the porters
and fishermen trying to get them ready for the next tide.

After 1945 the herring vanished, and took most of that old
East Neuk world with them. Today a neat car park takes up
most of the front, there is a Fisheries Museum and a wonderful
fish restaurant. I felt suddenly grateful for change, and also
impatient: the nostalgia-arithmetic of gains-and-losses had
become pointless, it was time to move on. Time to get back
and vote.

There has to be an end to elegies for the dead. The world of
the little white rose and all its accompanying heartbreak is gone
for good. Yet in 1999 a war was still going on. Even during
Scotland's moment of returning identity, her most important
since the Middle Ages, the new day had come like the angel of
dusk, overcast and bloodstained. A Southern war leader could
still count on that deeper-swimming inheritance, and by evoking it drive the emerging concerns of Scotland off the air and

the front pages. This was for a different style of empire, agreed; yet one still imbued in popular instinct with all those Churchillian institutions, with the profile of greatness and an engrained longing for another fine hour upon the world stage. Part of us knows we need to be free from all that. However, there is another part which clings to it with a narcotic love: 'Deprived of our Parliamentary links with London, our traditional association with the British Army, the British Navy and Air Force, we would be a laughing stock, an uppity little hive of blethering broadcasters . . . It simply doesn't bear thinking about' (*Scotland on Sunday*, Neil Drysdale,18 April).

I left the coast after Leven and struck across inland, on a more direct route to the bridge. It goes by Raith, Puddledub and Auchtertool, where my mother used to be taken on summer holidays from Kirkcaldy. The country there has a briefly wilder, uncultivable aspect, the favoured terrain of Scottish identity since romanticism. It was in scenes like those that the exiled State took to being a traveller, a nobly self-destructive savage, a denizen of some nether world. He can be found (recently) in urban sub-class squalor, but was most often placed in a Highland fastness . . . 'wild country where he's safe', like Douglas Dunn's Gaberlunzie man ('18th–20th century, Origin obscure', *Scots National Dictionary*) –

> Among bracken, in his hideouts of fern –
> Gaberlunzie, half-life, national waif,
> Earth-pirate of the thistle and the thorn.

I found myself driving too fast along the winding up-and-down hill road, in sheer haste to get away him. We've had more than enough of all that. There should an allotted space for it in the new Museum of Scotland, preferably ill-lit and difficult to get to. Perhaps it might be juxtaposed to a brashly illuminated section on 'Traditional Associations with the British Army'. Both half-lives could then continue supporting one another in retiral.

Returning over the road bridge in the lightening rain I noticed the Millenium Clock properly for the first time. It was set up on the old rail bridge to signal the days and hours remaining before 2000. On 6 May, there were only two hundred and thirty-nine to go. Not long enough for a new beginning. Turning right towards Newton and Uphall I saw that the wreck had now been towed away from the lay-by.

A vague imperial heritage may stand still, and occasionally proclaim a new age in order to stick in its chosen place. But ex-dependencies have to be more decisive. They have to learn what they are by self-definition bad at: responsibility. And unlike the interminable Empires they come out of, they do not have an age to do this in. If they fail to free themselves, then some fatality like Blair's war, some bit of traditional wreckage or set of blindly sentimental habits will always be dragging them backwards. Failures of state are already being supplemented by a nostalgia-industry, suppurating with dear old links and customs in common.

It's good not to be obsessed by 'vileinye of hatred' against England. But the way to use such fortune is not by being terribly good in England's sense. It should lead to a more intransigent assertion of rights, through different politics and principles. A civic nationalism needs to be constitutional; but for that very reason it can never be placatory or submissive. Meekness and docility will never avert the perils of ethnicity. Civic and juridical warfare is much more likely to – founded as these are upon a profounder demand for equality of status, and recognition.

The phrase 'villainy of hatred' was also used in Henderson's *Elegies for the Dead*, as 'the great word of Glencoe's son', Alasdair

MacIain. In 1745 the latter urged his men to forswear all such hatred against former enemies, at Newliston House, two miles south of my road home to Livingston. Crossing Ecclesmachan ridge southwards one leaves Tam Dalyell's Binns on the right and looks down to Newliston (near Kirkliston) on the left. M. passes its lodge gates every day on her way to work (with Marshall's Chunky Chicken factory across the road). It was formerly the home of the Dalrymples of Stair, a great legal dynasty responsible for *The Institutions of the Laws of Scotland*, one of whom had ordered the massacre of 1692. MacIain urged his Glencoe men to look after it rather than loot it, in the name of a more civilized and reconciled Scotland. After Culloden MacIain paid for his vision with many years in prison, but John Buchan surely gave the right verdict on this (the same as Henderson's): 'The last word – and a great word – was with Glencoe', in an expression of native and unimposed generosity.

At the Polling Station in Livingston the rain had stopped. The numbers built up, and there were knots of people making sure they knew what to do with the coloured voting papers under the new system. As we came out and walked quietly down the road I felt I had been on it for a very long time. It had mostly been quiet, like this. As Neal Ascherson had written of another threshold, eighteen months before, 'Quietly, without trumpets, Referendum Day began'; and now here we were, returned from the hill and into the house at last— no longer gaberlunzies, the unclassifiable waifs of a half-forgotten realm.

The trumpets lie ahead, when much of the present heritage has been demolished, and made over into a building-site. Scotland's way has been too quiet, for far too long. But no one will stop walking down that road, just because we have a government of sorts. In fact they ought to march, or even run, towards the sound of clangour and the promise of dissidence At the time no one had yet heard James Macmillan's great fanfare for a small orchestra, which was to usher in the Parliament on 1 July. On 6 May there was only a longing for something like it. Just beyond this sound-horizon lies the folklore which counts most, the unimaginable music of the future. We have not come this far, through so much defeat and disappointment, in order to curl up inside an uppity hive of blethering British whingers, curmudgeonly husks who can go on surviving in defeat only because the English have not spoken yet.

I wish *they* would get on with it too. Like the Scots, they no longer have all the time in the world. Europe will not wait for either of us.

Appendix:
'De Facto Independence'

[Evidence given to the House of Commons Select Committee on Scottish Affairs (24 June 1998)]

Comparing Like with Unlike

Comparisons are an essential tool of social thinking. The conditions we actually live in are so complex, so many apparently contradictory things happen every day, that I doubt if one can have much grasp of any society without comparing it to somewhere else, at least implicitly. However, the very importance of this factor means one has also to be careful with it. Comparison with mistaken or inappropriate models can lead to wrong conclusions, and (where policy is involved) to mistaken strategies.

I make these academic points with some feeling, in the case of Scotland. Here a positive mania has grown up for what I suspect are really miscomparisons. Few political speeches are now pronounced which do not refer to the budding European Union, Spain and Germany as sound indicators of the way things might (or more often, should) go under the Scottish Parliament next year. Catalonia is easily the prizewinner in this *concours d'élégance*. In fact President Pujol came to Scotland to rub the point in, and shortly thereafter Donald Dewar went out to Barcelona to confirm it. The official message is that there is no reason why the Scots should not follow the Catalan example, as a non-state autonomous region. But avoidance of trouble and strife always appears to be the true point at issue. Nations without political nationalism and independent statehood are good; those with them are bad, or at any rate represent a risk best avoided. Sound examples of risk-avoidance are German federalism, Spanish nationality policy and Belgian consociationalism. Grand Euro-blueprints for Regionalism are also frequently invoked in the same cause.

Unfortunately, such examples are partial and dubious. I doubt very much if any conclusion can be drawn from them regarding current developments in the United Kingdom – including the kind of autonomy envisaged for the new Scottish Parliament. What the comparisons omit is something fundamental: the sheer oddity and anachronism of the United Kingdom state, which actually make it quite hard to set convincingly alongside anything else in present-day Europe, at other than a superficial level.

Some may feel that the advent of Blair has altered this, because he says almost every day that all is or will be made radically new: the past is now behind us, trust New Labour to keep it there, and so on. Long may it be so! But then again – *would that it were so!* The wish must be pretty widespread and powerful, or else Blair wouldn't be where he is, and such speeches would not achieve the effects they obviously do. However, wishing does not make things so. Nowhere is this clearer than in matters relating to Scotland's resumption of self-government.

Earlier sessions of the Scottish Affairs Committee have heard from authorities like Paul Heywood, Charles Jeffrey and Uwe Leonardy about the regional and national arrangements of the new German and Spanish states. Perhaps I might overview these in terms of a metaphor. All post-war nation-states and state-nations have had to adapt themselves to certain common tidal movements. I mean influences like the Cold War, then the post-Cold War thaw, 'globalization', deregulation, democratization and (in Western Europe) the institutional development of European Union. Some new states which have recreated or reformed themselves over this period have set up formidable hydraulic works to try and control or influence such movements, like the new constitutions of Germany, Republican Italy, post-Franco Spain, the French Fifth Republic and Belgium. The most impressive of such works are the Spanish and German ones, and naturally it tends to be they which are referred to in arguments over the belated and piecemeal changes now under way in the United Kingdom.

A Moribund Constitution

> Britain is a term which has a very uncertain future. The Scots, who in the sixteenth century were quite largely responsible for promoting the concept of 'Great Britain', and who were later instrumental in translating it into the lexicon of monarchical and state polity, are now only too anxious to escape it . . . As a source of symbolic capital, Britain's credit- seems to be exhausted.
>
> Raphael Samuel, 'Unravelling Britain', in *Island Stories* (1998), p. 41.

I will not try to repeat any of the institutional points made earlier. But it may be worth stressing another aspect of the comparison which has been less touched upon. This is what one could call the moral constitution. Constitutional arrangements are not just bits of institutional machinery, they are meant to secure the popularity, prestige and standing of the state responsible for them. Unless they 'work' in this moral or ideological sense they are not likely to be successful or last very long. Looked at in this perspective, how does the United Kingdom compare?

Uniquely badly, I would suggest. The British Constitution is not just unusually old and largely unaltered in the face of the big tidal movements of post-1950 – it is also unusually dependent upon these same 'moral' factors. 'Good will' is notoriously more important for it than other systems. It used to function largely via the informal, consensual attitudes of a governing class or élite ('good sense', etc.) and the acquiescence of those governed. This was the soul of the Old Constitution, and since no new formal one seems likely to take its place, that soul or animating spirit had better be kept in working order too. Is it?

Take Spain as the point of contrast here. Over the period from the 1970s to the present, 'Spanish' has become a much more positive and acceptable identity-denomination. The post-1975 reforms the Committee have looked at were meant to produce this effect, and they have been successful. Spanish democracy has been established, and stably established in the sense that it has now survived both an attempted coup, the epidemic of sleaze which overtook the Gonzalez régime, and the recent change of government from Left to Right. The contrast with the *Hispanidad* of the 1960s could hardly be greater.

This is the same Spain which has become 'Independent-in-Europe' (a phrase which seems appropriate before this Committee). Catalans, Basques, Galicians, Andalusians and the other autonomous communities have both shared in and contributed to these movements. They wanted the reformed multinational state to be democratic, and politically part of Europe, as a guarantee of their own new status as well as of liberal norms. They have not been disappointed. In the same decades, Spain even managed to invent a new Monarchy for itself. Not only did the new order survive the Tejero *coup d'état*, the new monarchy helped it do so, and became genuinely popular as a consequence – even in Catalonia.

And in Great Britain? Virtually the diametric opposite: this is a contrast every bit as striking as any formal or institutional one. British democracy, by universal agreement, has sharply declined and lost prestige over the same twenty-year period. The constitutional inflexibility of the Thatcher-Major era was accompanied by a steeply accentuated centralization, relieved only by frantic attempts at the reform of local government ('local' here defined essentially as meaning whatever did not affect or concern the Constitution, national identity and Britishness). In retrospect Local Government Reform can be seen as a curious, somewhat crazy substitute for the serious and high-level constitutional change which Britain really needed. Its final flourish was the reappearance of the Middle Ages in the shape of the Poll Tax, and the profoundly undemocratic palace coup against Margaret Thatcher in 1990.

At the same time as 'Britishness' was suffering these body blows, the Union Monarchy was undergoing a startling transformation. The main symbolic instrument of Britishness sank into a kind of prolonged moral collapse – via sundry incidents I don't need to remind people of here – and this slide went on until the extraordinary phenomenon of Princess Diana's death and the popular reaction to it last year. Since then Tony Blair and his government have been trying to 'stabilize' the decline, and rehabilitate the institution as part of their 'Cool Britannia' and Millenial-Britain campaigns. Thus Public Relations has been called upon to redress the long balance of decline and (in the case of the Crown) its precipitous fall from popular grace.

The Spanish Union-state bore all the Spanish countries forward into Europe. By contrast, though Great Britain has not of course literally withdrawn from European Union, it did so to speak 'morally withdraw' for quite substantial periods of time. It is showing signs of doing so again today. It grudgingly went along with things like the Single European Act and then Maastricht, becoming Europe's perpetual foot-dragger and complainer, forever contrasting a supposed European corporatism with the more bracing world climate of free-trade globalization and entrepreneurial individualism. In this key European direction the prestige of 'Britishness' has never been lower. Indeed the fag-end of the Tory period of government lapsed into the general anti-European trance of 'Euro-scepticism'. At times this appeared to be anticipating an actual exit by plebiscite, and hence a new version of right-wing or isolationist British identity.

Shortly thereafter, the Empire which had formerly been a wider-world alternative to Europe was formally wound up in Hong Kong. The New Labour régime embarked upon another Public Relations campaign of attitude-change: their morally rejuvenated Youthful Britain is urged to be more willingly and joyously in Europe, and even in the new Common Currency (though not quite yet . . .). As I suggested before, it is possible to be happy about such a marked change of tone and attitude, while still doubting its efficacy. There is such a lot to be made up for.

Let me sum up in this way. On the institutional plane, what does the United Kingdom have to compare with the great Spanish and other hydraulic works – with regulatory mechanisms like the *Tribunal Constitucional* and other Supreme Courts designed to manage conflicts? On the basis of the previous evidence before this Committee, little more than a pile of sandbags. Without prematurely disparaging the proposed Judicial Committee of the Privy Council (*Scotland's Parliament*, 4.17) it cannot help looking like a strange island substitute for the written-constitutional dams and sluice-gates which the

United Kingdom has, once more, decided to dispense with. How that substitute functions is likely to depend (as ever) upon 'good will' – see the same White Paper document, clauses 4.14 to 4.16. That means it is bound to depend on keeping in good repair the same broader ideological consensus and morale – the historical 'British identity'.

But this is just what is in the deepest trouble. I suspect that trouble may be terminal. Even as a trademark 'British' seems to be on the skids. 'Britishness' has passed from being one of the soundest properties on the international ideas-mart (liberal, trustworthy, decent, first among equals, 'Mother-of' this-and-that, Progressive haven, etc.) to being a down-market leftover – not quite a slum, but heading in that direction. The Spain one should perhaps look to for a relevant comparison here is not that of the present, but rather the tumbledown post-imperial state of earlier in the century. Whereas intra-Spanish conflicts have so far taken place in a context of enhanced and growing Spanish identity – the worth of being 'Spanish' and its positive link to Europe – the intra-British conflicts in prospect here look like continuing in a context of growing doubt, scepticism, or worse.

It may be objected that the Spanish comparison is a bit one-sided. Perhaps, but even if one takes the others mentioned – Germany, Italy, France, Belgium – the contrast is still remarkable. Germany has already been considered by the Committee. The fates of *italianità* and Belgium's composite identity have certainly been less glorious than that of restored Spanishness. On the other hand, both these states have done something about it. They have tackled the question directly by bold attempts at constitutional remoulding, with determination and on an impressive scale. In Rome the Prodi government is at present devoting itself to writing a new and more federalized Republican constitution – something at least half-analogous to contemporary Spain. As for the Belgian communal constitution, it has been like a perpetual building-site for decades. No multi-national state since the later Hapsburg Empire (1890s–1914) has been so devoted to ingenious new devices for reconciling national interests (with lots of difficulty, but thus far without disaster). Even the Fifth Republic, in spite of its strongly centralizing, Jacobin tradition, has at least sought to cover its tracks by implementing formal decentralization – and combined it with an unremitting Europeanism.

Reverting to the metaphor of tidal movements – it may indeed be that the new gravitational pressures of the 1960s–1990s period have damaged or lessened all of these old identity-formations. Nation-states and State-nations alike are no longer what they were. Nor, on the other hand, have they ceased to be what they were. And it must at once be added that some have responded differently and better than others.

The one which has clearly suffered most is that which chose to change nothing at all: the UK. For eighteen years after 1979 the British state behaved like a stick-insect – not just immobile but deliberately and almost religiously so. It chose a path of vigorous but very narrow social and economic adaptation to a somewhat idealized free-trade and laissez-faire world, assuming that this had no relevance whatever to its historic constitutional arrangements. Thus the overarching state became divorced from its nation – or, in this case, from its four different nations.

The advancing 'divorce' of Scotland may then be seen as originating from such long-term conditions. The largest national minority in the archipelago happened to have a long and remembered history of separate statehood, its own self-managing civil institutions (carefully safeguarded in the Treaty of Union), discernibly different low and high cultures, a flourishing identity folklore (real and/or invented), a mainly uncontested frontier with the majority, and no lack of conceit about itself. Yet these conditions alone might not have provoked effective political separatism. The *sufficient* conditions for that came only with the decay and then the virtual psychological collapse of the wider identity-framework – a state structure to which, as Raphael Samuel notes in the essay quoted above, the Scots had very heavily contributed, and to which in a sense they felt themselves indebted.

But for precisely that reason they feel it falling apart, perhaps more clearly than England does. The 'divorce' is coming, and they are already preparing themselves. Like the Welsh, they always took 'Britain' much more seriously than the English. Indeed 'Britishness' to some extent protected them from 'Englishness', by offering a very crude balance-mechanism for the preservation of multiple identities. The decline of that old defence-mechanism has administered a profound seismic shock, and the shock simply has to be manifested in a recovered political voice. This is probably already happening, through the marked rise in support for the SNP in the Holyrood Parliament.

There is an interesting implication here. It is not devolution which is the famous 'slippery slope' – it is the defective constitutional support-structures of the United Kingdom identity and state themselves. It is (so to speak) that into which we are being devolved. These structures were not timeless wonders. They represented a quite specific and rather narrowly-based polity, which has been unable to rebuild itself in time for the challenges of the post-Cold War period. The task has been left too late, and then finally rushed into more on the level of rhetoric than of patient constitutional reality. There is still insufficient motivation and interest in the process among the British majority – that is, the 80% or so of the dominant *ethnos*, England. They are quite naturally liable to be puzzled by what is happening – having been encouraged to think that 'fairness'

and 'give-and-take' should always be the answer to difficulties
of that sort, rather than 'constitution-mongering' (as I think
Harold Macmillan once called it). Hence they are likely to
blame the Scots for 'the trouble', as in the past they usually
blamed the Irish.

Once these sufficient conditions are assembled, then everything can alter overnight. All the other circumstances
mentioned (autonomy, culture, differential identities, etc.)
assume new or renovated meaning. They quickly come to
appear as stand-alone signs of separateness, linked to gathering
confidence rather than becalmed within the ambiguity or
dependence of the older multinationality. One 'instinct' seems
to take over from another. But this shift does not come out of
party-political policies or ideology, or from a welling-up of popular sentiment or memory – from 'conversions' in the
conventional sense. It only seems to. The political nationalism
of the SNP was only one among the older spectrum of Scottish
identity-conditions, and never in itself came near producing
such an earth-movement. But on the other hand, once that
shift starts, it quickly benefits and can place itself in the (apparent) vanguard of a movement already under way. How rapidly
a sense of fatality is attached to a movement like this!

In 1997 the heirs to 'Thatcherism' suddenly launched a
reform programme. A Scottish Parliament, the Welsh Assembly
and the new devolved settlement in Northern Ireland followed
one another in quick succession. The advantage of 'British
empiricism' was that such moves could be made rapidly. They
have taken just one year, while the restructuring of Spanish
political life (1975–78) took three. The disadvantage is that no
one can have much idea what their longer-term impact will be
like. By comparison with continental post-war practice these
changes have been carried out 'the wrong way round'. British
constitutionalism meant that the Centre simply altered the

periphery, without redesigning itself. God was not required to adapt to what was, at bottom, just another range of local governments. The assumption has been that things will work out, 'settle down', etc., on a basis of pragmatic common sense – the old common denominator of British identity.

Can they? Without being particularly apocalyptic or doom-laden, it is surely possible to doubt this. Governmental rhetoric notwithstanding, these changes are not 'radical'. They are piecemeal, tentative and still regulated by a persisting non-radicalism at the centre. They are examples of minimal reforms rather than maximal. True, there are now supposed to be some central changes on the way (the House of Lords, Lord Jenkins's electoral reform, etc.) but these do not so far look like an over-all written constitution. In terms of the metaphor, they represent more sandbags and surface-drainage channels rather than dams and sluice-gates, appearing 'radical' only because they follow upon eighteen years of glaciated immobilism. Their most visible effect is likely to be the stabilization of a New Labour and Liberal-Democrat régime in long-term office, rather than the reorientation and stabilization of the Constitution itself. Only in rhetoric can they be thought of as a reconstruction of British identity and its multinational will-power or consensus. Is the rhetoric so loud because the real shifts are so feeble?

Across the Watershed

Recent opinion polls seem to indicate that something seismic is taking place in Scottish political opinion. Many, perhaps most, of those young Scots in their kilts getting drunk in Paris are convinced that Scotland should and will become independent within the next decade or so. And this has nothing whatever to do with football . . . Of course, we still don't know exactly how solid is this new constituency for Scottish independence; it could be merely an expression of cultural Scottishness which will evaporate as the hard practical choices emerge in the campaign for the Scottish parliament next year. Or it could be that since the September referendum Scotland already feels that it is another country, and that the momentum will propel Scotland into some form of independence in Europe. This is a question we simply cannot begin to answer at this stage in national development . . .

Iain Macwhirter, *The Scotsman*, 11 June 1998

But of course, we do have to 'begin to answer the question', and this Committee is trying to do so. So what conclusions should be drawn from the picture presented so far? Apart (i.e.) from the obvious one – that people should not have been drawing so many superficial conclusions already from comparisons between Scotland and Catalonia, or between Britain and Spain?

As far as Scotland is concerned, I would suggest it is now quite difficult to foresee any result except what I would define provisionally as '*de facto* independence'. This is a contradiction in terms, of course. By the criteria of international-relations 'realism' a population is either independent (hence 'recognized', represented, etc.) or it is not. But Realism never fully reckoned with the British Constitution.

Least of all could it reckon with a later evolutionary phase of this beast in which the Constitution would be in a sense trying – in its own inimitably piecemeal way – to manage its own break-up. This is an increasingly attractive theory of what is now occurring. Indeed, as part of the recent Northern Ireland Agreement, Her Majesty's government has gone so far as to obligingly redefine 'Sovereignty' for some of its subjects.

Those lucky enough to be born in Northern Ireland are to become the true and effective sources of the magic authority, at least as deployed within their own territory. For them, Sovereignty will no longer be drawn exclusively from the Crown and the Houses of Parliament. (See *The Belfast Agreement*, 1998, p. 2, 'Constitutional Issues'). I don't think it needs a pedant to see something rather fishy here. Or is this the Middle Ages again? Can there really be two classes of subject/citizens under a single state-roof?

The Agreement appears as one of the greatest vindications of politics in our time – but 'politics' directed on to constitutional issues, and towards defining or 'spelling out' such fundamental points, more or less in the way dismissed as quite unnecessary at the Union or central-power level. The odd new conditions of the British-Irish condominium or protectorate imply there will be two constitutions at work for the Northern Irelanders – two, or perhaps two-and-a-half if one takes the influence of the newly reformed Eire constitution as well, plus the Agreement document's declaration that these particular subject-citizens can now 'identify themselves as Irish or British, or both, as they may so choose'.

But coming back to Scotland, and to this Committee's problem, it is surely possible that another constitution will soon be added to the list. Day to day debate about future Anglo-Scottish relations tends to assume that Westminster 'gave' self-government to Scotland in a post-election fit of 'radical' generosity. But no future historian is likely to write it that way. I suspect he or she may end up reframing the same events something like this –

In the course of the 1980s the Scots, via bodies like the Campaign for a Scottish Parliament and the Constitutional Convention, designed a new constitution for the country on foundations quite distinct from those of the old 1688–1707 Union. This constitution was built around the *Claim of Right* signed by most native leaders in 1988. That document (like the *Belfast Agreement* ten years later) located constitutional authority in the will of the people, and inevitably became the primary reference-point for all the subsequent conflicts and judicial disputes between Edinburgh and London after 1999. The 1997 legislation largely accepted the Convention's 1980s plan – and by implication, much of the context in which the plan was made, i.e. the process by which the Scots had designed their own form of government and legislature, and the national norms and ideas informing that process.

Having done almost nothing to reform the former state, Union governments soon discovered they had few institutional or judicial resources to deal with the constant controversies, demands and protests which emerged from Holyrood – aggravated by those from Belfast, and increasingly from Cardiff, as the Welsh Assembly grew restive about its lack of legislative power. Having created a 'slippery slope' (as the polemicists of the day liked to put it) the multinational government could find no way of either climbing back or even staying in one place. With an 'absence of mind' like that which formerly characterized its overseas hegemony, it now found itself colluding in practice with the growth of virtual Scottish independence. Thus at first the pre-formed Scottish constitution simply emerged as the quasi-official rationale of a restored statehood. In the end this was almost welcomed by a Westminster régime now itself far more concerned with problems of English identity, and with the renegotiation of a more satisfactory Anglo-Euro agreement. Just as the Czechs of the one-time Czechoslovakia had found a separate Slovakia less of a nuisance than an incessantly complaining Slovak 'partner', the English discovered that not having Scots on their backs was not just tolerable but in some ways preferable.

Thus did the strange *de facto* independence of the post-2000 period turn into the *de jure* independence of 2010, creating the situation familiar today. At that time there was simply no other status solution available. The transformation of the rapport between Scotland and England (which had always been the axis of the old UK) led to that wider mutation first clearly prefigured in the famous 'Strand Three' of the Peace Agreement of 1998. There 'a British-Irish Council' had been established to reorganize 'the totality of relationships among the peoples of those islands'. Even then (although not phrased in quite those terms) it was foreseen that the former Great Britain would transform itself into an archipelago-system of effectively independent polities, meeting regularly to discuss or decide questions of common interest. Only at a later stage was it conceded that the precondition of such a new order had to be all-round independence-in-Europe, and the final liquidation of the old United Kingdom apparatus of state . . .

Tom Nairn,
Graduate School in Social Sciences,
University of Edinburgh.

Notes

Introduction

1   *Break-up* came out in 1977, and was followed by a paperback edition with a new introduction in 1981. The publisher was New Left Books, which metamorphosed into Verso Books shortly afterwards. The most important notices of the original were those by Ernest Gellner in *The Political Quarterly* vol. 49 (1), 1978, republished as 'Confessions of a New Edinburgh Sinner' in the collection *Spectacles and Predicaments* (1980); and Eric Hobsbawm's in *New Left Review*, 1977.

2   See *Faces of Nationalism: Janus Revisited* (Verso Books, London & New York, 1998).

3   Unless, of course, it sought simply to join the rest of Ireland in its present constitutional Republic. This is the course finally counselled by none other than Conor Cruise O'Brien, for so long an unflinching defender of Protestant political rights. In the last chapter of his *Memoir: My life and themes* (1998), 'The Union on the Eve of the Millennium', he recognizes that the Union may very well *in extremis* cast out its Northern Ireland relations: 'Many unionists now see the disintegration of the Union as something already in progress, and are considering what options are now open to them in these dire circumstances'. He believes the most sensible course would be simply to join the Republic, as far as possible on their own terms – terms of democracy and established minority rights, naturally. These would be readily, even

eagerly, conceded – and would be (though O'Brien omits to point this out) hugely better than what they have ever enjoyed within the British Union.

4 As the book goes to press, the initiative has been shelved along with everything else which depended upon the Peace Process, and the setting-up of a cross-community Parliament in Northern Ireland. Thus even the most clearly modern and forward-looking expression of a post-imperial identity has in the end been allowed to depend upon the retrograde intransigence of a founding Protestantism – that 'primordial' *Geist* so decisively analyzed in Linda Colley's great history, *Britons* (1995).

1 Blair's Britain

1 Tim Hames, *The Times* 12 February 1999, p. 22.

2 In 1988 I published a pre-lapsarian tract entitled *The Enchanted Glass: Britain and its Monarchy* (Cape, London), which reappeared with an update in 1994, under the Radius (Random House) imprint.

3 This was one of the late A.J.P. Taylor's insights, in his *The Hapsburg Monarchy* (1941 & 1981).

4 A substantial extract from it appears as Chapter 2, 'The Nation', in Gopal Balakrishnan's reader, *Mapping the Nation* (Verso Books, London & New York, 1996), pp. 39–78. Bauer's idea was, in Benedict Anderson's words of introduction: 'The importance of the Hapsburg Empire was . . . that it formed a contingent historical shell of practices and institutions out of which a socialist federation of nationalities would emerge – on the road towards the eventual withering away of all states'. Since nationality was in the long run more important than the state, it had to be kept and cultivated separately – and a contingent imperium-shell was simply one way of pursuing this objective.

5 Professor Anthony Giddens has made important contributions to the forecasting industry since New Labour triumphed, as in *The Third Way: the renewal of social democracy* (Polity Press, Cambridge, 1998) and his 1999 BBC Reith Lectures on Radio 4. But these forecasts seem increasingly to coincide with New Labour helmsmanship rather than

inspiring it – see for example Patrick Kane's interview with him in the Glasgow *Sunday Herald* of 21 February 1999, 'Blair's Brain Baulks at Separatism': '. . . I've come round to the idea that it's worth trying to find an accommodation between older nations, like Scotland and England, or Catalonia and the rest of Spain. I would like to see . . . a wider identity still sustained by Britain. It's a change of view for me.' But the change has exactly paralleled those in the Blairite brain-cells inclined (as described here) to reimpose the 'wider identity' through a post-devolutionary strengthening of central authority – a retreat to Leviathan, rather than any authentic third way out of its grasp.

2   The Return of Scotland

1   This is not the same as harmonious. The metaphorical extended 'family' of the nation may be quarrelsome, as 17th century Scotland certainly was, yet also close and capable of unity against external threats, and also of astonishing communal enterprises like the Darien Company and expedition in 1698 (only nine years before the Union).

2   In Christian terms this could be interpreted as like the blood of loss; although in the case of Scotland, I suppose the 'Christ-nation' would then have to be held guilty of auto-crucifixion, a problem I gladly turn over to students of Divinity.

3   *Scotland on Sunday* (8 November 1998), an edited extract from the pamphlet *The Battle Between Social Justice and Separatism*, by Gordon Brown and Douglas Alexander (1998). Later in the year similar pronouncements were made by both authors around the first Scottish election and its results. Since they have nothing farther to say after Devolution, except that there is nothing farther to be said (beyond 'sensible policies' etc.), they have ended by expressing the platitudes of Britishry ever more loudly and woodenly.

4   *Dante's Drum-kit* contains a superbly bitter meditation on Scotland's modern militarism, 'Dressed to Kill', pp. 129–145: 'The glory that was kilt and riflegrease, The grandeur that was bayonet and rum . . .
     Ironic sepoy. *Whaash my nashun?*
     No answer. Silence's oration.'

5   Most people who now write critically of earlier develop-
    ments and the intelligentsia are products of the 1960s, with
    correspondingly little grasp of just what things were like
    before. I'm glad to say they simply possess no effective
    measuring rods for ancestral despair or the drunken, sub-
    arctic provincialism which preceded them around 1950. The
    text which to this day best encompasses that era is Hamish
    Henderson's *Elegies for the Dead in Cirenaica* (1948), a lyrical
    and humane retrospect upon the heroic world of the 51st
    Highland Division in Africa and Sicily, when kilt and rifle-
    grease resumed an honourable purpose, before reverting
    back to that of the reinstated *Sunday Post*. A line from the
    book's 'First Elegy', 'There were no gods and precious few
    heroes' later became the title of Christopher Harvie's radical
    new history of Scotland in the 1980s.
6   It was as if Joe had once again beaten his drum in Edinburgh
    High Street and called forth the folk, but this time to give
    the cold shoulder to such a condescending parade of surro-
    gate nonsense. In 1950 something anti-official and assertive
    of rights was *done*; in 1996 something ultra-official and bla-
    tantly placatory was *being allowed* – in order to limit farther
    assertion of the same rights.
7   A particularly glorious example was *Scotland on Sunday*'s
    Christmas editorial for 1998: 'Best foot forward for polls vic-
    tory'. It points out that when it ought to be riding high, after
    delivering Devolution, New Labour was visibly faltering and
    out of touch, as if reality had moved on, and away from it.
    This will not do. An alliance of Blairism, big business and
    departure-lounge girners is the only way to stop the rot.
    Hence – 'The lesson Labour must learn if it is to triumph in
    May 1999 is that it has the best tunes. Devolution is what
    Scotland wants and that is what Labour has given it. The
    argument is not about independence . . . *that* must be the
    agenda for the forthcoming election campaign.' (27
    December 1998). It was indeed. In fact it produced the most
    despicable election broadcast in British TV history, where a
    'family portrait' of the United Kingdom, like the sort most
    houses have on the sideboard or in the front hall, was seen
    being literally 'smashed up' by frenzied delinquents.
8   The negotiations (it is interesting to recall) were not

conducted 'round a table' at all, but in the manner of the recent conferences on Bosnia, Palestine and Northern Ireland – i.e. with delegations meeting separately and occasionally sending messengers to one another.

9   Clerk's memoir is quoted by David Daiches at length in *Scotland and the Union* (1977), Chapter 8, 'The Commission and After', and was most recently edited and commented on by T.C. Smout as 'Sir John Clerk's Observations on the Present Circumstances of Scotland, 1730' in the *Miscellany of the Scottish History Society*, vol. X, Edinburgh, 1965.

10   A very good succinct account of this can be found in Mark Kishlansky's history of the later Stuarts, *A Monarchy Transformed: Britain 1603–1714* (1996), Chapter 13.

11   The most priceless manifestation of this trend was a *Scotsman* article of 14 November 1998, 'Our History is Bunk', by Oxford historian Niall Ferguson. This is a plea for 'the old feeling of Britishness' especially dear to Scots abroad who think 'the Scots have at best an apology for a national history', which they were right to sell out in 1707. 'When we see Scots acting independently . . . the results are usually an embarrassment', he goes on. But they can still make damn' fine Britishers (e.g. Gordon Brown and Robin Cook).

12   In two important *Scotsman* feature articles Ian Bell has made this point strongly (27th February and 1st March). Because a constitutional dilemma is the critical problem, prolonged delays could envenom politics in both Scotland and England and produce a fag-end of British limbo for both peoples. Interestingly, a few weeks after that Michael Ignatieff gave a lecture in Edinburgh arguing, in very similar fashion, that at all costs Scotland should avoid the Quebec situation of indeterminate stalemate with repeated referenda and rising frustration on both sides (address at Edinburgh University, 2 March 1999).

13   See the *Scotland Act* (1998) Clause 37: 'The Union with Scotland Act 1707 and the Union with England Act 1707 have effect subject to this Act' – *Acts of Union*: 1706 c.11 & 1707 c.7(S).

14   Perhaps the best expression of this recently was Jim Sillars's 'No Nation for Nationalists', in *Scotland on Sunday* (31 May 1998). According to this attack the SNP should not have

allied itself with Labour to win the referendum, and thus
'turned the gas down' on Independence: 'Make no mistake,
devolution and independence are opposites ... (and) ... the
Scotland Bill "sets up a body not worthy of the name of parliament".' This sets the stage for a magnificent defeat – a
referendum staged by the other side, to exorcise
Independence for good (and thereby permanently restore
the bad old days).

15 Douglas Dunn, 'An Address on the Destitution of Scotland',
St. Kilda's Parliament (1981).

3 The Last Days of Sovereignty

1 I am greatly indebted to many discussions with Benedick
Wellings on this subject. His thesis on *English Identity* at
Edinburgh University helped me to understand the related
question of British identity, and its meaning for the Scots. He
is now continuing to work on the subject at the Australian
National University in Canberra.

2 This argument has been developed most importantly in a
collective study, *A Union of Multiple Identities: The British Isles,
c.1750–c.1850* (Manchester University Press, 1997), edited
by Laurence Brockliss and David Eastwood. See in particular the valuable concluding comparison between the
assimilative techniques of the British and the French states:
'From dynastic union to unitary state', pp. 191–208. The
chapters on Ireland in the same book make it clear how the
machinery of political fusion was at its weakest there. The
agrarian revolution and capitalist farming were retarded until
the period of nationalism was well advanced, in the later
19th century, and the Gladstonian unitary state was unable to
realign such basic social conditions of development.

3 Lord Russell is a historian, and Education spokesman for the
Liberal-Democratic Party, here writing in the *Times Literary
Supplement* (In Search of the Constitution, 4091, 7 March
1999).

4 A 'palimpsest' was a re-used piece of parchment of skin,
before the invention of modern paper. New messages were
overwritten on the original to save writing-space, but sometimes the primary document showed through (and can be

recovered today by scanning techniques).

5   The Binns is an evocative, living museum of one important
    family's history from pre-Union times to the present, and
    tells the story of national ruling-class survival better than
    any theory could. It is open to the public in the summer, only
    a few miles from **Edinburgh** or the **Forth Road Bridge**, on
    the road to Linlithgow. On a recent excursion there I noticed
    that each single room contained a portrait of the present
    Laird and Member of Parliament.

6   Mr Dalyell was sent South to Eton College, a common mis-
    fortune during the days of Scotland's estrangement from its
    state. But his family was only following the dictates of James
    VI. James was terribly keen on élite amalgamation, realizing
    right at the start that a fusion of ruling classes was the best
    way for his family to keep the throne. Gentlemen could get
    together, be 'cymented by love' (etc.) far more easily than
    societies or religious faiths.

7   In 1998–99 there was indeed a proposal under way to prevent
    the lapse, in the form of the 'British-Irish Council, (or
    'Council of the Isles').

8   It is sometimes objected that, because everyone else in the
    UK will be affected by such a change, they must be given
    some say in deciding it. The same objections were made on
    behalf of Russia during the break-up of the USSR, and they
    were equally futile. In practice a 'say' for the commanding
    majority would amount to their right to forbid the change of
    status altogether – which they would almost certainly do.
    The way would then be open for force to be legitimated and
    used, as did happen in the ex-USSR (Chechnya) and ex-
    Yugoslavia (Bosnia and Kosovo).

9   It is important to stress that the same standards should be
    read as including whatever minorities find themselves within
    the dominant configurations. Just as 'Britain' did not cancel
    out the peripheral peoples, its successors cannot take democ-
    racy to entail suppression of their own residual (or new)
    minorities. But that is surely what *constitutional* democracy
    means, as distinct from head-count authoritarianism.

4   Devolution or 'Virtual Liberation'?

1   These quaint terms have much of the old régime's soul in
     them. 'Consultation' means something like: 'softening them
     up' (for whatever Power has decreed must come next), while
     'settling down' seems to imply the more protracted process
     whereby, after a relatively short time, the imposed order
     comes to appear traditional or even immemorial, and hence
     immune to farther interference (save in the mind of utopi-
     ans, fanatics, etc.). Poor old provinces. It is probably a sign of
     régime desperation that they got little consultation and next
     to no settling-down time at all.
2   The *Financial Times*'s Christmas Eve edition of 1997 did
     make Blair 'Man of the Year' but hinted that 'There has
     been a disjunction between vaulting rhetoric and prosaic
     reality. The unanswered question is whether the mood
     music is the precursor for radicalism; or whether it is enough,
     for New Labour, like Mr Clinton's New Democrats, merely
     to win a second term'. The level-headedness of this
     approach has been maintained in the paper's later commen-
     tary on the government. The same issue published a piece
     by Max Wilkinson on the Millennium Dome plans, which he
     suggested shrewdly might disclose how 'Truth . . . can no
     longer be distinguished from the language in which it is
     packaged. The 1951 Festival of Britain commemorated
     actual achievements, while the great Greenwich tent will be
     devoted to virtual or aspirational ones'.
3   See above, Chapter Two, 'The Return of Scotland'.
4   Edited by Laurence Brockliss and David Eastwood,
     Manchester University Press (1997).
5   In a recent article David McCrone has strongly underlined
     the function of warfare – and above all of World War I – in
     the formation of the British State. This function undoubt-
     edly retained something of its efficacy until only fifteen
     years ago, with the war for the Falklands in 1982. On the
     other hand it was always double-edged: each dose of mili-
     tarism emphasized the statist character of 'Britain' and the
     national character of contributions to the state's glory (espe-
     cially in Scotland). See 'Unmasking Britannia' in *Nations and
     Nationalism*, vol. 3, no. 4 (1997).

6 The *locus classicus* for reflection on the English-British connection has become Linda Colley's *Britons* (1993), a dazzling
account of how the wars against France and the earlier stages
of empire-building favoured the building of an extruded
identity which (for a time) embraced the non-English
nationalities. However, two other recent studies have
emphasized the depth of proto-national formation in
England itself, before this feat was accomplished. Liah
Greenfeld's *Nationalism: Five Roads to Modernity* (1992)
assigned a template-function to Englishness as the pioneer
of modern nation-statehood. Then Adrian Hastings's *The
Construction of Nationhood: Ethnicity, Religion and Nationalism*
(1997) has convincingly portrayed the ethno-religious intensity and durability of the template. The unresolved dilemma
of Englishness seems thus to be a contrast between this
unique depth of field – from the 16th to the 19th century –
and the final lack of focus inseparable from the extruded
developmental mode of later British imperialism.

7 As the book goes to press I find a front-page story in *The
Times*: 'Ministers seek to avert backlash over devolution', by
their chief political correspondent Roland Watson (26 July
1999). The aim of new Whitehall guidelines over inward
investment to the United Kingdom, Mr Watson explains,
'. . . is to stop devolution turning English voters against the
Government'. The English voters are already 'feeling overlooked', three weeks after the inauguration of Scotland's
Parliament. In the context of rumblings about an English
Parliament and the 'lack of clout' of English regions, the
conventional formulae for equal real redistribution in the
multinational state-area (like the Barnett Formula) suddenly
appear unfair. Such stories now appear practically every day
(the previous day, the same paper had reported at length on
Lord Archer's attempt in the House of Lords to get *different
time-zones* in the Crown lands – supposedly more convenient to his South-Eastern voters in the forthcoming elections
for a London Mayor.

8 Campbell, from a Glasgow Loyalist family associated with
the UVF paramilitary organization, had cut a Catholic boy's
throat in the street and left him to bleed to death. He was
given a life sentence. After the furore surrounding Ms

Mowlam's initiative in Scotland (practically unnoticed in London) the decision had to be rescinded, and Campbell is still serving his sentence.

9 On this theme see *The Economist*, 3 January 1998, 'Little Countries: is it better nowadays to be a small nation than a big one?' (pp. 63–5). I have also tackled this theme in some essays in *Faces of Nationalism: Janus Revisited* (London, Verso Books, 1998).

10 How significant micro-states can be has been borne in upon London opinion in the most comical fashion, when it was revealed that the Treasurer (and main financial contributor) to William Hague's reborn Conservative party, Paul Ashcroft, had derived his millions from an offshore banking operation in Belize. In fact he turned out to be the Belizean representative at the United Nations, *and* founder of one of that tiny country's main political parties. Again Musil and all latter-day imitators were confounded by reality. And all jokes about Britain looking more and more like 'a banana Republic' stood automatically rehabilitated.

5   On Not Hating England

1 A collective study, *The Scottish Electorate* (1999, Alice Brown, David McCrone, Lindsay Paterson and Paula Surridge) gives some idea of the previous situation, culminating in the 1997 general election. But it was in time to detect signs of the change in intentions for the referendum vote, when – 'Perhaps surprisingly there are few differences among the religious groups in their intended vote, with a majority of both Catholic and Protestant identifiers intending to vote Yes-Yes.' (p. 124). The figures were Catholic 60%, Protestant 55%. A year later the Primate of Scotland, Cardinal Winning, was actively defending the prospect of Scottish independence in Brussels!

2 Another paradoxical implication of this is that it was of course the very strength of 'Old Labour' in West-Central Scotland which had determined the Blair government's original move towards devolution. Since Scottish Labourism had during the eighties and nineties become converted under nationalist pressure to Home Rule, and it was necessary to 'do

something for Scotland', a Scottish Parliament was the sole available answer in 1997. The prevalent belief was that Labour hegemony would continue unchallenged in the Glasgow area, and that a thoroughly grateful Party and electorate would afterwards dominate the new assembly *and* go on sustaining New Labour at Westminster. Such blind Britishness reposed in fact on a characteristic 'occlusion' of all that did not fit into its habitual world-view – an attitude with many different expressions, and discussed in other parts of this book.

3   In 'Dressed to Kill' Douglas Dunn writes:
>   For someone born in '42
>   This subject sticks like rancid glue –
>   All those wars, before and since . . .
>   Rinse hands, and rinse, re-rinse, re-rinse,
>   But still the blood just won't wash off
>   As if the world can't get enough.
>   No, by Jingo, no, I'm not
>   A patriotic *British* Scot . . .
>   *Dante's Drum-kit* (1993), pp. 143–4.

4   *The Dunciad* (1976). Alongside many others, the writer was chided in it for his already misguided 'tendencies'. Owen Dudley Edwards replied at the time with a counter-mock-epic on the theme of Labourite self-importance, which was broadcast on BBC Scotland, but (alas) remains unpublished.

5   A Dundee newspaper more widely read than any other in the Scotland of the Imperial Captivity. Its populist parochialism and safe Britannic conservatism made it a byword for all that seemed inveterately and unalterably Scottish. It is still published by D.C. Thomson Ltd, who also brought out a range of comic and children's papers read all over the UK, like *Dandy*, *Beano*, *Hotspur* (and many others). Having been raised on Thomsonite hay, the present author was misguided enough to declare at one moment (1968) that liberating his homeland would depend, ultimately, upon 'strangling the last Minister (of the Presbyterian Kirk) with the last copy of the *Sunday Post*'.

6   Some recent revelations in *The Herald* have shown this is almost literally true. Papers released under the thirty-year rule show how Labour Secretary of State William Ross strove

to keep Home Rule legislation at bay until the 1970s, when
(following on the SNP's electoral successes of 1974) it could
no longer be postponed.

7   The Barclay brothers are Scottish property millionaires living
in the Channel Island of Brecqhou, off Sark, who have in
recent years diversified as press barons, most famously with
the Scotsman group (which they bought from its previous
Canadian owners) and the now-defunct *European*. Their
views are rigidly neo-liberal, anti-European and of course
anti-nationalist.

8   At the time of writing there seems no way of estimating the
significance of the deeply-rooted clash between Brown and
Blair which resulted in the latter's victory in 1994. In spite of
the great amount of speculation and argument over their
rivalry, this may have to await farther disclosures or revelations, or even the memoirs and papers of the protagonists.
However, there is one school of speculation which insists on
the manifest weakness of the English component within
the deteriorating British Socialism of the 1980s and '90s.
After the electoral failures of Kinnock and Smith, it was
urgently necessary to redress the weakness by (at least) not
having another Scot. Blair, by contrast, was a practically
identikit *British* individual in the sense most acceptable to
English sensibility. Thus a subjacent national conflict may
have been modulated (though not exactly resolved) by the
residual rules of British identity. But is this ever likely to
happen again?

9   This was recognised by Channel 4 Television at Christmas
time, 1998, when a 'Christmas Message' from Mr and Mrs
Lawrence was broadcast on 25 December to coincide with
the usual Queenly message going out on other channels. It
was a short and moving programme describing their son's
murder and the police mishandling of it, and appealing for a
different approach by both the law and the media.

10 'Anyone for an Inclusive Britain?', *Scotland on Sunday*, 8
November 1998.

11 Around 1992 the SNP fundamentalist leader Jim Sillars had
castigated Scottish voters for their inconstancy and fearful-
ness, by calling them 'ninety-minute patriots': fervent in
momentary enthusiasm, they would go home and vote

British the day after, still lacking in the confidence to run things for themselves.
12   See the Appendix to this volume, above, where the contrast is discussed at greater length.

6   The Unmasking of Scotland

1   Sandel, *op. cit.* p.
2   Jean-François Revel, *L'absolutisme inefficace* (*Impotent Absolutism*), Plon, Paris (1992) pp. 150–1.
3   I quote from the text as published in the *International Tribune*, April 1999, as recorded on the Movement for a European Constitution website http://www.euraction.org

Index